19/4/01×
£1·50.
£3

Patrick Taylor

The Daily Telegraph

GARDENER'S
— GUIDE —
TO BRITAIN
& IRELAND
1998

D0993711

PATRICK TAYLOR

The Daily Telegraph
GARDENER'S
—GUIDE—
TO BRITAIN
& IRELAND
1998

DORLING KINDERSLEY

LONDON • NEW YORK • SYDNEY • MOSCOW

A DORLING KINDERSLEY BOOK

DEDICATION
For Laura, with much love

First published in 1992
This 7th edition published 1998 by
Dorling Kindersley Ltd,
9 Henrietta Street, London WC2E 8PS
Visit us on the
World Wide Web at http://www.dk.com

Text copyright © 1998 Patrick Taylor

Illustrations © Open Books Publishing Ltd
except pages 36 (© Robin Loder) and 279 (© Faith Raven)

This book was devised and produced by
Open Books Publishing Ltd, Higher Folly Cottage,
Higher Folly, Crewkerne TA18 8PN, Somerset, UK

Designer: Andrew Barron and Collis Clements Associates

Maps: John Gilkes

Computer consultants: Michael Mepham and Roger Davies

All rights reserved. No part of this publication may be
reproduced, stored in a retrieval system, or transmitted in
any form or by any means, electronic, mechanical,
photocopying, recording or otherwise, without the prior
permission of the copyright holders.

A CIP catalogue record for this book is available from the
British Library

ISBN: 07513 0513 8

Text film output by Wandsworth Typesetting Ltd, London
Printed in Italy by Graphicom srl, Vicenza

CONTENTS

INTRODUCTION & ACKNOWLEDGEMENTS

THIS IS the seventh edition of *The Daily Telegraph Gardener's Guide to Britain* – and the first to include Ireland, involving the addition of a further 32 pages, and providing the opportunity for a radical revision of the whole book. Not only did I travel all over Ireland inspecting possible gardens for the Irish section but I also went all over the United Kingdom, reconsidering old places and searching for new ones.

The addition of the gardens of the Republic of Ireland gives me special pleasure. They share some of the traditions of gardening in mainland Britain but have a marvellous beauty all of their own. The climate, especially on the south and west coast, provides exceptional conditions for growing a huge range of plants – I have never seen trees growing in greater splendour than at places like the Fota Arboretum near Cork and at Muckross in County Killarney. Although it would be true to say that the woodland garden in the tradition of William Robinson is the type of Irish garden most widely seen there is *much* else to admire. Relatively youthful gardens such as those of Helen Dillon in Dublin and of Jim Reynolds at Butterstream, for example, show a brilliant use of plants and and an exhilarating decorative sense. Historic estates, going back to the early 17th century, display every style of garden. Irish gardens are not sufficiently known and I urge my readers to go and enjoy them. I came to them rather late in life and I now feel rather foolish that I did not take the trouble to visit them earlier on.

My search for delights in England, Scotland and Wales has continued and there are some marvellous new places appearing in the book for the first time. These range widely and among them are the austerely enchanting Stone Lane Gardens in Devon, the dazzling and fastidious exuberance of the Old Vicarage at East Ruston in Norfolk, the palatial splendours of Witley Court in Worcestershire and the rare pinetum at Scone Palace in Perthshire. I have also discovered some exceptional new nurseries like Bob Brown's Cotswold Garden Flowers, Pleasant View Nursery with its marvellous collection of salvias, and the alpine treasures of Christie's Nursery in Scotland. I travelled thousands of miles and was constantly reminded how fortunate we are today. Never before has there been so

Illustration:
The gravel garden at Beth Chatto's garden

much good gardening going on either in Britain or Ireland. The standards are marvellously high and the potential pleasures for garden visitors enormous.

May I set out, once again, how the book works? Opening times have been checked to the last possible moment, but things change – and if you have set your heart on seeing a place do check by phone beforehand. Dates showing opening seasons are inclusive – Apr to Sept means from the 1st April to the 30th September. Try to arrive at least 45 minutes before closing time. I have indicated those places where the house is also open but I do not give separate opening times – it should not be assumed that they are the same as those for the garden. It is sometimes possible to make arrangements to see gardens at other times by appointment; do *not* turn up unannounced and assume the kind owner will let you in. Many nurseries are one-man, or more often one-woman, places and the proprietor may have to desert his or her post. Do check by phone before making a special journey.

Once again I have received invaluable help from my wife, Caroline. She has edited the text and read proofs with a piercing eye – I am profoundly grateful to her. I am also grateful to my daughter Sophie who kindly pointed out that I had confused, for six editions, the rivers Taw and Torrington. On my Irish excursions I had magnificent help from Ailbhe de Buitléar of Gardens of Ireland, John Lahiffe of the Irish Tourist Board and Mo Durken of the Northern Irish Tourist Board – heartfelt thanks to them all.

At Dorling Kindersley Christopher Davis, David Lamb, Louise Abbott and Lee Griffiths smoothed out the publishing process with Jeeves-like calm.

Lastly, it is the owners of gardens and nurseries who make the irreplaceable contribution to this book. I am lucky enough to have come to know many of them well and without their friendly and generous help I could not possibly have done this book.

Patrick Taylor
Wells, Somerset

SOUTH-EAST ENGLAND

Kent
London
Surrey
Sussex

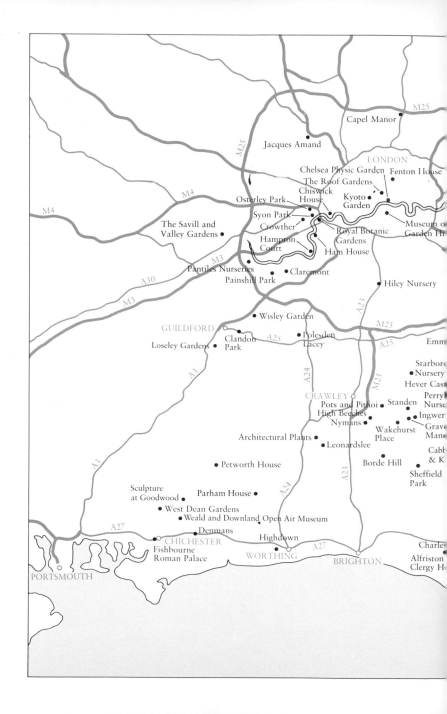

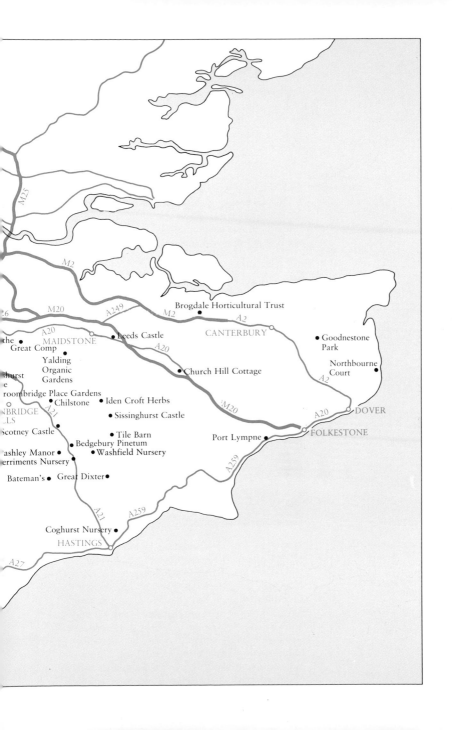

Brogdale Horticultural Trust

M25

M2

M20

A249

M2

A2

CANTERBURY

A20

MAIDSTONE

Leeds Castle

the
Great Comp

Goodnestone
Park

Yalding
Organic
Gardens

Church Hill Cottage

Northbourne
Court

hurst
e

A2

roombridge Place Gardens

Chilstone

Iden Croft Herbs

M20

A20

DOVER

NBRIDGE
LS

A21

Sissinghurst Castle

FOLKESTONE

cotney Castle

Tile Barn

Port Lympne

ashley Manor
erriments Nursery

Bedgebury Pinetum

Washfield Nursery

A259

Bateman's

Great Dixter

A21

A259

Coghurst Nursery

HASTINGS

A27

ALFRISTON CLERGY HOUSE

East Sussex

The Tye, Alfriston,
Polegate BN26 5TL
4m NE of Seaford by B2108
Tel: 01323 870001

Owner: The National Trust

Open: Apr to Oct, daily
except Tue and Fri (open
Good Fri) 10–5 or dusk if
earlier. 1/2 acre. House open

ALTHOUGH THE garden surrounding this beautiful medieval hall house is quite small it has all sorts of virtues and many ideas for owners of gardens with limited space. It has a wide range of different styles – from brick-edged borders of cottage-garden exuberance to a charmingly austere parterre of standard box trees clipped into umbrellas and underplanted with pinks. A herb garden has square beds with low hedges of santolina and there is a proper kitchen garden. A trickling stream runs along one side of the garden and beyond there are views of the countryside and the downs.

JACQUES AMAND LTD

Middlesex

Illustration: Fritillaria michailovskyi

The Nurseries, 145 Clamp
Hill, Stanmore HA7 3JS
NW of London off the
Uxbridge Road (A410)
Tel: 0181 427 3968
Fax: 0181 954 6784

Open: Mon to Fri 9–5, Sat
9–4; Sun 9–1.30 (closed Sun
in Dec and Jan)

JACQUES AMAND specialises in bulbs of which he sells one of the best selections in the country, and regularly wins medals at RHS shows and elsewhere. Although he also carries a few shrubs such as dwarf rhododendrons and some herbaceous perennials, especially those that are suitable for woodland gardens, like *Jeffersonia diphylla* and *Mertensia virginica*, it is the bulbs that are the great glory of the place – very many alliums, fritillaries, lilies and narcissi are stocked, and less usual plants such as trilliums of which an exceptional range is listed. Well illustrated complimentary catalogues, full of useful information on cultivation, are produced in spring and autumn from which orders by post may be made. There is a special spring display area.

ARCHITECTURAL PLANTS

West Sussex

Cooks Farm, Nuthurst,
Horsham RH13 6LH
2m S of Horsham by A281
and minor roads
Tel: 01403 891772
Fax: 01403 891056

Open: Mon to Sat 9–5

ARCHITECTURAL PLANTS has a completely distinctive house style. It sells plants that have strong, architectural shapes and contribute to the structure of the garden. Angus White, the founder, says that his garden was as fascinating to look at in the winter as 'a wet breeze block' and he wanted exotic, preferably evergreen plants that would give winter liveliness. This nursery is his answer. His elegantly produced list is colour coded – green means that the plant is perfectly hardy; orange means that a plant will survive in the right site in the southern counties; and red means that the plant will survive only on the Atlantic coast or the privileged islands. The list is full of rarities – like the cartwheel tree (*Trochodendron aralioides*) or the Mexican strawberry tree (*Arbutus glandulosa*) – and packed with information. A mail order service is provided but it is much better to go to Cooks Farm and see the exotics in splendid action.

BATEMAN'S

East Sussex

Burwash, Etchingham
TN19 7DS
1/2 m S of Burwash by
A265
Tel: 01435 882302

Owner: The National Trust

Open: 4 Apr to 1 Nov, daily
except Thur and Fri (open
Good Fri) 11–5.30. 10 acres.
House open

RUDYARD KIPLING lived here, in the handsome early 17th-century house, from 1902 to 1936 and himself designed many of the existing features of the elegant garden. The site is flat but it is animated by attractive decorative ingredients and a strongly designed layout. Above the house a beautiful tunnel of pears and clematis trained over broad arches is underplanted with bergenias, spring bulbs, geraniums and Corsican hellebores. A path leads down one side of the house and occasional 'windows' cut in a yew hedge give glimpses of the country beyond. In the formal garden a curved seat in a bower of clipped yew overlooks a long rectangular pool. At the end of the pool a rose garden has flagged paths and flower beds with a shady double pleached lime walk. The whole place has the air of a quintessentially English garden of the Edwardian period; the sort of thing dreamed of by homesick men in Poona.

BEDGEBURY NATIONAL PINETUM

Kent

nr Goudhurst,
Cranbrook TN17 2SL
4 1/2 m S of Goudhurst
by B2079
Tel: 01580 211044
Fax: 01580 212423

Owner: The Forestry
Commission

Open: Daily 10–dusk.
300 acres

BEDGEBURY PINETUM has a splendid site in a broad and deep valley. An ornamental lake at the bottom provides the right conditions for moisture-loving plants such as swamp cypresses, of which there are some handsome specimens, and on the slopes of the valley conifers are grouped either by kind – spruces, junipers, cypresses and so on – or by place of origin – the Chinese glade, the American glade or the Japanese glade. Conifers are obviously the main meal here but the menu is varied with some deciduous trees and many rhododendrons. The appearance of evergreens varies subtly through the growing year – the changing colour of foliage and fruit – and a visit is rewarding in any season. At the visitors' centre there is a marvellous display of different cones. Bedgebury holds National Collections of junipers, of yews and of Lawson cypress cultivars. In the autumn an added interest is the outstanding range of mushrooms that flourishes here. Open throughout the year, there is always something to admire.

BORDE HILL

West Sussex

Haywards Heath
RH16 1XP
1 1/2m N of Haywards
Heath by minor roads
Tel: 01444 450326
Fax: 01444 440427

Owner:
Borde Hill Gardens Ltd

Open: Daily 10–6. 7 acres
garden, 200 acres woods

BORDE HILL is famous for trees and shrubs but near the house there are handsome borders and formal planting. These have recently been enriched by a new rose garden and herbaceous borders. That is all very decorative but the serious matter at Borde Hill is the splendid collection of ornamental woody plants. It was started in 1892 by Colonel Stephenson Clark who was one of the financers of the great plant-hunting expeditions to the Chinese Himalayas between the wars. Thus, the garden is wonderfully rich in magnolias and rhododendrons (particularly species) which relish the light, slightly acid soil. But the collection is wide-ranging and there are also very good conifers in Warren Wood and rare deciduous trees, particularly American species, in Little Bentley Wood. The agreeably undulating site makes it a most attractive place in which to admire some marvellous plants.

BROGDALE HORTICULTURAL TRUST

Kent

Brogdale Road,
Faversham ME13 8XZ
1m SE of Faversham
Tel: 01795 535286
Fax: 01795 531710

Owner: The Brogdale
Horticultural Trust

Open: Easter to 25 Dec,
daily 9.30–5.30; 26 Dec to
Easter, daily 10–4. 150 acres

BROGDALE HAS the National Collection of fruit, with over 4,000 varieties disposed in 30 acres of orchards. It is a marvellous enterprise, preserving, for example, over 2,000 old cultivars of apples alone. Guided tours of the orchards are offered and fruit is for sale in season. In spring the display of blossom is one of the most spectacular garden sights. Special events of a fruity kind are organised throughout the year, reaching their climax with the great Apple Celebration held in October. There are plants for sale, with an emphasis on fruit.

CABBAGES & KINGS

East Sussex

THERE IS no other garden like this and it offers a valuable inspiration for gardeners. Subtitled 'The Centre for Garden Design', it is an intimate display garden showing an astonishing range of features most

Wilderness Farm, Hadlow
Down TN22 4HU
5 1/2m NE of Uckfield by
A26 and A272, 1/2m S of
Hadlow Down by
Wilderness Lane
Tel: 01825 830552
Fax: 01825 830736

Open: Easter to Sept, Fri,
Sat, Sun and Bank Hol
Mon 10–6. 1 acre

fastidiously laid out. The garden designer Ryl Nowell devised it to show clients and interested gardeners exactly how she solves design problems. In a small area are beautifully made paths, steps, terraces, pools and sitting places, embellished with strong planting from which anyone can learn. Everywhere there are examples of the emphatic, simple planting which good designers use – sheaves of *Stipa gigantea* emerge from lapping waves of *Cotoneaster horizontalis* 'Variegatus' or *Potentilla* 'Gibson's Scarlet', and hummocks of clipped yew embrace a bench. If visiting the garden is rather like guzzling an excessively rich meal, indigestion is nevertheless kept at bay by the strength of the design and, glimpsed over the garden walls, the exquisite views of surrounding countryside.

CAPEL MANOR

Middlesex

Bullsmoor Lane,
Enfield EN1 4RQ
14m N of Central London
by A10; Jnct 25 of M25
Tel: 0181 3664442
Fax: 01992 717544

Owner: Capel Manor
Horticultural and
Environmental Centre

Open: Daily 10–5.30 (last
tickets 4.30, earlier in
winter). 30 acres

DISPLAY GARDENS such as this can be both entertaining and instructive. Here, a series of historical gardens includes a Tudor-style knot, a formal 17th-century garden and a recently planted prickly maze of holly taken from William Nesfield's design for the great exhibition in 1851. A garden for the physically disabled is full of ideas and a 'Sensory Garden' rich with the scent of herbs and the sounds of water is designed for the visually impaired. Demonstration gardens – woodland, water and courtyard – give ideas for design and planting. The magazine *Gardening from Which?* has sponsored a trial garden and the National Gardening Centre has a permanent exhibition of horticultural equipment. This is a satisfying mixture of both practical information and inspiration, fizzing with horticultural endeavour.

CHARLESTON

East Sussex

Illustration opposite: Venus
among the cow parsley at
Charleston

CHARLESTON MAY fairly be described as the country seat of the Bloomsbury set. Vanessa and Clive Bell, and Duncan Grant, lived here, and the whole place, now most sympathetically restored, is redolent of Bloomsbury. The 17th-century house has a

nr Firle, Lewes BN8 6LL
6m E of Lewes by A27
Tel: 01323 811265 (visitors);
01323 811626
(administration)
Fax: 01323 811628

Owner:
The Charleston Trust

Open: Apr to Oct, Wed,
Sun and Bank Hol Mon 2–6
(Jul and Aug 11.30–6).
1 acre. House open

south-facing garden walled in brick and flint. Gravel paths and mixed borders run round the walls and the planting is cheerfully colourful – the horticultural equivalent of Omega workshop textiles. Apple trees erupt from borders and a long box hedge has been clipped into undulating waves, echoing the smooth surface of the downs that rise above the house. Everywhere there are decorative touches – a pottery mask overlooking a little pool, mosaics of broken china (Bloomsbury and older) on a terrace, busts dotted along a wall. Outside the walled garden, by a wild orchard, Ophelia floats on the edge of a pool and Venus lurks in a grove of cow parsley. All this gives a vivid picture of the charms of Bloomsbury life.

CHELSEA PHYSIC GARDEN

London

66 Royal Hospital Road,
SW3 4HS
Tube: Sloane Square
Tel: 0171 352 5646

Owner: Trustees of Chelsea
Physic Garden

Open: Apr to Oct, Sun 2–6
and Wed 12–5; also during
Chelsea Festival week.
4 acres

WHEN ONE has got over the astonishment of finding a 4-acre walled garden – with full Secret Garden character – in the middle of London, there is still plenty to marvel at. Founded as a garden of medicinal herbs in 1673 it became, especially under the directorship of Philip Miller in the 18th century, an important botanic garden. It still possesses a large collection of herbs, a range of 'order' beds and a research area. But there are magnificent trees including male and female *Ginkgo biloba*, a cork oak (*Quercus suber*) and a splendid olive tree (which in fine years produces big crops) and all sorts of other tender things relishing the protection of the old walls. The garden holds the National Collection of cistus and has some good plants for sale.

CHILSTONE GARDEN ORNAMENTS

Kent

CHILSTONE MAKE high-quality composition stone garden ornaments and architectural pieces, many of which are meticulous copies of fine originals. The firm has recently moved to new quarters at Victoria Park, where many of the ornaments are disposed about a handsome woodland walk. In the display garden to

Victoria Park, Fordcombe
Road, Langton Green,
Tunbridge Wells TN3 0RE
3m W of Tunbridge Wells
on A264
Tel: 01892 740866
Fax: 01892 740249

Open: Mon to Fri, 9–5, Sun
10–4.30

one side a large selection from the stock is arranged in
lovely profusion – colonnades, sprinkling fountains,
impassive sphinxes, stately urns and the busts of
emperors. Some of these are now richly encrusted with
moss and the patina of age – making them all but
indistinguishable from 18th-century originals.

CHISWICK HOUSE

London

Burlington Lane,
Chiswick W4 2RP
4m SW of Central London
by A4 and A316
Tel: 0181 742 1225

Owner: London Borough of
Hounslow

Open: Daily, 7.30–dusk.
62 acres. House open

LORD BURLINGTON built Chiswick House as a
pleasure dome in 1723–9 and surrounded it with
appropriate gardens. These have now been taken in
hand by English Heritage, and a thoroughly
worthwhile restoration programmme is beginning to
have splendid results. The house itself, domed and
portico'd, dominates the formal garden with its avenue
of cypresses interspersed with grand urns. To one side,
a circular sunken pool is surrounded by orange trees in
pots and overlooked by a temple. At a little distance
from the house a Victorian garden has a dazzling
conservatory, arabesques of clipped box, lush bedding
schemes and an avenue of mop-headed acacias.

CHURCH HILL COTTAGE GARDENS

Kent

Charing Heath,
Ashford TN27 0BU
8m NW of Ashford by A20;
400 yards from Red Lion
pub towards Charing Heath
Church
Tel: 01233 712522

Open: Feb to Nov, daily
except Mon (open Bank
Hol Mon) 10–5

AN ATTRACTIVE development in recent years is that of the small nursery alongside the owners' private garden where the plants may be seen in cultivation. The nursery here specialises in herbaceous perennials, with excellent collections of penstemons, named varieties of pinks, herbaceous sages, unusual verbenas and violas. The garden next door to the nursery permits the distinctive virtues of these and other plants to be seen and savoured. A winding stream is edged with waterside plants, and herbaceous beds are given an occasional note of emphasis by some well-placed ornamental tree – a golden acacia or a variegated maple, for example. New beds of ferns and of hostas have recently been developed.

CLANDON PARK

Surrey

West Clandon,
Guildford GU4 7RQ
3m E of Guildford off A25
Tel: 01483 222482
Fax: 01483 223479

Owner: The National Trust

Open: Daily 9–dusk.
8 acres. House open

THE MANSION at Clandon Park, built of brick and stone in about 1730, dominates the garden. Under its south facade a neat parterre of box hedges, topiary box cones and summer bedding is flanked by raised hedges of clipped hornbeam. Across the lawn, a damp and ferny flint grotto houses a cluster of shivering nymphs, almost certainly dating from the late 18th-century landscaping of the garden. To one side of this, in the shade of an immense oak, there is a charming oddity: a carved and painted Maori house brought here in the 1890s by the 4th Earl of Onslow who had served as Governor of New Zealand. Half way up the drive, rather tucked away and easy to miss, is a Dutch garden enclosed in tall yew hedges and laid out in a geometric pattern of hedges of box, lavender and variegated euonymus, with pyramids of white roses rising above.

CLAREMONT LANDSCAPE GARDEN

Surrey

Portsmouth Road,
Esher KT10 9JG
14m SW of Central London
by A3
Tel: 01372 469421

Owner: The National Trust

Open: Jan to Mar, daily
except Mon 10–5 or dusk if
earlier; Apr to Oct, Mon to
Fri 10–6, Sat, Sun and Bank
Hol 10–7 (closed 14 Jul and
closes at 2 from 15 to 19
Jul); Nov to Mar 1999,
daily except Mon 10–5 or
dusk if earlier. 49 acres

THE LANDSCAPE garden at Claremont had virtually disappeared from view, drowned in a sea of rhododendron and laurels, until the National Trust took it in hand in 1975. Some of the greatest figures in landscape design worked here from 1720 onwards – Sir John Vanbrugh, Charles Bridgeman, William Kent and 'Capability' Brown. What has now been restored is chiefly the work of the first three, and what the visitor now sees – never mind garden history – is an enchanting garden of woodland, beech alleys rising steeply uphill, a vast turf amphitheatre which looks down on a lake with an island temple designed by Kent, and beautiful stands of sweet chestnuts. This is not a garden for lovers of flower power. On summer weekends it fills with picnickers relishing an Elysian oasis threatened on all sides by suburbia.

COGHURST NURSERY

East Sussex

Ivy House Lane, nr Three
Oaks, Hastings TN35 4NP
3 1/2m NE of Hastings by
A21, A259 and minor roads
Tel: 01424 756228

Open: Mon to Fri 12–4.30,
Sun 10–4.30

CAMELLIAS ARE the main thing at Coghurst and the nursery has one of the best collections in the country, including many that are available commercially nowhere else. Well over 300 varieties include a particularly choice range of cultivars of the autumn-flowering *C. sasanqua* and the tender *C. reticulata*. Even if you do not have acid soil, camellias are among the most marvellous of plants for pots, making lovely winter ornaments. Coghurst also sells a limited range of rhododendrons – including many evergreen azaleas – mostly cultivars but with a few choice species. Catalogues are issued (two 2nd-class stamps) and smaller specimens may be sent by post.

CROWTHER OF SYON LODGE

Middlesex

Busch Corner, London
Road, Isleworth TW7 5BH
3 1/2m SW of central
London by A315
Tel: 0181 560 7978
Fax: 0181 568 7572

Open: Mon to Fri 9–5, Sat
to Sun 11–4.30; also by
appointment

CROWTHER PIONEERED dealing in antique garden ornaments and architectural fragments, and their premises at Syon Lodge are a treasure trove of wonderful things. Here, displayed in a crowded garden, is a bewildering and constantly changing profusion of temples, seats, statues, urns and fountains. All are decorative and some are distinguished – and expensive – works of art. Many of them have grand provenances and are the sort of things around which a new garden might be designed. There are very few places anywhere in the world where such a range of garden ornaments of this quality can be found for sale. Displayed all together in such quantity the ever-changing stock gives the place a dream-like quality, like a scene from an elegant surrealist film.

DENMANS

West Sussex

Fontwell,
nr Arundel BN18 0SU
5m E of Chichester on A27
(NOTE: The road is dual
carriageway at this point
and access is only from the
west-bound lane)
Tel: 01243 542808
Fax: 01243 544064

Owner: John Brookes

Open: Mar to Oct, daily
9–5. 3 1/2 acres

THIS UNUSUAL garden was started in 1946 by Mrs J.H. Robinson and has for many years now been run by the well-known garden designer and writer John Brookes. The entrance is through a huge glasshouse which houses a large collection of tender plants. Gravel paths meander across a walled garden in which profuse herbaceous planting is given structure by huge clipped mounds of variegated box, a handsome strawberry tree and the bold foliage of rhus and rheum. Beyond, in the main garden, sweeping beds have mixed plantings and 'rivers' of gravel have striking groups of mulleins, grasses and phormium. There are many unusual plants here, and an attractively bold sense of design with the creative use of interesting foliage. The garden has an altogether distinctive character, with many lessons for gardeners. A nursery sells some good plants, mostly herbaceous but with a carefully chosen selection of shrub roses. The potential of most of the plants may be seen handsomely displayed in the adjacent garden, so a visit will be doubly rewarded.

EMMETTS GARDEN

Kent

Ide Hill,
Sevenoaks TN14 6AY
1 1/2m N of Ide Hill by
B2042
Tel: 01732 750367/750429

Owner: The National Trust

Open: Apr to Oct, Wed to
Sun and Bank Hol Mon
2–6. 6 acres

THIS IS the highest point in Kent and the garden has splendid views of the North Downs. Frederick Lubbock, a friend of William Robinson, lived here and put into practice Robinson's idea of arranging hardy exotic plants in a naturalistic setting. A formal rose garden hedged in thuja, and a rock garden, are the only tamed parts of what is essentially an informal garden of wild character merging imperceptibly with the surrounding woodland. The acid soil allows many azaleas, camellias, eucryphias, rhododendrons, stewartias and other ericaceous plants. Excellent trees and shrubs are to be seen everywhere – *Kalmia latifolia*, magnolias, maples, dogwoods – and there are also real rarities, such as the American fringe tree, *Chionanthus virginicus*. In spring the slopes of the densely wooded valley are carpeted with bluebells. In autumn there is a wonderful display of colour from azaleas, cercidiphyllums, maples and others. The fine undulating site and profusion of good plants make it a wonderful place to explore.

FENTON HOUSE

London

Windmill Hill,
Hampstead NW3 6RT
In Hampstead village.
Tube: Hampstead.
Tel: 0171 435 3471

Owner: The National Trust

Open: 1 to 22 Mar, Sat and
Sun 2–5; Apr to 1 Nov, Sat,
Sun and Bank Hol Mon 11–5,
Wed to Fri 2–5. 1 acre.
House open

A COMPLETE COUNTRY garden, of traditional English style, in the middle of Hampstead village reminds the visitor of the former rural character of this part of London. Fenton House, built in the 1690s in fine brickwork with beautiful detailing, looks out over a formal garden in which a gravel path is edged with standard-trained Portugal laurels in tubs, and borders are given formality with rhythmic plantings of clipped lavender or Irish yews. At the far end, yew hedges conceal hidden borders and elegant benches. At a lower level, parallel to this, an orchard bursts into life in spring, with fruit blossom and many bulbs naturalised in the long grass – anemones, narcissi and snake's head fritillaries.

FISHBOURNE ROMAN PALACE GARDEN

West Sussex

Fishbourne PO19 3QR
1 1/2m W of Chichester
by A259
Tel: 01243 785859

Owner: Sussex
Archaeological Society

Open: Mar to Jul, Sept to
Oct, daily 10–5; Aug, daily
10–6; 8 to 28 Feb, Nov to 13
Dec, daily 10–4; remainder
of year, Sun 10–4. 2 acres

THIS IS an unusual attempt to show what an aristocratic Roman garden would have looked like, based on archaeological examination of the site and on Roman garden practice. The original garden was enclosed by a verandah with a colonnade; in this area a low box hedge is shaped into a geometric pattern and some characteristic Roman plants (such as acanthus) are used. A representative collection of plants grown by the Romans, culled from classical sources, is to be seen and a display area shows typical features of gardens of the period – such as an out-of-doors dining room. Roman garden design was rediscovered in the Renaissance and is the foundation of European garden aesthetics. In the adjoining museum are mosaics of great beauty and a detailed model of the palace and the garden, showing how it appeared in its original state.

GOODNESTONE PARK

Kent

nr Wingham,
Canterbury CT3 1PL
7m E of Canterbury by
A257 and minor roads; or
A2 and B2046; signposted
from Wingham
Tel: 01304 840107

Owner: Lord and Lady
FitzWalter

Open: Apr to Oct, Mon,
Wed to Fri 11–5, Sun 12–6.
6 acres

THE CHARMS of this garden are revealed only gradually, but they are real and the place has memorable character. At first glance the visitor may think – 'oh dear, another old country house garden about to go to seed.' The entrance to the garden takes the visitor past the 18th-century mansion with traces of an old formal garden and specimen trees. A stupendous ancient sweet chestnut is suddenly revealed – and behind the house are equally ancient but rather battered cedars of Lebanon of tremendous presence. The trump card of the place is the series of exuberantly planted walled gardens between house and church, which borrow the church tower as an eyecatcher for their central vista. Apart from excellent mixed borders there is a splendid kitchen garden with a central walk flanked by beds of old roses, peonies and delphiniums. Some of the planting shows crafty colour planning – in one corner a sprightly arrangement of yellows and apricots includes asphodels, yellow daylilies, Moroccan broom, *Fremontodendron californicum*, orange pokers, the rose 'Buff Beauty' and a pale orange honeysuckle.

GRAVETYE MANOR

West Sussex

nr East Grinstead
RH19 4LJ
4m SW of East Grinstead
by B2110
Tel: 01342 810567
Fax: 01342 810080

Owner: Peter Herbert

Open: Perimeter walk only,
Tue and Fri 10–5; private
garden by house for use of
hotel and restaurant
customers *only.* 30 acres

THIS WAS the house and garden of William Robinson, the greatest and most influential of late-Victorian gardeners. Thanks to a brilliant restoration carried out by the present owner, visitors may now see a properly Robinsonian garden in all its splendour. The gabled 17th-century manor house, now an unashamedly comfortable hotel with one of the best restaurants in England, looks south across a valley. South and west of the house are formal gardens with many of the plants that Robinson loved. On the northern wooded slopes things become wilder with azaleas, camellias and magnolias planted among the trees. South of the house, sweeping down to a lake made by Robinson, is a meadow dazzling in spring with naturalised bulbs where in summer the grass is allowed to grow long. Although in a densely populated part of England, Gravetye is at the heart of a large Forestry Commission wood and has preserved to a remarkable degree the wild and naturalistic atmosphere that Robinson cherished.

GREAT COMP

Kent

Comp Lane, St Mary's
Platt, nr Borough Green
TN15 8QS
7m E of Sevenoaks off A25;
signposted on B2016, off
A20/A25 between
Sevenoaks and Maidstone
Tel: 01732 882669/886154

Owner: Great Comp
Charitable Trust

Open: Apr to Oct, daily
11–6. 7 acres

THERE IS something enticing about the design of the garden at Great Comp – paths lead the visitor on, curving out of sight round bold plantings. The atmosphere is essentially informal, an impression which is only sharpened by the occasional straight line and touch of formality. Against a background of deciduous woodland a very wide range of ornamental trees and shrubs relishes the acid loam. Spreading out south of the house a generous apron of impeccable lawn is fringed with tall conifers, oaks and willows and, as it reaches the woodland, bordered with beds of heathers. Paths lead off into the wilder woodland (and a temple lost in the woods) and thence back towards the house. Everywhere there are excellent trees and shrubs set off by well-chosen underplanting – the larger campanulas, geraniums, hostas, lilies, and violas. This is not a garden which depends on superficial fripperies – but capitalises on the very skilful use of carefully chosen plants.

GREAT DIXTER

East Sussex

Northiam, Rye TN31 6PH
11m N of Hastings off A28
Tel: 01797 252878
Fax: 01797 252879

Owner: Christopher Lloyd

Open: Apr to mid Oct, daily except Mon (open Bank Hol Mon) 2–5. 5 acres. House open

THE DISTINGUISHED gardener/writer Christopher Lloyd is the genius of this place. Edwin Lutyens restored the timbered 15th-century house, and also planned the garden upon which Mr Lloyd has put his lively stamp. Billowing yew topiary dates from Lutyens's time but most of the planting is of a more recent date. Here are Christopher Lloyd's virtuoso mixed border which he constantly improves; sheets of spring flowers in the orchard; a meadow garden; and, wherever you look, fastidiously chosen plants of all kinds planted with a crafty eye for colour. Mr Lloyd does not treat his garden as a shrine – it is more like a horticultural test ground. A recent experiment involved booting out a Lutyens rose garden and installing a late summer 'tropical garden' rich in bold shapes and brilliant colours which engulf the visitor. No gardener could visit Great Dixter without making discoveries and rekindling the zest for gardening. There are good plants for sale, of which there is a catalogue (£1.00), and they are sold by mail order.

GROOMBRIDGE PLACE GARDENS

Kent

THE HOUSE at Groombridge is a wildly romantic and slightly gloomy 17th-century brick mansion suspended ethereally above a moat. Behind the house are gardens of formal inspiration with a parterre, an avenue of yews clipped into pillars, an oriental garden and a mysterious 'drunken garden' of misshapen yew and juniper topiary. At some distance from all this, across a field, is the 'Enchanted Forest', which is not a California-style cemetery but an ambitious and beautifully executed woodland garden packed with ideas. It is a place worth watching to see if this early promise is maintained.

Groombridge, Tunbridge Wells TN3 9QG
4m SW of Tunbridge Wells by A264 and B2110
Tel: 01892 863999
Fax: 01892 863996

Owner: Blenheim Asset Management

Open: Apr to Oct, daily 10–6. 164 acres

HAM HOUSE

London

THE EARLY 17th-century brick house was modernised in the smartest taste in the 1670s by the Duke and Duchess of Lauderdale who took as much interest in the garden as they did in the house. The garden decayed until in 1976 work was started by

Ham,
Richmond TW10 7RS
SW of Central London off
A307 at Petersham,
Tel: 0181 940 1950

Owner: The National Trust

Open: Daily except Thur
and Fri 10.30–6 or dusk if
earlier (closed 25–26 Dec
and 1 Jan). 18 acres. House
open

the National Trust on its restoration. This was helped by the survival of late 17th-century documentation – plans and plant lists – which enabled an authentic reconstruction. The formal walled garden south of the house is divided into spacious grass plats with a maze-like wilderness of hornbeam, winding paths and hidden pavilions. To one side a further walled garden has a large orangery (now a tea-room) with, sprawling in front of it, a vast *Paliurus spina-christi*, the thorned tree from which Christ's crown of thorns was supposed to have been made. In the east court on the other side of the house a parterre of gravel paths and box hedges is arranged in racy lozenges of lavender and santolina and overlooked by shady tunnels of yew and pleached hornbeam.

HAMPTON COURT

Surrey

East Molesey KT8 9AU
6m SW of Central London
at Hampton Wick where
A308 and A309 meet
Tel: 0181 781 9500
Fax: 0181 781 9509

Owner:
Historic Royal Palaces

Open: Daily, dawn–dusk.
30 acres. Palace open

THIS IS one of the most famous places in England and has much to interest the gardener. It was started by Thomas Wolsey in the early 16th century and became a royal palace, which it remains. In the late 17th century Sir Christopher Wren added grandiose extensions to the Tudor palace and was involved in the design of a new garden. Part of his garden 'wilderness' survives: a yew maze – the earliest known hedge maze in England. South of the palace, the original royal privy garden has been triumphantly restored, showing exactly what King William III would

Illustration opposite: The Privy Garden at Hampton Court

have seen in the late 17th century. Views of the Thames are framed by Jean Tijou's exquisite wrought-iron screen of the same date. Nearer the palace there is a colourful (some say *too* colourful) sunken pond garden and a reconstructed Tudor knot. In the vinery is a 'Black Hamburgh' grape-vine planted in 1768 and still productive. To the east of the palace old topiary of yew and holly rises above spring and summer bedding schemes, and three noble lime avenues radiate from a semi-circle of clipped yew and holly.

HEVER CASTLE

Kent

nr Edenbridge TN8 7NG
3m SE of Edenbridge by
minor roads
Tel: 01732 865224
Fax: 01732 866796

Owner: Broadland
Properties Ltd

Open: Mar to Nov, daily
11–6. 50 acres. Castle open

HEVER HAS everything a proper castle should have – a romantic moat, whimsical topiary, an infuriating maze and an excellent garden. The setting of old woodland is very fine and in spring there are some good rhododendrons and azaleas. The enormous Italian garden was designed chiefly to show off the collection of classical statuary collected by William Waldorf Astor who bought the estate in 1903. Much of the statuary is artfully arranged in enclosures running along the Pompeian Wall which is planted to great decorative effect. Facing it, on the shady north-facing side, is an immense pergola draped with vines, clematis and roses, behind which there is a series of grotto-like niches, dripping with water, where ferns, hostas and other moisture-loving plants thrive. Much of the

garden is flamboyantly grand – a swashbuckling Italianate loggia with fountains and naked nymphs, for example – but there are more intimate moments and much attractive planting. In 1997 a new water maze was added, in the tradition of those Italian renaissance water works which unexpectedly springled the unwary.

THE HIGH BEECHES

West Sussex

Handcross RH17 6HQ
1m E of Handcross off
B2110
Tel: 01444 400589

Owner: High Beeches
Gardens Conservation Trust

Open: Apr to Jun, Sept to
Oct, daily except Wed 1–5;
Jul to Aug, Mon and Tue
1–5. 20 acres

AFTER WALKING round this exquisite woodland garden it is hard to believe that it is only 20 acres in area. Winding paths, shifting views and the subtle lie of the gently undulating land give such a rich diversity of scenery. The High Beeches formerly belonged to the Loder family of Leonardslee and Wakehurst; in 1966 the Hon. Edward and Mrs Boscawen came here and have added immensely to it. The emphasis is as much on the quality of the landscape as on the distinction of the planting. There are marvellous camellias, magnolias, maples and rhododendrons and many other groups of woody plants, including a National Collection of stewartias. But there are also many herbaceous plants – drifts of naturalised willow gentian, irises and primulas – and a 4-acre meadow, unploughed in living memory, with 15 species of grass, many cowslips and orchids.

HIGHDOWN

West Sussex

Littlehampton Road,
Goring-by-Sea BN12 6NY
3m W of Worthing by A259
Tel: 01903 501054

Owner:
Worthing Borough Council

Open: Apr to Sept, Mon to
Fri 10–6, Sat, Sun and Bank
Hol Mon 10–8; Oct to Mar,
Mon to Fri 10–4. 9 1/2 acres

SIR FREDERICK Stern, who lived at Highdown and died in 1967, was a banker whose passionate hobby was gardening. The making of the garden here is vividly described in his book *A Chalk Garden*, a 20th-century gardening classic. On his death Highdown was left to Worthing Borough Council and there is still much to admire. The site is a steep, south-facing slope with occasional chalk cliffs, and the layout is informal with occasional formality such as the avenue of *Prunus serrula*, with its glistening, peeling bark, at the entrance. The garden is of especial interest to those who want to know more about the splendours and miseries of gardening on chalk. Stern was able to discover here exactly what flourished in chalk; for example, maples from China and Europe did very well but those from Japan and the USA did not. Although the garden is rich in woody plants there are marvellous groups of herbaceous perennials and bulbs – agapanthus, anemones, hellebores, irises, narcissi and peonies – which provide floriferous underplanting.

HILEY NURSERY

Surrey

Illustration:
Bidens ferulifolia

25 Little Woodcote Estate,
Wallington SM5 4AU
Off Woodmansterne Lane
Tel: 0181 647 9679

Open: Wed to Sat 9–5

BRIAN HILEY specialises in rare perennials and tender plants and has an excellent eye for a good plant. Some groups are very deeply represented: he has a particularly good collection of penstemons – species and cultivars – and an exceptional list of sages, woody and herbaceous. But throughout his list there are rare and well-chosen things, not all of them herbaceous – felicias, the mysterious *Hieracium candidum*, a creeping loosestrife *Lysimachia henryi* and several kinds of phygelius and of polemonium. A catalogue is issued (three 1st-class stamps) and there is a mail order service but plants are often propagated in numbers too small to allow them to be listed. Brian Hiley's own 1-acre garden next door, stuffed with excellent plants, is open on Wednesday and Saturday and by appointment.

IDEN CROFT HERBS

Kent

Frittenden Road,
Staplehurst TN12 0DH
In Staplehurst village,
8m S of Maidstone by A229
Tel: 01580 891432
Fax: 01580 892416

Open: Feb to Sept, Mon to
Sat 9–5, Sun and Bank Hol
Mon 11–5; Oct to Jan, daily
except Sun 9–5

IDEN CROFT still sells a vast range of herbs but it also has an excellent ornamental garden. There are well-planted herbaceous beds, a garden specially designed for the blind, partially sighted or disabled – with sitting places and plenty to feel and smell – and an atmospheric walled garden. Iden Croft holds the National Collections of mint and origanums, and has large collections of lavender and thymes. Many other culinary herbs are sold, as well as a good selection of herbaceous perennials. There is a mail order service (plant list, four 1st-class stamps).

W. E. Th. INGWERSEN LTD

West Sussex

Birch Farm Nursery,
Gravetye, East Grinstead
RH19 4LE
2 1/2m SW of East
Grinstead by B2110 and
minor roads
Tel: 01342 810236

Open: Mar to Sept, daily
9–1, 1.30–4; Oct to Feb,
Mon to Fri 9–1, 1.30–4

ANYONE WHO has not heard of Ingwersen has probably not heard of alpine plants either. This famous family firm offers 1,800 different plants for sale, grown to exemplary standards and often rare. The elegantly produced list (50p stamps) has wonderful groups of alliums, campanulas, dianthus, primulas, dwarf rhododendrons, saxifrages and violas. Among the bulbs are excellent colchicums, crocuses, fritillaries, narcissi and species tulips. The nursery is on sacred ground, too, for this was formerly part of William Robinson's Gravetye estate.

KYOTO GARDEN

London

Holland Park W14
In the middle of Holland
Park, W of the centre of
London
Tube: Holland Park

Owner: The Royal Borough
of Kensington and Chelsea

Open: Daily 8–sunset.
1 acre

INTO THE sedate setting of Holland Park the Kyoto Garden made an exotic arrival in 1991. Designed by Japanese garden designers, it is of the type known as a 'tour garden', with all the ingredients one expects – a pool fed by a rocky cascade, stepping stones, Japanese maples, raked gravel, snow lanterns and an atmosphere pregnant with meaning even if one cannot unravel its significance. On its sloping site and backed by fine old trees, it is a welcome and exhilarating presence – a refreshing oddity in urban conservatism.

LEEDS CASTLE

Kent

nr Maidstone ME17 1PL
4m E of Maidstone by A20
and B2163; Jnct 8 of M20
Tel: 01622 765400
Fax: 01622 735616

Owner: Leeds Castle
Foundation

Open: Mar to Oct, daily
10–5; Nov to Feb, daily
10–3. 500 acres. Castle open

DISTANT VIEWS of Leeds Castle are enchanting – the wildly romantic silvery 12th-century castle, apparently afloat on its vast moat. The Culpeper Garden, designed by Russell Page, is a series of box-edged beds overflowing with herbaceous plants underplanted among shrub roses. Further from the castle a yew maze, designed by Randall Cote and Adrian Fisher, has an extraordinary grotto embellished by Diana Rennell and Simon Verity with statues, rare stones and shells, the cave-like gloom pierced from time to time by circular skylights.

LEONARDSLEE GARDENS

West Sussex

Lower Beeding,
nr Horsham RH13 6PP
4m SW of Handcross;
bottom of M23 by B2110
Tel: 01403 891212
Fax: 01403 891305

Owner: The Loder Family

Open: Apr to Oct, daily
10–6 (10–8 May).
200 acres

S IR EDMUND Loder bought the estate of Leonardslee in 1889 and started to make his great woodland garden. The spectacular site – a shallow valley with a series of linked lakes running along the bottom – makes a superb place to grow ornamental trees and shrubs. Rhododendrons were Sir Edmund's first love and he raised the hybrid R. 'Loderi' which has produced some of the best garden varieties. But there are also especially choice collections of camellias and magnolias, including some of the largest specimens in the country. Evergreens – wellingtonias, Douglas firs, deodars and spruce – make a fine background for the brilliant spring flowering and the explosion of autumn colour. An interesting 'green' technique practised here since 1889 is the use of wallabies as grass cutters.

LOSELEY GARDENS

Surrey

T O LOVERS of food Loseley means delicious Jersey ice-cream and to lovers of architecture the name signifies, in Pevsner's words, the 'finest house of its date in the county'. Long, gabled and imposing, it was built in the 1560s by Sir William More whose descendants still live there. Having mastered the art of ice-cream making they have now turned their attention to the garden. Since 1993 the walled former kitchen garden has been transformed into an ambitious formal

Loseley Park,
Guildford GU3 1HS
3m SW of Guildford by A3
(Compton and Puttenham
exit) and B3000
Tel: 01483 304440
Fax: 01483 302036

Owner: Mr and Mrs
Michael More-Molyneux

Open: 4 May to 26 Sept,
Wed to Sat 11–5. 6 1/2 acres

layout. A very large collection of old shrub roses is disposed in box-edged beds – beautiful and superbly scented in season, though some herbaceous underplanting, *à la* Mottisfont Abbey, would greatly extend the interest; flowerless rose bushes are very dull. A garden of useful plants is planted in triangular beds edged with ropework tiles and, to one side, a fortissimo ornamental garden has brilliant colours – *Crocosmia* 'Lucifer', *Helenium* 'Moerheim Beauty', *Hemerocallis* 'Stafford' – and demure walks of tall 'Golden Hornet' crab-apples. To the east a Fountain Garden was being made when I visited in July 1997. Further delights are planned and the whole place is being transformed with great brio.

MERRIMENTS GARDENS

East Sussex

Hawkhurst Road,
Hurst Green TN19 7RA
12m SE of Tunbridge Wells
by A21
Tel: 01580 860666

Open: Daily 10–5.30

THIS FAMILY nursery was started in 1988 and a splendid 4-acre garden alongside was subsequently added to display its wares and is a marvellous addition. The nursery carries a general stock of shrubs, trees and climbers but of special interest to gardeners is the wide range of herbaceous perennials: named cultivars of dianthus, euphorbias, geraniums, excellent lobelias, penstemons, poppies, sages and violas. These are very well chosen and, in addition, there is a choice selection of ferns and grasses. An exceptionally good range of pots and ornaments is carried. A useful catalogue is published (£1.50) but there is no mail order. The well planned and richly

Illustration opposite:
Northbourne Court

planted garden – which covers an area of 4 acres – is worth visiting in its own right, and forms an attractive display ground for the wide range of plants that the nursery sells.

MUSEUM OF GARDEN HISTORY

London

Lambeth Palace Road
SE1 7LB
Immediately S of Lambeth
Bridge
Tube: Victoria or Waterloo
Tel: 0171 261 1891
Fax: 0171 401 8869

Owner:
The Tradescant Trust

Open: Mon to Fri 10.30–4,
Sun 10.30–5

JOHN TRADESCANT, father and son, immensely influential gardeners and collectors of exotic plants in the 17th century, lived and died in Lambeth. They are buried in the churchyard here, in a magnificent tomb. In the disused church an excellent museum of garden history has been formed, containing a permanent collection including a small gallery devoted to Gertrude Jekyll, and presenting temporary exhibitions, courses and lectures. In the churchyard a charming 17th-century garden has been made, with a knot of box hedges designed by the Marchioness of Salisbury with plants of a Tradescantian flavour.

NORTHBOURNE COURT

Kent

HISTORIC GARDENS that yield their secrets only to the cognoscenti are pretty boring to most garden visitors. The great early 17th-century terraces at Northbourne Court, however, make an immediate and delightful impression. They were built by Sir Edwin

Northbourne,
Deal CT14 0LW
In Northbourne village
near the church, 2m W of
Deal,
Tel: 01304 611281
Fax: 01304 614512

Owner:
The Hon. Charles James

Open: Jun to Aug, Sun 2–5.
2 acres

Sandys to be seen from his mansion, which was destroyed by fire in 1750. The terraces and fine brick garden walls survive, and there is much lively recent planting, some of it carefully planned to take advantage of sharp drainage and a southern exposure. An avenue of peonies ornaments the kitchen garden where there is a virtuoso arrangement of purple cotinus, purple sage and purple-headed artichokes, and everywhere there are old roses. This is not a place for great rarities – the irresistible character of the ancient garden layout is the rare pleasure here.

NYMANS GARDEN

West Sussex

Handcross, nr Haywards
Heath RH17 6EB
7m NW of Haywards
Heath by A272 and B2114
Tel: 01444 400321/400777

Owner: The National Trust

Open: Mar to 1 Nov, daily
except Mon and Tue (open
Bank Hol Mon) 11–6 or
sunset if earlier (Jun and
Jul 11–9). 30 acres

THERE ARE few gardens anywhere in England where rare and beautiful plants are grown in such an attractive setting, in which formality and informality are subtly interwoven. Nymans was acquired by Leonard Messel in 1890 when he began introducing a wide range of plants. He made a woodland garden in which magnificent trees and flowering shrubs – particularly camellias, eucryphias, magnolias and rhododendrons – are seen to great advantage. One of the best hybrid eucryphias, *E.* × *nymansensis*, had its origins here. In an irregularly shaped walled garden Messel laid out a pair of spectacular herbaceous borders, whose design was influenced by William Robinson. These are wonderful today, and in late summer their flowering season is prolonged by the subtle use of annuals. Surrounding the borders are choice ornamental trees such as dogwoods, *Koelreuteria paniculata* and styrax. There is much topiary of yew and box – geometric shapes and plump birds – and romantic ruins. Huge numbers of trees were lost in the great storm of October 1987 but the rose garden containing many old roses – in whose use Mrs Messel was a pioneer – has been restored and the pinetum replanted.

OSTERLEY PARK
Middlesex

Isleworth TW7 4RB
5m W of Central London
by A4
Tube: Osterley
Tel and Fax: 0181 560 3918

Owner: The National Trust

Open: Daily 9–7.30 or
sunset if earlier. 140 acres.
House open

THE PARK at Osterley survives only in part, but there are some good remaining garden buildings and some marvellous trees decorate the landscape. Block your ears to the roar of the Great West Road and something of the Elysian atmosphere of the past can be brought to life. The late Elizabethan mansion was rebuilt after 1761 by Robert Adam, who also designed the semi-circular conservatory against the old kitchen garden wall. A series of lakes to the south and east of the house glitter among splendid trees – old cedars of Lebanon, oaks, limes and London planes. The lake nearest the house has an octagonal Chinese pavilion on an island. The pleasure gardens have been undergoing their long-awaited restoration which is beginning to show its paces.

PAINSHILL PARK
Surrey

Portsmouth Road,
Cobham KT11 1JE
1m W of Cobham by A245;
Jnct 10 of M25
Tel: 01932 868113
Fax: 01932 868001

Owner: Painshill Park Trust

Open: Apr to Oct, daily
except Mon (open Bank
Hol Mon) 10.30–6; Nov to
Mar 1999, daily except
Mon and Fri (open Bank
Hol Mon) 11–4. 158 acres

THIS EXTRAORDINARY landscape garden is being restored by a private trust – one of the most worthwhile of all recent garden restorations. The garden was made by the Hon. Charles Hamilton between 1738 and 1773, when he ran out of money. It is a splendidly idiosyncratic pioneer in the large-scale creation of ornamental landscape. At the heart of the garden a long curvaceous lake with islands is overlooked by decorative buildings – an airy ten-sided Gothic pavilion, a fake ruined abbey and a ruined Roman arch. One of the islands has the remains of a dazzling grotto and is linked to the mainland by an

elegant Chinese bridge. Paths wind through woods and across meadows about the shores of the lake. In the westernmost part of the park a huge water wheel is revealed, and on the wooded slopes high above, a castellated gothic tower commands immense views horribly blemished by electricity pylons. The vineyard below the gothic temple has recently been replanted and the enchanting Turkish tent, high on its hill, is once more in place. Everywhere the landscape composes itself into delicious views and the place has an unforgettable exhilaration.

PANTILES PLANT CENTRE

Surrey

Almners Road, Lyne,
Chertsey KT16 0BJ
1 1/2m W of Chertsey; Jnct
11 of M25
Tel: 01932 872195
Fax: 01932 874030

Open: Daily 9–5.30 (Sun
9–5)

MANY PEOPLE willingly spend thousands of pounds on a new kitchen but might never think of buying expensive large trees or shrubs which will give instant character to a new garden. At Pantiles there is a wide selection of woody plants in whopping sizes: a 20ft-high *Magnolia grandiflora* 'Galissonière' (not the commonest tree in the world) will cost £3,000 but it will last your lifetime, getting lovelier all the time, which is more than you can say of a new kitchen. A new line of Tasmanian tree ferns, *Dicksonia antarctica*, which will stand up to −13°C in their native habitat, will make this lovely plant available to a much wider range of gardeners. A catalogue is produced, and delivery and planting – a tricky business with a very large tree – can be arranged by the nursery.

PARHAM HOUSE

West Sussex

Pulborough RH20 4HS
4m S of Pulborough by
A283
Tel: 01903 744888
Fax: 01903 746557

Owner: Parham Park Trust

Open: Easter Sun to first
Sun in Oct, Sun, Wed, Thur
and Bank Hol Mon 12–6.
11 acres. House open

PARHAM, a grand Elizabethan house, is splendidly situated in an atmospheric old deer-park dotted with ancient oaks. The chief ornamental part of the garden lies in the walled former kitchen garden, divided by gravel paths. Here are some very effective herbaceous borders with carefully controlled colour schemes: a pair of blue borders enlivened with dashes of magenta *Lychnis coronaria*, pink diascias and purple penstemons; a gold border, given structure by repeated plantings of yellow potentilla, golden elder and juniper, yellow loosestrife and achilleas; and a long border, facing west, of hot, bright colours. It is very much a working kitchen garden, providing cut flowers, fruit and vegetables for the house. To the west, a lake is overlooked by a pavilion with, to one side, a fiendish maze with infuriatingly complicated rules.

PASHLEY MANOR

East Sussex

nr Ticehurst TN5 7HE
1 1/2m SE of Ticehurst by
B2099
Tel: 01580 200692
Fax: 01580 200102

Owner: Mr and Mrs James
A. Sellick

Open: mid Apr to Sept,
Tue, Wed, Thur and Sat
and Bank Hol Mon 11–5.
8 acres

THE APPROACH to Pashley Manor lies through beautiful parkland and the house, mid 16th-century half-timbered on one facade and early Georgian on another, sits well in its setting. The gardens have recently been revived with the help of the garden designer Anthony du Gard Pasley who has contrived elegant formal plantings near the house, with carefully judged colour associations, and a wilder garden of woodland character behind it. The kitchen garden has recently been redesigned, many old roses added, and improvements have been made to the waterside planting in the wild garden. All this is impeccably well maintained. The Sellicks have by no means completed their ambitious garden schemes and this will be a place to watch keenly in the future.

PENSHURST PLACE

Kent

Penshurst,
nr Tonbridge TN11 8DG
In Penshurst village, 5m W
of Tonbridge by B2176
Tel: 01892 870307
Fax: 01892 870866

Owner: The Rt Hon
Viscount De L'Isle

Open: 28 Feb to 27 Mar, Sat
and Sun 11–6; 28 Mar to 1
Nov, daily 11–6. 10 acres.
House open

THE SIDNEY family have been here since the 16th century but the house is much older and magnificently dominates the huge walled gardens with their lovely Tudor bricks that surround it. Although the planting is modern in this enclosure, the present pattern of beds, pools and walks closely resembles that shown in Kip's engraving of around 1700. Very few gardens preserve their essential layout from such an early date as this. The entrance leads past a border planted as a dazzling Union Jack, with the colours picked out in spring and summer bedding. Beyond it all sorts of ornamental schemes spread out: a charming orchard of apples and Kentish cobs; a garden of magnolias and golden Irish yews; a pair of herbaceous borders; a rose garden; a spring garden; and a pair of handsome borders designed by Lanning Roper and now being revamped.

PERRYHILL NURSERIES

East Sussex

Illustration:
Rosa 'Gertrude Jekyll'

Hartfield TN7 4JP
1m N of Hartfield, 8m W
of Tunbridge Wells by A264
and B2026
Tel: 01892 770377
Fax: 01892 770929

Open: Daily 9–5 (in winter
9–4.30)

A MARVELLOUS GARDEN could be made, using Perryhill as your only source of plants. It has well chosen representatives of the most valuable ornamental plants, both woody and herbaceous, and there is a small selection of fruit. With some plants, such as roses, there is an exceptional choice of the best kinds. Apart from that there is no attempt to specialise and in most groups you will find things not seen in the average garden centre. A useful catalogue is produced (£1.65), but there is no mail order.

PETWORTH HOUSE

West Sussex

Petworth GU28 0AE
In Petworth village
Tel: 01798 342207/343929
Fax: 01798 342963

Owner: The National Trust

Open: Pleasure grounds:
28 Mar to 1 Nov daily
except Thur and Fri (open
Good Fri) 12–6 (Jul and
Aug Bank Hol Mon 11–6).
Park: Daily 8–sunset (26 to
28 Jun 8–12). 700 acres.
House open

PETWORTH HAS an ancient gardening history: Elizabethan gardens here had a fountain and roses, and in the late 17th century formal gardens were made for the newly-built house. Today the park is the thing at Petworth, and is best appreciated by taking a long walk in it (for this, go to the Park, rather than to the House, car park). It was laid out from 1752 for the 2nd Earl of Egremont by 'Capability' Brown and is one of the best of all his surviving landscapes. It is big enough to reduce the mansion, seen from a distance framed in trees, to the stature of a garden ornament. Brown placed a Doric temple north of the house and an Ionic rotunda beyond it on a rise. Marvellous oaks, limes, sweet chestnuts and planes survive from Brown's time.

POLESDEN LACEY

Surrey

THE DAPPER early 19th-century house was owned by the great Edwardian political hostess, the Hon. Mrs Ronald Greville, and the garden has much of the blowsy charm of the age. A beech avenue leads up the hill and wonderful views of the valley are revealed from the house at the top. Beyond the house a very large formal rose garden, with such distinctive

nr Dorking RH5 6BD
5m NW of Dorking by
A246
Tel: 01372 458203/452048

Owner: The National Trust

Open: Daily 11–6 or sunset
if earlier. 30 acres. House
open

Edwardian varieties as 'Dorothy Perkins' and 'American Pillar', has at its centre a white marble well-head. South of the rose garden is a magnificent herbaceous border, backed by a wall festooned with climbing plants, which is an object lesson in bold but disciplined planting.

PORT LYMPNE GARDENS

Kent

Lympne, Hythe CT21 4PD
3m W of Hythe by A20 and
B2067; Jnct 11 of M20
Tel: 01303 264647
Fax: 01303 264944

Owner: John Aspinall

Open: Daily 10–5 or one
hour before dusk in winter.
15 acres

HIGH ABOVE Romney Marsh the gabled brick house was built by Sir Philip Sassoon to designs by Sir Herbert Baker before World War I, and completed after the war by Philip Tilden who, in collaboration with his patron, laid out the garden. Sassoon died in 1939 and subsequently the place deteriorated until John Aspinall bought it in 1973 and commissioned a complete restoration with advice from Russell Page. The garden is formal in spirit and decorative in execution, making full use of the lovely position. Compartments are hedged in yew or Leyland cypress and the chessboard garden and the striped garden present dazzling geometric patterns in bedding schemes. Beautiful herbaceous borders, a fig garden, vineyard, and terraces of roses and dahlias decorate the slopes. Within its carefully designed architectural setting the garden at Port Lympne has a brilliantly festive air.

POTS AND PITHOI

West Sussex

The Barns, East Street,
Turners Hill RH10 4QQ
E of Turners Hill on B2110,
5m E of Crawley by A264
and B2028
Tel: 01342 714793

Open: Daily 10–5 (in winter
10–4; closed 24 Dec–2 Jan
and Sat and Sun in Jan)

MOST GARDEN pots are mass-produced to fairly
commonplace designs but Pots and Pithoi sell a
unique range of hand-made Cretan pots in many
different designs and sizes. They are fired at a very
high temperature and are therefore resistant to frost.
The great attraction is their beautiful patina and the
liveliness of their design and decoration, with patterns
that are either incised or applied in delicate ribbons of
clay. These are the kind of pots that, without being in
the slightest pretentious, have tremendous garden
presence. There is a good catalogue and delivery can
be arranged. But a visit is really essential to appreciate
these rare pots.

G. REUTHE LTD

Kent

Crown Point Nursery,
Sevenoaks Road, Ightham,
nr Sevenoaks TN15 0HB
4m E of Sevenoaks by A25
Tel: 01732 810694
Fax: 01732 862166

Open: Mon to Sat
9.30–4.30

REUTHE IS famous for rhododendrons. Here is an
exceptionally wide range of species and hybrids
and a choice collection of evergreen and deciduous
azaleas – the catalogue runs to well over 30 pages of
them. The nursery sells other things, particularly
woody plants, but its real distinction lies in its
rhododendrons. It is essential to buy the informative
list (£1.50); mail order is available. The nursery is now
part of Starborough nursery (see page 55) to which all
correspondence should be sent.

THE ROOF GARDENS
London

99 Kensington High Street,
W8 5ED
Central London
Tube: High Street,
Kensington
Tel: 0171 937 7994
Fax: 0171 938 2774

Open: Daily 9–5 but
telephone beforehand as
sometimes closed for private
functions. 1 1/2 acres

THESE ARE the largest roof gardens open to the public in London. On the top of the old Derry & Toms department store, they are one of the most unexpected horticultural sights that the capital has to offer. This extraordinary place, complete with pink flamingoes, is delightful. It has well tended borders with substantial shrubs, secluded sitting places, thoughtfully planted pots, attractive paths of old York stone and herring-bone laid brick and a knock-out Moorish extravaganza with more than a whiff of the Alhambra – old coloured tiles, a scalloped canal with fountains and palm trees.

ROYAL BOTANIC GARDENS, KEW
Surrey

Kew, Richmond TW9 3AB
7m SW of Central London.
Tube: Kew Gardens
Tel: 0181 940 1171
Fax: 0181 332 5610

Owner: Trustees of the
Royal Botanic Gardens

Open: Daily 9.30–4
(9.30–6.30 summer
weekdays; Sun and Bank
Hol Mon in high summer
9.30–7.30). 300 acres

IT IS not the purpose of the Royal Botanic Gardens to be interesting to gardeners but this, despite itself, it effortlessly is. The landscape park with its great Chinoiserie pagoda (designed by Sir William Chambers in 1761) and many specimen trees going back to the 18th century is exquisite; its setting on the Thames wonderful. Most of the plants are wild species rather than garden varieties but it is a perfect place to come on any day of the year and discover new plants, impeccably labelled and well grown. The various glasshouses are immensely rich in non-hardy plants: the palm house designed by Richard Turner and

Decimus Burton; the Temperate House; and the Princess of Wales Conservatory with tender plants of different climates arranged in naturalistic settings. Among the hardy plants there are several reference collections of great interest to gardeners – they include heathers, bulbs, bamboos, grasses and several others. A new glasshouse showing the evolution of plants has recently opened. The atmosphere at Kew is livelier than it has been for many years and it is now one of the most attractive places in the country for gardeners to visit.

THE SAVILL AND VALLEY GARDENS

Surrey

Wick Lane, Englefield Green, near Egham SL4 2HT 3m W of Egham by A30 and Wick Road
Tel: 01753 860222
Fax: 01753 859617

Owner: Crown Property

Open: Savill Garden: daily 10–6 (winter10–4; closed 25–26 Dec). 35 acres. *Valley Garden:* daily, sunrise–sunset. 400 acres

SOME GARDENS set a fashion and affect the future style of gardening. The Savill Garden has had a strong influence on the tradition of woodland gardening. It was started in 1932 by E.H. (later Sir Eric) Savill who was Deputy Ranger of Windsor Great Park. He invented a natural style of woodland gardening which gave the plants appropriate habitats and made something that was beautiful. The well-watered site with many old trees – especially marvellous beeches and oaks – was an excellent place for such a garden. He planted large numbers of ornamental trees and shrubs – azaleas, camellias, dogwoods, magnolias, rhododendrons – and about the streams moisture-loving plants such as ferns, lysichitons, primulas and rheums. In addition to this there are fine formal gardens – herbaceous borders, a dry garden and rose gardens – which are maintained to rare old-fashioned standards. In 1947 Sir Eric turned his attention to the nearby Valley Garden, on a wonderful undulating site on the north bank of Virginia Water. Here the planting is of a similar style but, on a much larger site, the variety is much greater. You will find here several magnificent National Collections of plants, of great interest to gardeners – dwarf conifers, hollies, magnolias (no less than 34 species and 242 cultivars), mahonias, pernettyas, pieris and species rhododrons (over 500).

SCOTNEY CASTLE

Kent

Lamberhurst, Tunbridge Wells TN3 8JN
1m S of Lamberhurst by A21
Tel: 01892 890651

Owner: The National Trust

Open: Apr to 1 Nov, Wed to Fri 11–6 or sunset if earlier (closed Good Fri), Sat and Sun 2–6 or sunset if earlier, Bank Hol Mon 12–6 or sunset if earlier. 19 acres

THE GARDENS at Scotney Castle are a piece of irresistibly romantic picturesque landscape gardening made in the middle of the 19th century by Edward Hussey, with advice from William Sawrey Gilpin. At the same time Hussey built a new house high on a hill, benefitting from wonderful views down towards the moated medieval castle which became an exotic eyecatcher for his landscaping schemes. Walks descend the precipitous and rocky hill, with superb trees and shrubs; the flowers of azaleas, rhododendrons, and the new foliage of maples, are dazzling in spring. In the castle forecourt there is a pretty herb garden designed by Lanning Roper and, nearby on an island, a bronze by Henry Moore seems strangely at home in the wild planting.

SCULPTURE AT GOODWOOD

West Sussex

Goodwood,
Chichester PO18 0QP
E of Goodwood House,
1/2m NE of Chichester by
A27 and minor roads,
Tel: 01243 771114 (recorded
directions); 01243 538449
(enquiries)
Fax: 01243 531853

Owner:
Wilfred and Jeannette Cass

Open: Mar to Nov, Thur,
Fri and Sat 10.30–4.30.
20 acres

ONCE YOU have run the gauntlet of the remote-controlled security gate and whacking £10 admission charge you will find yourself in an enchanted world. Disposed in youthful woodland is a marvellous display of contemporary British sculpture, most of which is for sale – ranging in price from a few thousand pounds to almost a million pounds. The artists range from Grand Old Men (such as Sir Anthony Caro) to the young, or youngish, Turks of the day such as Bill Woodrow and Andy Goldsworthy. Apart from the frequent intrinsic beauty of the exhibits there is much to admire in their placing in the woodland. Some are glimpsed vaguely in glades, some form eyecatchers or embrace paths and others, most beautifully of all, are positioned in clearings at the very edge of the woodland, drawing the eye to the lovely rural landscape beyond. Some of the works are created in situ, giving them a special relevance to their context. If you are fairly rich, and in the market for a marvellous piece of sculpture to animate your garden, this is a lovely place to clinch a deal.

SHEFFIELD PARK

East Sussex

Uckfield TN22 3QX
Midway between East
Grinstead and Lewes off
A275
Tel: 01825 790655

Owner: The National Trust

Open: Mar, Sat and Sun
11–6; Apr to 15 Nov, Tue to
Sun and Bank Hol Mon
11–6 or sunset if earlier; 18
Nov to 20 Dec, Wed to Sun
11–4. 100 acres.

THERE IS something dream-like about Sheffield Park. Both 'Capability' Brown and Humphry Repton had a hand in the design but the present appearance of the gardens is due chiefly to Arthur Soames who bought the estate in 1905. James Wyatt's gothic palace of 1775–8 sits on an eminence at the head of a broad valley, with a series of four descending lakes extending far into the distance. On the banks trees and shrubs are arranged in bold groups with subtle contrasts, conifers and deciduous trees artfully mingled. The hinterland surrounding the lakes is laced with paths and full of marvellous trees and shrubs, with the occasional dazzling piece of herbaceous planting, such as a path fringed with gentians. The garden is exquisitely laid out and a slow walk at any time during the long opening season offers some of the most beautiful garden scenes the visitor may ever see.

SISSINGHURST CASTLE GARDEN

Kent

THE HISTORY of this garden is quickly told – it was made by Vita Sackville-West and Harold Nicolson from 1930 onwards, and became the most admired English garden of its time. Few great gardens live up to their reputation so effortlessly as this one. Whatever superlatives have been heaped on it, Sissinghurst never disappoints and each visit will reveal new pleasures.

Illustration opposite:
Sissinghurst Castle Garden

Sissinghurst,
nr Cranbrook TN17 2AB
2m NE of Cranbrook off
A262
Tel: 01580 712850

Owner: The National Trust

Open: Apr to 15 Oct, Tue
to Fri 1–6.30, Sat, Sun and
Good Fri 10–5.30 (NOTE:
Timed entry system means
visitors may sometimes have
to wait). 10 acres. House
open

The National Trust was fortunate to inherit two
brilliant gardeners, Pamela Schwerdt and Sibylle
Kreutzberger, who had worked with Vita Sackville-
West before her death in 1963. They maintained the
garden to perfectionist standards until their retirement
and their successor, Sarah Cook, seems every bit as
good. Within the disciplined enclosures of old brick
walls, cool hedges of yew and linking paths and vistas,
here is a profusion of fastidiously chosen plants in
which an immense collection of old roses provides a
recurring theme. One of the many refreshing things
about Sissinghurst is the way in which virtuoso
changes in mood are effortlessly achieved – from the
hot oranges and reds of the Cottage Garden, for
example, to the austere yew alley that separates the
formal gardens from the orchard. Despite Vita
Sackville-West's aristocratic spirit, it would be quite
wrong to think of Sissinghurst as something far from
the interests of everyday gardeners. In terms of
practical gardening – the pruning, training and feeding
of plants, for example – the highest standards were
maintained, and are still a delight to observe. Certainly
Sissinghurst has the power to enchant but it is also an
unending source of practical inspiration for gardeners
of every kind. Sissinghurst has become a garden icon,
but it is still buzzing with life.

STANDEN

West Sussex

East Grinstead RH19 4NE
2m S of East Grinstead off
B2110
Tel: 01342 323029

Owner: The National Trust

Open: 25 Mar to 1 Nov,
Wed to Sun and Bank Hol
Mon 12.30–6. 10 acres.
House open

STANDEN HAS a memorable position, high on an
eminence with views across the Medway Valley to
Crowborough Beacon. Below the house, which was
designed by Philip Webb, the land falls away on south-
facing slopes. An enclosed formal garden is hedged in
beech and yew and has square beds edged in catmint
with an Irish juniper at each corner and a crab apple at
each centre, surrounded by rugosa roses. The rest of
the garden consists of terraced lawns and paths that
amble through groups of shrubs and trees – azaleas
and rhododendrons with maples rising above. The
quarry garden above the house displays a fine
collection of ferns. A wonderful tulip tree and a very
large Scots pine at the foot of a sloping lawn frame
distant views of cornfields surrounded by woodland –
a marvellous scene.

STARBOROUGH NURSERY

Kent

Illustration: Styrax japonica

Marsh Green,
Edenbridge TN8 5RB
Tel: 01732 865614
Fax: 01732 862166

Open: Daily except Sun
10–4 (closed Jan and Jul)

Sᴛᴀʀʙᴏʀᴏᴜɢʜ ꜱᴘᴇᴄɪᴀʟɪꜱᴇꜱ in acid-loving woody plants – many of them rarely seen in nurseries. There are good selections of acers, camellias, daphnes, magnolias, pieris, rhododendrons, stewartias, styrax, viburnums and a choice selection of climbing plants; among all these are many rare and lovely things. A catalogue is published (£1.50) and mail orders are fulfilled. The nursery is in the same ownership as G. Reuthe (see page 47).

SYON PARK AND GARDENS

Middlesex

Brentford TW8 8JF
On the N bank of the
Thames between Brentford
and Isleworth
Tel: 0181 560 0881
Fax: 0181 568 0936

Owner: The Duke of
Northumberland

Open: Mar to Oct, daily
10–6; Nov to Feb, daily
10–dusk (closed 25–26
Dec). 30 acres. House open

Iᴛ ɪꜱ surprising to find a complete great country estate so near to the centre of London. It has been owned by the Percy family, later Dukes of Northumberland, since 1594 and the approach to the house runs through classic ancient parkland. The house, with grand rooms by Robert Adam, faces a wide avenue of limes. The chief pleasure gardens lie to one side of the house and are dominated by one of the finest conservatories you will see anywhere, built by Charles Fowler in 1827 in beautiful golden Bath stone. There is an excellent collection of trees – acacias, catalpas, holm oaks and sweet chestnuts, and rarer things such as sweet buckeye (*Aesculus flava*). A long narrow lake is edged with trees including some good swamp cypresses. A very large garden centre has a good stock in all departments and a fine selection of garden pots.

TILE BARN NURSERY

Kent

Illustration:
Cyclamen repandum

Standen Street, Iden Green,
Benenden TN17 4LB
In hamlet of Standen Street,
1/2m S of Benenden
Tel: 01580 240221

Open: Wed to Sat 9–5

THIS IS the kind of nursery that makes converts of even the most unyielding. It specialises in cyclamen and stocks all the most garden-worthy species and varieties of these charmingly seductive plants, several of which are very hard to come by. An excellent list is produced (s.a.e.) giving valuable information on their cultivation – indeed it constitutes a perfect guide to the subject. Plants are sold by mail order but visitors are welcomed and a few additional bulbous plants are available to callers only.

WAKEHURST PLACE GARDEN

West Sussex

nr Ardingly, Haywards
Heath RH17 6TN
1 1/2m NW of Ardingly on
B2028
Tel: 01444 892701

Owner: The National Trust

Open: Daily except 25 Dec
and 1 Jan, Nov to Jan 10–4;
Feb and Oct 10–5; Mar
10–6; Apr to Sept 10–7.
170 acres

ALTHOUGH THERE is an attractively planted walled garden and some good borders (albeit with a botanical slant – one is devoted to monocotyledons) Wakehurst Place is really about trees and shrubs. It is the country department of the Royal Botanic Garden at Kew and it is full of wonderful things. By the house the site is relatively flat and the house looks out onto pools and a water garden fringed with maples and moisture-loving plants. Further away the ground sweeps down into the Himalayan Glade and the precipitous ravine of Westwood Valley and its lake, and beyond that, to more woodland. There are wonderful collections of azaleas, magnolias and rhododendrons in the Himalayan Glade and the Westwood Valley and particularly fine groups of conifers in the Pinetum. The lie of the land adds immensely to the beauty of the trees and this is a wonderful place in which to spend a few hours walking, looking and learning.

WASHFIELD NURSERY

Kent

Illustration:
Helleborus orientalis

Hawkhurst TN18 4QU
1m SW of Hawkhurst by
A229
Tel: 01580 752522

Open: Wed to Sat 10–5

WONDERFUL HERBACEOUS perennials are the strongest point of this exceptional nursery. The presiding genius behind it, Elizabeth Strangman, is an authority on hellebores and has bred some exquisite hybrids of *Helleborus orientalis* in which she aims for 'purity of colour and full rounded flower'. Here are other great treasures – epimediums, hardy geraniums, kniphofias, pulmonarias – all chosen among the very best species and cultivars. Some of these are from seed collected in the wild by the nursery's botanist friends, and thus true, unadulterated forms. A good catalogue is produced (s.a.e. and four 1st-class stamps) but there is no mail order.

WEALD AND DOWNLAND OPEN AIR MUSEUM

West Sussex

THIS IRRESISTIBLE place, which could so easily have teetered over into Disneyfication, is a model of how the past may be brought vividly to life. It is a collection of historic rural buildings, from the Middle Ages to the 19th century, from the Weald and Downland areas of southern England, moved to a beautiful site and disposed in a convincingly realistic manner. Of special interest to gardeners are those whose gardens have been recreated. The 15th-century Bayleaf Farmhouse has a little garden fenced in wattle

Singleton, Chichester
PO18 0EU
6 1/2m N of Chichester by
A286
Tel: 01243 811348
Fax: 01243 811475

Owner: Weald and
Downland Open Air
Museum

Open: Mar to Oct, daily
10.30–6; Nov to Feb, Wed,
Sat and Sun 10.30–4 (also
open in Christmas Holidays
Dec 26 to 4 Jan, daily
10.30–4). 60 acres

Illustration opposite:
Bayleaf Farmhouse

with primarily culinary or medicinal plants, and a few ornamentals, disposed in rectangular beds. This seems convincingly authentic and certainly very pretty, but not all the plants are of the period; *Catananche caerulea* is unknown before the end of the 16th century and it is hard to imagine a Wealden yeoman munching 'Lollo Rosso' lettuce. Walderton House, of the 17th century, has pale fencing, an orchard, and a pattern of rectangular beds filled with vegetables and herbs. The garden of the 19th-century Toll Cottage skilfully evokes a cottage garden of that period with brick path, picket fence and beds of vegetables dotted with hollyhocks, bachelor's buttons, lavender and roses. As you raise your head from the entrancing buildings and gardens to admire the beautiful natural setting you see that this, too, is threatened – a line of electricity pylons marches purposefully across the land, bringing you sharply back to the 20th-century.

WEST DEAN GARDENS

West Sussex

West Dean,
Chichester PO18 0Q2
6m N of Chichester by
A286
Tel: 01243 818210
Fax: 01243 811342

Owner: The Edward James
Foundation

Open: Mar to Oct, daily
11–5. 90 acres

THE FLINT and stone early 19th-century gothic house by James Wyatt belonged to Edward James, patron of surrealism, though the only surrealistic touch in his garden is a curious fibreglass truncated beech tree. The garden is set in a beautiful valley and at its heart is an immense pergola designed by Harold Peto, draped in clematis, roses and wisteria and underplanted with agapanthus, daylilies, ferns, geraniums and lamium. This, and the fine beds on its southern side, have recently been superbly restored and replanted. Marking one end of it is a pretty gothic flint summerhouse, its floor curiously paved with horse's teeth, and at the other end a sunken garden with a pool, ornamental grasses, a sea of *Alchemilla mollis*, ferns and roses. The magnificent walled kitchen garden, with Edwardian glasshouses, has been brilliantly restored – the glasshouses brim with melons, tender foliage plants and all the exotic produce of the Edwardian age. Beyond the garden, handsome parkland with fine old trees, especially conifers, in St Roche's Arboretum, spreads across folds in the South Downs – of which there are fine views from the circuit walk. Always interesting, West Dean, with dynamic new gardeners has become outstanding.

WISLEY GARDEN

Surrey

nr Ripley,
Woking GU23 6QB
6m NE of Guildford by A3;
S of Jnct 10 of the M25
Tel: 01483 224234
Fax: 01483 211750

Owner: The Royal
Horticultural Society

Open: Daily 10–7 (Suns for
RHS members only).
250 acres

WISLEY IS where the Royal Horticultural Society shows the gardening public how it should be done. Here are the highest standards of practical horticulture deployed over an immense range of different kinds of gardening, in the setting of a splendid old site rich in fine trees and a very large number of other plants, all impeccably labelled. There is a pinetum, an alpine house, a vast and beautifully kept rock garden, trial grounds of various kinds and practical display areas. A huge shop contains the largest selection of new gardening books in Britain (a valuable mail order service is provided for books), and a large plant centre sells plants of high quality, many unusual, but there is no catalogue and no mail order. Changes are afoot in the garden, with a master plan devised by the landscape architect Hal Moggridge who is imposing gentle but firm harmony on earlier muddle. In addition, many of the best garden designers are making new contributions, including Penelope Hobhouse whose 'Country Garden' should be finished in 1999.

YALDING ORGANIC GARDENS

Kent

Benover Road, Yalding,
nr Maidstone ME18 6EX
5m SW of Maidstone on
B2010
Tel and Fax: 01622 814650

Owner: Henry Doubleday
Research Association

Open: May to Sept, Wed to
Sun and Bank Hol Mon
10–5; Oct, Sat and Sun
10–5. 10 acres

NOTHING HELPS the organic gardening movement so effectively as a good display garden. The Henry Doubleday Association, which also owns the garden at Ryton in the Midlands (see page 206), has now expanded in the south-east with this ambitious new place. A series of recreated historic gardens shows the distinctive styles of gardening of their time: from medieval plots to such characteristically 20th-century types as the organic allotment, the wildlife garden and a garden planned to withstand drought. There is much lively ornamental planting here and skilful design – and the vigorously growing plants are a tribute to organic techniques. Yalding is a garden of ideas, and the philosophy behind it is that of the responsible stewardship of resources and respect for ecology. Many gardeners have been won over to organic methods and Yalding will make more converts.

SOUTH-CENTRAL ENGLAND

Berkshire
Buckinghamshire
Hampshire
Oxfordshire
Wiltshire

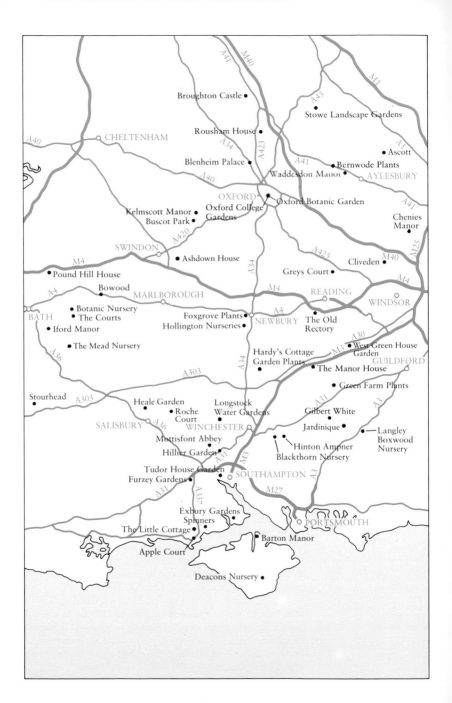

APPLE COURT

Hampshire

Hordle Lane,
Lymington SO41 0HU
3 1/2m W of Lymington by
A337
Tel: 01590 642130
Fax: 01590 644220

Open: Feb to Oct, daily
except Tue and Wed 9.30–1,
2–5; Jul to Aug, also open
Tue and Wed

THIS VERY attractive nursery and garden have some outstandingly good plants – hostas (over 80 varieties), American daylilies, ferns and ornamental grasses. In the charming, fairly recently made garden that forms part of the nursery many different examples of the nursery's specialities may be seen performing, including hostas, finely displayed in a shady walk. A catalogue is produced (four 1st-class stamps) and a mail order service is provided but a visit to the garden where so many of the plants sold are displayed so handsomely and imaginatively is particularly worthwhile.

ASCOTT

Buckinghamshire

Wing, nr Leighton Buzzard
LU7 0PS
2m SW of Leighton
Buzzard by A418
Tel: 01296 688242
Fax: 01296 681904

Owner: The National Trust

Open: Apr to 7 May and 1
to 30 Sept, daily except
Mon 2–6 ; 13 May to 30
Aug, Wed and last Sun in
each month 2–6.
39 acres. House open

THIS IS a rare garden, in which the distinctive late Victorian character is cherished and made into something special. The house was a hunting box on the Rothschilds' Mentmore estate, and the gardens were made at the end of the 19th century. Behind the house, lawns are terraced gently down towards a long double herbaceous border hedged with variegated holly and golden yew. From the middle of these borders a path leads to rose beds and a splashing fountain of Venus designed by Thomas Waldo Story. To the east there are great topiary pieces in golden and common yew and a unique topiary sundial. From the terraces marvellous views of the Vale of Aylesbury are seen in the distance.

ASHDOWN HOUSE

Oxfordshire

Lambourn,
Newbury RG16 7RE
3 1/2m N of Lambourn by
B4000
Tel: 01488 72584

Owner: The National Trust

*Open: House and
immediate surroundings:*
Apr to Oct, Wed and Sat
2–5 (closed Easter
weekend); *Woodland:* all
year, Sat to Thur
dawn–dusk

Illustration opposite:
Ashdown House

Ashdown house is an exquisite 17th-century mansion perched high on what we used to call the Berkshire Downs (until the county boundaries were changed). It was built as a hunting lodge by Lord Craven and as a refuge from the plague for the 'Winter Queen', King Charles I's sister, Elizabeth of Bohemia, who died in 1662 before the house was finished. Kip's early 18th-century engraving shows it looking remarkably as it does to this day. Then it was at the centre of great hunting rides cutting through woodland. Today it is embellished with a convincing period parterre of box and gravel, a broad avenue of limes, and lawns. Visitors to the house (guided tours only) are taken to the roof from which there are wonderful views clearly showing, after over 300 years, the original pattern of rides. The woodland surrounding the house is open throughout the year – marvellous for a winter's walk. The charm of the place is the exhilaration of the high, windy woodland with, at its centre, the delicate refinement of the house. There is not a flower in sight.

BARTON MANOR

Isle of Wight

Whippingham,
Cowes PO32 6LB
Next to Osborne House,
1m SE of Cowes by A3021
Tel: 01983 292835
Fax: 01983 293923

Owner:
Mr Robert Stigwood

Open: Jun to Aug, Mon to
Fri 10–5. 20 acres

Formerly part of the Osborne House estate, the Barton estate, with its gabled stone manor house, was a particular interest of Prince Albert, who laid out the gardens and planted the splendid grove of cork oaks (*Quercus suber*) at the entrance. Today a large part of it is run as a commercial vineyard but the gardens have been very well restored to preserve their Victorian character. By the house there are herbaceous borders and a secret garden of roses and winding paths. An avenue of bushes of St John's Wort leads down to a lake with a romantic 19th-century thatched boat house. Here are many good trees (especially willows, relishing the moist ground) and the banks are dazzling with daffodils in spring. In summer a National Collection (over 100 species and cultivars) of red hot pokers (*Kniphofia*) may be seen doing its dazzling stuff. A more recent addition is a maze of rose hedges now showing its paces.

BERNWODE PLANTS
Buckinghamshire

Kingswood Lane,
Ludgershall,
nr Aylesbury HP18 9RB
1m SE of Ludgershall on
Wotton Road; 11m W of
Aylesbury by A41
Tel and Fax: 01844 237415

Open: Mar to Oct, daily
except Mon (open Bank
Hol Mon) 10–6

BERNWODE PLANTS has a distinctive identity – the lovely plants sold by Derek and Judy Tolman are carefully chosen to be 'rare, old-fashioned and desirable'. The emphasis is on herbaceous plants and the selections of many groups of plants are among the best you will find. There are achilleas, aquilegias, campanulas, euphorbias (probably the largest for sale in the country), hardy geraniums, a marvellous range of Michaelmas daisies, mints, a selection of old cultivars of pinks, a wide range of primulas, very many violas and several perennial wallflowers. A new selection of old apple cultivars is now stocked. No gardener could visit this nursery and come away empty handed. An excellent catalogue (£2.00) is available and orders are fulfilled by cheap courier.

BLACKTHORN NURSERY
Hampshire

Kilmeston,
nr Alresford SO24 0NL
6 1/2m SE of Winchester
by A272
Tel: 01962 771796

Open: 6 Mar to 27 Jun, Fri
and Sat 9–5

AT THE Blackthorn Nursery there are some very rare and desirable plants which you will not often see offered for sale. The nursery specialises in herbaceous perennials and alpines but among a short list of woody plants is an excellent selection of daphnes. Among the herbaceous plants are a magnificent range of epimediums (about which an excellent leaflet is available), several euphorbias, marvellous hellebores, and ferns. There is no mail order but a good catalogue is produced (three 1st-class stamps).

BLENHEIM PALACE
Oxfordshire

Illustration opposite:
The Italian garden at
Blenheim Palace

THE PARK at Blenheim has an immensely long history: in the 12th century it was the site of Henry II's Rosamond's Bower – and her well still exists; new gardens were laid out by Henry Wise early in the 18th century, and Sir John Vanbrugh who designed the immense palace, also had a hand in them; in the 1760s the park was landscaped by 'Capability'

Woodstock OX20 1PX
In Woodstock, 8m N of
Oxford by A44
Tel: 01993 811325
Fax: 01993 813527

Owner: The Duke of
Marlborough

Open: Park: daily 9–4.45;
Formal gardens at Palace:
mid Mar to Oct, daily
10.30–4.45. 2,000 acres
(including parkland). Palace
open

Brown; and in the early 20th century new parterres by
the palace were designed by the French designer Achille
Duchêne – fortissimo exercises in the grand formal
manner. The water parterre has arabesques of box
outlining pools, and classical statuary; the Italian
parterre has a magnificent central fountain, topiary of
golden yew and pots of oranges and agapanthus.
Everywhere ingredients from different periods are
harmoniously interwoven with, at their heart, the
palace and its vista leading north across Vanbrugh's
bridge to the immense Column of Victory surmounted
by a statue of the Duke of Marlborough clasping a
winged victory 'as an ordinary man might hold a
bird'. Brown's park, disposed on gently undulating
land about the vast serpentine lake that he made by
damming the river Glyme, is one of his masterpieces –
a subtle and satisfyingly rural contrast to the
extravagant architecture of the palace.

THE BOTANIC NURSERY

Wiltshire

Atworth,
nr Melksham SN12 8NU
9m E of Bath by A4 and
A365
Tel: 01225 706597 (office);
0850 328756 (mobile)
Fax: 01225 700953

Open: Daily except Tue
10–1, 2–5

TERENCE AND Mary Baker's nursery specialises in
lime-tolerant plants of which it has an excellently
chosen range. Those who garden on alkaline soil will
find a wide selection of plants that will flourish in
their gardens. The nursery concentrates on no
particular groups of plants but what it has is carefully
selected – for example a list of species foxgloves of
which it holds the National Collection. Although their
catalogue (£1) is full of good, and unusual, plants, the
Bakers are always on the lookout for something new,
and many items are available in insufficient quantities
to be listed. As the nursery no longer offers a mail
order service a visit is essential.

BOWOOD

Wiltshire

THE HOUSE – partly designed by Robert Adam – is
a splendid 18th-century confection and very much
in keeping with the park which is chiefly of the same
period. The park, with its great serpentine lake,
spreads out below the house and is enlivened by a
wonderfully picturesque cascade concealed in the

Calne SN11 0LZ
2 1/2m W of Calne by A4
Tel: 01249 812102

Owner: The Earl and
Countess of Shelburne

Open: Apr to Oct, daily
11–6. 100 acres. House
open

woods, a hermit's cave and an elegant pillared temple.
All this is at some distance from the house but there is
no point in going to Bowood if you cannot be
bothered to walk. This is the work partly of
'Capability' Brown and, later, of Humphry Repton,
and it is one of the very best landscape parks of its
kind. There are marvellous trees at Bowood, and the
mid 19th-century pinetum is exceptionally good, with
some of the finest specimens of conifers in the country
– magnificent cedars of Lebanon, pines, firs and giant
redwoods. Immediately alongside the house there are
19th-century formal gardens with beds of roses,
balustrades, vases, clipped Irish yews and a vast
languishing nude figure by David Wynne.

BROUGHTON CASTLE

Oxfordshire

THIS SPECTACULAR house is really a 14th-century
moated and fortified manor house, set in exquisite
parkland, and occupying a beautiful site next to the
church. Within the castle walls there are very
distinguished borders showing a fastidious sense of
colour harmony. Running along a wall overlooking the

Broughton,
nr Banbury OX15 5EB
2m SW of Banbury by
B4035
Tel: 01295 262624 or 01869
337126
Fax: 01295 272694

Owner: Lord Saye and Sele

Open: 18 May to 14 Sept,
Wed and Sun 2–5; Jul and
Aug, also Thur 2–5 and
Bank Hol Sun and Mon
2–5; also groups by
appointment. 3 acres.
Castle open

moat a mixed border is planted in yellow, cream and
blue with much grey and variegated foliage. My Lady's
Garden has a pattern of *fleur de lis* clipped in box and
a Victorian centrepiece well planted with the rose 'De
Rescht', *Convolvulus sabatius* and ivy. Disposed
around the walls, overflowing mixed borders are
planted with many shrub roses in a colour scheme of
pink, mauve and white. They look superb against the
grey stone and are an object lesson in charming, and
appropriate, design and planting – generous
abundance softening the stern castle walls. Visitors to
the castle may go out onto the roof, from which there
is a bird's eye view of this garden and the surrounding
parkland; it is one of the loveliest views you will ever
see and should certainly not be missed – unforgettable
in June but marvellous in any season.

BUSCOT PARK

Oxfordshire

EAST OF the house, running through woodland
towards a lake, is a water garden you will never
forget. Designed by Harold Peto before World War I, it
is in the form of a canal that drops down the incline in
gentle steps, dips under occasional little bridges,

Faringdon SN7 8BU
3m NW of Faringdon on
A417
Tel: 01367 242094 (not
weekends)

Owner: The National Trust

Open: Apr to Sept, Wed to
Fri and every 2nd and 4th
Sat and Sun (including
Easter) 2–6. 20 acres.
House open

widens and contracts, and from time to time bursts
forth in exuberant fountains. The water garden is
edged with stately clipped hedges of box, and the
flanking path is punctuated by Irish yews, statues and
urns. Approaching the lake the visitor sees on its far
bank a gleaming temple and an ornamental bridge. To
one side of the water garden a pattern of exhilarating
avenues is punctuated by handsome eyecatchers. On
the far side of the house, by the kitchen garden, are
strongly designed borders in yellow and, within the
walls, tunnels of pleached hop hornbeam and Judas
trees underplanted with spring bulbs followed by waves
of many different daylilies – an admirable and
instructive piece of modern design.

CHENIES MANOR

Buckinghamshire

Chenies,
Rickmansworth WD3 6ER
4m E of Amersham on
A404
Tel: 01494 762888

Owner: Lt. Col. and Mrs
MacLeod Matthews

Open: Apr to Oct, Wed,
Thur and Bank Hol Mon
2–5. 3 acres. House open

THE MANOR is a lovely early Tudor brick house and
the garden is an excellent setting for it. The formal
gardens are chiefly behind the house, with a white
garden with plump topiary birds of yew, a cool tunnel
of pleached lime, and a virtuoso little sunken garden,
intricately planted, in which spring tulips are followed
by an elaborate summer bedding scheme. Beyond this,
a parterre has a large yew maze and a physic garden
has beds of medicinal and culinary herbs laid out
round a decorative old octagonal well-house. To one
side of the house an ornamental kitchen garden has
gravel paths edged with catmint or box, currants and
gooseberries grown in cordons, beautifully tended
vegetables and a turf maze in an orchard. The garden
is impeccably well kept and gives the impression of
bursting with life.

CLIVEDEN
Buckinghamshire

Taplow,
Maidenhead SL6 0JA
2m N of Taplow on B476;
Jnct 7 of M4 and Jnct 4 of
M40
Tel: 01628 605069
Fax: 01628 669461

Owner: The National Trust

Open: 28 Mar to 1 Nov,
daily 11–6 ; Nov to Dec,
daily 11–4. 375 acres.
House open

THE MANSION at Cliveden rises on a bluff above the snaking Thames. A giant terrace looks south to a vast parterre of box and santolina beyond which the land falls away in wooded slopes that run down to the river below. To the north of the house the pleasure gardens have excellent herbaceous borders and, beyond the walls, a hidden rose garden. To one side of the eye-stopping Fountain of Love is the magical Long Garden with serpentine box hedges, whimsical topiary and stone figures from the Commedia dell'Arte. In the woods by the house, are exceptional garden ornaments – exquisite statues, urns and garden buildings.

THE COURTS
Wiltshire

CONCEALED BEHIND village walls, a pleached lime alley leads up to an ornate 18th-century Bath stone house at the heart of a highly decorative garden in which yew topiary and Irish yews give firm

Illustration opposite:
The Courts

Holt,
nr Trowbridge BA14 6RR
In Holt village, 3m SW of
Melksham by B3107
Tel: 01225 782340

Owner: The National Trust

Open: Apr to 1 Nov, daily
except Sat 1.30–5.30. Also
by appointment out of
season. 7 acres

structure. Among the less known of the National Trust's gardens, it has great character. The essential layout dates from just before World War I when the architect Sir George Hastings lived here. Good shrubs and ornamental trees half conceal an ornamental pool smothered in season with water-lilies, and a billowing hedge of two varieties of holly forms the eastern boundary to a meadow garden. Cherries, dogwoods and maples give dazzling autumn colour which may be enjoyed by visitors as the garden stays open until late in the season. This is a vision of a cottage garden seen through aristocratic eyes. The whole garden has recently been given a good wash and brush-up.

DEACONS NURSERY

Isle of Wight

Godshill PO38 3HW
In Godshill village,
9m S of Cowes by A3020
Tel: 01983 840750/522243
Fax: 01983 523575

Open: Apr to Sept, Mon to
Fri 8–4; Oct to Mar, Sat
8–12

DEACONS NURSERY specialises in fruit trees and bushes, of which it has an immense collection – around 250 varieties of apples alone, for example, which may be ordered on a choice of five rootstocks. There is virtually no fruit that is hardy in Britain which is not stocked, and many of the varieties, especially the old kinds, are very difficult to find elsewhere. Although visitors are welcome, virtually all the business of this nursery is conducted by mail order and an exceptionally informative catalogue is produced (31p stamp).

EXBURY GARDENS

Hampshire

nr Southampton SO4 1AZ
In Exbury village, 14m from
Totton (W of
Southampton) by A326 and
B3054
Tel: 01703 891203
Fax: 01703 243380

Owner: E.L. de Rothschild

Open: Mar to Oct daily
10–5.30 or sunset if earlier.
200 acres

THE CLIMATE is particularly mild at Exbury. Lionel de Rothschild came here in 1919 and started to build up the collection of rhododendrons, many bred by him, which was to make the garden famous. His son has continued the tradition and has added many new varieties which may be seen growing in this huge garden. Edmund de Rothschild is a regular exhibitor and prize winner at RHS shows. But even for those not interested in rhododendrons there is much to see throughout the season, especially superb old specimens of trees. There is an excellent plant centre with a good range of the ericaceous plants found in the garden.

FOXGROVE PLANTS

Berkshire

Foxgrove Farm, Enborne,
nr Newbury RG14 6RE
1m W of Newbury
Tel: 01635 40554

Open: Wed to Sun and
Bank Hol Mon 10–5 (closed
Aug)

THIS LITTLE nursery has won several medals at
RHS shows and elsewhere. Its speciality is smaller
herbaceous plants and although the stock is small the
plants are particularly well chosen. There are large
selections of campanulas, geraniums, primulas
(including some pretty auriculas), saxifrages,
snowdrops (of which a special list is published) and
violas. Louise Vockins has an eye for a good plant and
the visitor is likely to find something unfamiliar and
worth buying.

FURZEY GARDENS

Hampshire

THIS GARDEN was started in 1922 on rough grazing
land which benefitted from some good old trees
and a rich natural vegetation which in many parts of
the garden has been preserved. The site is sloping, the
soil is acid and the garden is full of excellent plants,

Minstead,
nr Lyndhurst SO43 7GL
9m W of Southampton by
A336
Tel: 01703 812464/812297
Fax: 01703 812297

Owner: Furzey Gardens
Charitable Trust

Open: Daily 10–5 or earlier
in winter (closed 25–26
Dec). 8 acres

many of them unusual. The layout is informal, with grassy walks descending the hill and winding between groups of shrubs. Herbaceous plantings fringe the paths. In spring an immense number of bulbs – narcissi, dog's tooth violets and fritillaries – is followed by rhododendrons, many of them rare and tender. The garden is outstanding in autumn with brilliant foliage colours from such shrubs as enkianthus and witch hazel, and large specimens of *Liquidambar styraciflua* and the scarlet oak (*Quercus coccinea*).

GREEN FARM PLANTS

Hampshire

Illustration:
Asphodelus aestivus

Bury Court, Bentley,
nr Farnham GU10 5LZ
N of Bentley village off the
Well road
Tel: 01420 23202
Fax: 01420 22382

Open: Wed to Sat 10–6

JOHN COKE and Marina Christopher's beautifully kept nursery is well worth seeking out because they possess a connoisseur's eye for a good plant and there are many things here that you will not easily find elsewhere. They have now moved to spectacular new premises in beautiful old farm outhouses, with an excellent garden designed by Piet Oudolf displaying his highly original way with herbaceous plants. But, although there is much more space, the style of the nursery, and its personal character, remain the same. It specialises in the smaller decorative shrubs and hardy herbaceous plants. Everything chosen has something distinguished about it, which gives the range the feeling of a house style. There are not immense numbers of any particular genus but there are fastidiously chosen groups of plants such as cimicifugas (a much under-appreciated plant), cistus, eryngiums, penstemons, poppies and sages. But this is not just plant-collector's paradise – all these are thoroughly garden-worthy plants. There is no mail order but a catalogue is produced (three 1st-class stamps).

GREYS COURT
Oxfordshire

Rotherfield Greys, Henley-
on-Thames RG9 4PG
3m W of Henley-on-
Thames by A423
Tel: 01491 628529

Owner: The National Trust

Open: Apr to Sept, daily
except Thur and Sun 2–6
(closed Good Fri).
9 acres. House open

THE HOUSE, partly Tudor and partly Georgian, commands unforgettable views over the valley of beech woods, and downland. Passing through a white garden and a garden of old roses underplanted with pinks, a path leads under a great canopy of *Wisteria sinensis*. In the former kitchen garden paths are edged with *Rosa gallica* 'Versicolor' or espaliered fruit trees. Here, a pergola veiled with vine and honeysuckle leads to the Archbishop's Maze. Turning back towards the house, by the Cromwellian Stables, a brilliant little enclosed garden has knots of box hedges and topiary, London pride edging the paths, beds burgeoning with herbaceous plants, and walls of pleached laburnum.

HARDY'S COTTAGE GARDEN PLANTS
Hampshire

Priory Lane, Freefolk,
Whitchurch RG28 7NJ
2m E of Whitchurch
signposted from the B3400
Tel: 01256 896533
Fax: 01256 896572

Open: Mar to Oct, daily
10–5

THE STRENGTH of this nursery lies in the harmony of its range of plants rather than in great botanical curiosities. I once saw a consignment of Hardy's plants on their way to a show, and jumbled together before being loaded they resembled an excellent little herbaceous border. The stock is chiefly herbaceous and the emphasis is on good garden plants rather than dazzling rarities. Campanulas, euphorbias, geraniums, penstemons and phloxes are well represented. A few woody plants – such as an unusual range of lavateras – are also stocked. But the value of this place is Rosy Hardy's sure eye for a good plant. There is not a dud in the place. A catalogue is produced (s.a.e and five 1st-class stamps) and there is a mail order service.

HEALE GARDEN AND PLANT CENTRE

Wiltshire

Middle Woodford,
nr Salisbury SP4 6NT
In the Woodford Valley, 4m
N of Salisbury by minor
roads, signed from A345
and A360
Tel: 01722 78504

Owner: Mr Guy Rasch

Open: Daily 10–5. 8 acres

O N LOW-LYING land on the banks of the Avon, Heale House is an irresistibly decorative confection of rosy brick and stone dressings. The garden has a character all of its own and there are few places in England where a gardener is likely to have more fun. The 'landing stage' by the house and the scalloped fish ponds and rose terraces west of the house were designed by Harold Peto in 1910 for the Hon. Louis Greville who installed a Japanese garden with scarlet bridge and fragile tea-house after a tour of diplomatic duty in Japan before World War I. Nearby is a walled vegetable garden with broad tunnels of espaliered apples, clipped mounds of box surrounding a pool, and a beguiling mixture of fruit, vegetables and masterly ornamental planting. Everywhere in the garden there are roses – particularly old shrub roses – an unforgettable sight in late June; but there is always something to admire at other times. An excellent plant centre, expanding all the time, sells exceptionally good plants including the beautiful 'Terrace' roses, apparently unique to Heale, which have so far resisted identification. A catalogue is produced but there is no mail order.

THE SIR HAROLD HILLIER GARDENS AND ARBORETUM

Hampshire

T HIS IS one of the greatest collections of woody plants in the country and had its origin as the private arboretum of Sir Harold Hillier. The arboretum holds the National Collection of oaks – an extraordinary collection of no less than 140 species

Jermyns Lane, Ampfield,
nr Romsey SO51 0QA
3m NE of Romsey by A31
Tel: 01794 368787
Fax: 01794 368027

Owner:
Hampshire County Council

Open: Apr to Oct, daily
10.30–6; Nov to Mar, daily
10.30–5. 166 acres

and over 70 cultivars, by far the largest collection in
the country. Several other National Collections are
held of which the most interesting to gardeners are
those of cotoneaster (over 200 species and over 50
cultivars), dogwoods (40 species and over 50 cultivars)
and a dazzling range of pines (over 100 species and
over 90 cultivars) But the riches of the place are so
enormous and so various that there is little point in
beginning to list them. A visit at any time of the year
will be splendidly rewarded and this is a marvellous
place for even expert gardeners to learn more in the
most enjoyable way; for beginners it is an essential part
of gardening education.

HINTON AMPNER

Hampshire

Bramdean,
nr Alresford SO24 0LA
1m W of Bramdean village
by A272
Tel: 01962 771305

Owner: The National Trust

Open: 15 and 22 Mar, 28
Mar to Sept, Sat, Sun, Tue,
Wed, Bank Hol Mon
1.30–5.30. 8 acres. House
open

THIS IS an exciting place to visit – an excellent old
garden, redesigned in the 20th century and now
given new life. The estate formerly belonged to Ralph
Dutton, Lord Sherborne, who rebuilt the house, an
18th century brick mansion, and laid out a new garden
incorporating older features such as a superb lime
avenue planted in 1720. It is a marvellous site and
Dutton opened views into the beautiful surrounding
parkland. Within the garden he laid out all sorts of
decorative schemes – a cherry garden with formal
hedges of box and yew, a yew walk backed with shrub
roses, a leafy and mysterious dell, a sunken garden,
yew topiary and much else. Everywhere there is a
brilliant use of ornaments – statues and urns – which
direct the gaze and emphasise a vista.

HOLLINGTON HERB GARDEN

Berkshire

Woolton Hill,
Newbury RG15 9XT
5m S of Newbury off A343
Tel: 01635 253908
Fax: 01635 254990

Open: Mar to Sept, Mon to
Sat 10–5.30, Sun and Bank
Hol Mon 11–5; Oct to Feb,
restricted opening, please
phone

ALTHOUGH THIS marvellous place certainly sells
herbs, it is misleading to call it a herb garden
because it is of much wider interest that that. In a
handsome old walled former kitchen garden Simon and
Judith Hopkinson have laid out a series of borders,
knots, parterres and raised beds to show their plants in
action. All this – beautifully designed and executed – is
bursting with ideas for gardeners, well worth visiting in
its own right; the garden has over the years assumed as

much importance as the nursery which still sells excellent plants. Apart from a very wide range of herbs there are shrubs and trees with scented foliage, scented climbers and many old shrub roses. In 1996 an entirely new garden was made – the Paradise Herb Garden – a formal layout stuffed with strongly textured plants surrounding four gurgling fountains and ending in a 60ft carpet of thyme. A very good catalogue is produced (four 1st-class stamps) and there is a mail order service.

IFORD MANOR

Wiltshire

Iford, nr Bradford-on-Avon
BA15 2BA
7m SE of Bath by A36. 2m
SW of Bradford-on-Avon
by B3109 and Westwood
Tel: 01225 863146
Fax: 01225862364

Owner:
Mrs Cartwright-Hignett

Open: Apr and Oct, Sun
2–5; May to Sept, daily
except Mon and Fri 2–5.
2 1/2 acres

THE ARCHITECT and garden designer Harold Peto came here in 1899 to an Elizabethan manor house with an early 18th-century front in an idyllic position on the steep wooded slopes of the Frome valley. Here he laid out a formal garden on old terraces, embellished with the collection of classical statuary and architectural fragments that he had been collecting for years. Steep flights of steps link the terraces with their pools, fountains, loggias, colonnades, urns and figures. He wrote in his *Boke of Iford*, 'old buildings or fragments of masonary carry one's mind back to the past in a way that a garden of flowers only cannot do.' But the planting was also important. Columnar cypresses add to the Italian atmosphere, and many trees and shrubs flower among the statues. The formal garden contrasts with its rural surrounds, and idyllic views open out over cattle grazing in meadows. In the woods above the garden a Japanese garden is being recreated by the present owners who have done an immense amount of restoration. It is a garden of unique character, an Italianate vision transposed to the English countryside, well deserving of the care it receives and a marvellous treat to visit.

JARDINIQUE

Hampshire

Kemps Place,
Selborne Road,
Greatham, Liss GU33 6HG
On W side of Greatham
village, 5 1/2m NE of
Petersfield by A3 and B3006
Tel: 01420 538000
Fax: 01420 538700

Open: Tue to Sat 10–5; also
by appointment

IT MAY take you a moment or two to recover from the tweeness of the name but when you have regained your composure you will find there is plenty to admire here. Jardinique sells garden ornaments and furniture, some antique and some not, staddle stones, wheelbarrows, watering cans, cisterns, old garden tools and pots – indeed all the lovely paraphernalia of gardening. You would be unlikely to discover an overlooked Jan van Nost Venus here but there is much that is attractive and affordable, blurred by the patina of age, of exactly the kind you may enviously admire in long-established gardens.

KELMSCOTT MANOR

Oxfordshire

THE GABLED manor is 16th-century, handsomely set on the edge of the village by the wooded banks of the infant Thames. It is famous as the country house of William Morris, and the garden preserves an atmosphere of simple rural charm. A historic survey, drawing on a wealth of material, has been carried out,

Kelmscott GL7 3HJ
In Kelmscott village, 6 1/2m
NW of Faringdon by A417,
B4449 and minor road
Tel: 01367 252486
Fax: 01367 253754

Owner: The Society of
Antiquaries

Open: Apr to Sept, Wed
11–1, 2–5. 1 1/2 acres

as a result of which the garden is resuming the appearance it had in Morris's time. Already new paths and box-edged beds have been made, with the addition of period plants. In the front garden standard roses have been replanted (using David Austin's English Roses) so that it now resembles the picture seen in Morris's *News from Nowhere*. Always a place of historic charm, Kelmscott is now developing a delightful garden thoroughly in keeping with the irresistible allure of the house.

LANGLEY BOXWOOD NURSERY
Hampshire

Rake, nr Liss GU33 7JL
5m NE of Petersfield, by
B2070 (formerly A3);
turning on W side of road
at beginning of dual
carriageway
Tel: 01730 894467
Fax: 01730 894703

Open: Mon to Fri 9–4.30,
Sat phone first

WITH THE renewed interest in formal gardens, box has become deservedly fashionable. In all its forms it is a wonderful plant and Elizabeth Braimbridge's passionate devotion to it is inspiring. She has gathered together, deep in Hampshire woodland, the greatest range commercially available in this country. Here is the curious and wonderful sight of queues of topiary teddy-bears, pyramids, spheres, corkscrews and preening peacocks. In addition to topiary she also sells many cultivars of *Buxus sempervirens* and other species which, with their often strikingly ornamental foliage, make highly decorative plants even without clipping. It is enough to make box fanatics of us all. Mrs Braimbridge holds the National Collection of box. An outstandingly informative catalogue is produced (four 1st-class stamps), and mail order is available.

THE LITTLE COTTAGE

Hampshire

Southampton Road,
Lymington SO41 9GZ
On N edge of Lymington,
on the A337 opposite Toll
House Inn
Tel and Fax: 01590 679395

Owner: Lyn and Peter Prior

Open: Jun to Sept, Tues
10–1, 2–6; also by
appointment. 1/4 acre

FEW GARDENS cram in so many decorative devices as this little plot which bursts with Hidcotean ambitions. It is an awkward site on a busy main road which Lyn and Peter Prior have since 1985 craftily divided into seven distinct compartments, each one with its own colour combinations. Every dinky vista has its eyecatcher and there is some resoundingly successful planting. The entrance, with an avenue of lollipops of variegated euonymus and a colour scheme of gold and blue, is enchanting – yellow daylilies, blue irises and geraniums, gold variegated ivy, periwinkles and hostas. The colours of ornaments, gates and garden buildings are as carefully considered as that of the plants themselves. To some gardeners' taste some of the colour schemes may be over the top. But the whole point about visiting gardens is not just to confirm your own horticultural prejudices but to enjoy other people's ideas. The occasional jolt to the sensibilities never did anyone any harm – indeed for some gardeners it is a bracing spiritual tonic. Also, there is a valuable lesson from which all owners of small gardens could learn – a strong sense of design is the essential ingredient of success.

LONGSTOCK WATER GARDENS

Hampshire

Longstock,
Stockbridge SO20 6EH
1 1/2m NE of Longstock
village
Tel: 01264 810894
Fax: 01264 810439

Owner: John Lewis
Partnership

Open: Apr to Sept, 1st and
3rd Sun in each month 2–5.
8 acres

THERE IS nothing in Britain quite like these mesmerising water gardens. A maze of little islands is linked by bridges and separated by streams and pools. Close-mown turf paths run along the waterside which is handsomely planted with bold drifts of herbaceous plants – geraniums, ornamental grasses, hostas, irises, ligularia and Asiatic primulas. Gold, grey and silver carp and orfe twist and sparkle in the water. Excellent trees such as swamp cypresses, Himalayan birches and *Liquidambar styraciflua* provide large-scale interest and in the background are fine woodland and ramparts of rhododendrons. Seats are placed here and there and the place, which is exquisitely maintained, exudes calm. Provided for the recreation of the staff ('partners') of the John Lewis Partnership, the public is occasionally admitted. No one should lose an opportunity to see this rare garden.

THE MANOR HOUSE

Hampshire

THE NAME of Gertrude Jekyll seems to be on almost every gardener's lips these days but very few of her gardens survive and fewer still have been restored with such care and affection as this. The Wallingers came in 1984, long after the Jekyll garden

Upton Grey,
nr Basingstoke RG25 2RD
In the centre of Upton Grey
village, 6m SE of
Basingstoke by minor
roads; Jnct 5 of M3
Tel: 01256 862827
Fax: 01256 861035

Owner:
Mr and Mrs J. Wallinger

Open: May to Jul, Mon to
Fri by appointment

had disappeared, and have now reinstated her original scheme with meticulous care. To one side of the entrance drive the wild garden has sinuous mown paths in long grass, rambling roses, thickets of bamboo and a flag-fringed pool. Behind the house the formal garden has a virtuoso Jekyll 'plat' – two squares of geometrical beds edged with grey stachys and brimming with swoony double pink peonies and the double pink rose 'Caroline Testout'. Terraces overlook it and the supporting dry-stone walls are rich with aquilegias, corydalis, hart's tongue ferns and valerian. Steps lead down to a terraced bowling green and tennis lawns hedged in yew. This is one of the very best Jekyll gardens from which to learn her principles which may be put into practice in any garden.

THE MEAD NURSERY

Wiltshire

Illustration:
Malva moschata 'Alba'

Brokerswood,
nr Westbury BA13 4EG
3m W of Westbury between
Woodland Park and Rudge
Tel: 01373 859990

Open: Feb to Oct, Wed to
Sat and Bank Hol Mon 9–5,
Sun 12–5

STEPHEN AND EMMA Lewis-Dale started their nursery in 1992 and have built up an admirable range of plants. The heart of their stock is herbaceous perennials with several of the smaller shrubs like artemisias, lavender, sages and thymes that make such valuable companion plants. An interesting range of hardy alpines is also displayed. You would have to possess the best-stocked garden in the world, or be impossible to please, to come away empty-handed. Some well-planned display areas show the plants performing. No mail order but a very good catalogue is issued (five 1st-class stamps) which, every year, seems to offer new and exciting plants.

MOTTISFONT ABBEY GARDEN
Hampshire

Mottisfont,
nr Romsey SO51 0LJ
4 1/2m N of Romsey
signposted off A3057
Tel: 01794 341220/340757

Owner: The National Trust

Open: 28 Mar to 28 Oct,
daily except Thur and Fri
12–6 or dusk if earlier;
during the rose season (13
to 28 Jun), daily 11–8.30.
21 acres. House open

MOTTISFONT IS known for its Rose Garden in which an immense collection of shrub roses, with an emphasis on the older varieties, is arranged in the old walled kitchen garden. Here is housed the National Collection of pre-1900 shrub roses. Unlike many rose gardens, however, this is beautifully designed; box-edged beds are divided by lawns and gravel paths, and the beds are enriched by all kinds of herbaceous plants which maintain interest when the roses are not performing. Visiting gardeners will not only meet many unfamiliar roses but will discover an immense amount about their ornamental use in the garden. All this is a tribute to Graham Stuart Thomas who rediscovered so many old roses and supervised the making of this garden. Nearer the house, partly medieval stone and partly Georgian brick, there are other things worth seeing: a pleached lime alley designed by Geoffrey Jellicoe, with carpets of chionodoxa in the spring; a dashing box parterre with summer bedding; and, down by the river Test which flows through the grounds, a stupendous London plane tree, one of the most memorable trees you will ever see. The National Collection of planes is kept here.

THE OLD RECTORY
Berkshire

Burghfield,
Reading RG3 3TH
In Burghfield village, 5m
SW of Reading
Tel: 01189 833200

Owner: Mr A.R. Merton

Open: Feb to Oct, second
and last Wed in month 11–4
(parties by appointment in
writing). 4 1/2 acres

THIS WONDERFUL garden gets in only by the skin of its teeth because it is open so rarely, but it is so good that it would be worth planning a visit to these parts to coincide with its opening. Immediately behind the handsome brick house a marvellous cedar of Lebanon, the supreme garden ornament, is given full breathing space on a lawn. A pair of brilliant borders, separated by a crisp turf path and backed by yew hedges, leads towards a pool with a statue of Antinous, fringed with maples, bold foliage planting and flowering shrubs. All about the house are beautifully judged plantings (including some magnificent pots) and there is a splendid kitchen garden. On open days a plant *souk* appears in the yard and many good plants are sold. Esther Merton, who made this garden, died in 1995 but her garden continues. She was a great gardener whose name pops up repeatedly among those who love plants and gardens – usually in the form of 'Oh, yes, this was given to me by Mrs Merton, she found it on the Great Wall of China.'

OXFORD BOTANIC GARDEN
Oxfordshire

THIS WALLED garden, with its lovely early 17th-century entrance gate, was founded in 1621, the first botanic garden in England. It still preserves its character of a 'repository of curious plants' but it is extremely attractively laid out and very well

High Street,
Oxford OX1 4AX
In the centre of Oxford,
near Magdalen Bridge
Tel: 01865 276920

Owner:
University of Oxford

Open: Daily except Good
Fri and 25 Dec 9–5 (in
winter 9–4.30); *greenhouses*
2–4. 4 1/2 acres

maintained. There are botanical 'order' beds' but there are also many ornamental trees and shrubs, some of them unusual (like the beautiful Himalayan birch, *Betula utilis* var. *jaquemontii*). Although much of the planting is severely botanical, the ornamental aspects of horticulture are certainly not neglected: there are excellent borders, and fine trees are well placed. Everything is impeccably labelled so it is an admirable place in which to learn about plants. To one side of the entrance, running parallel to the High Street, is the 'Penicillin Garden', a parterre of roses and hedges of box and yew, designed by Dame Sylvia Crowe to celebrate Oxford's greatest medical discovery and to make the connection with the ancient physic garden.

OXFORD COLLEGE GARDENS

Oxfordshire

A LL OXFORD colleges have some sort of garden, presenting to outsiders enticing green views glimpsed through iron railings or gates. A few of these are well worth visiting – hidden gardens of sometimes surprising size. **Magdalen College** (High St; *Open:* 2–6) has a deer park which gives the adjacent early 18th-century New Building something of the air of a rural seat; in front of it is an immense and beautiful London plane. Behind it, Addison's Walk, a shady tree-lined path loved by the 18th-century philosopher, skirts Magdalen Meadow, a lovely pasture which in spring is alive with snake's head fritillaries. **New College** (Holywell Street; *Open:* 11–5) in its Garden Quad, screened by handsome iron gates and railings, has bold borders with a jolly gallimaufry of colours against the sombre stone, given shape by crafty repeated plantings. In other parts of the college there are further signs of imaginative and skilful gardening; for example, bold pairs of distinguished shrubs such as *Carpenteria californica* flanking the entrance to a quad; all this, no doubt, the doing of Robin Lane Fox, the gardener-writer who is a New College don. **St John's College** (St Giles; *Open:* 1–5) has an attractive view of the garden through the gate from Canterbury Quad; here is a grand lawn, with good trees, fringed with borders. A path to one side leads to a rock garden. **Wadham College** (Parks Road; *Open:* 1.30–4.30) has a long mixed border and an exceptional old copper beech.

POUND HILL HOUSE

Wiltshire

West Kington,
Chippenham SN14 7JG
8m NW of Chippenham by
A420 and B4039 and minor
roads
Tel: 01249 782822
Fax: 01249 782953

Owner:
Mr and Mrs Philip Stockitt

Open: Tue to Sun and Bank
Hol Mon 2–5. Plant centre
same days but 10–5; also
parties by appointment.
2 acres

THIS IS the kind of garden that corresponds to
many people's ideal. It fits the pretty 16th-century
stone farmhouse perfectly, it is full of charm, it has
much variety of both plants and of design and it is not
so large and so lavish as to be beyond the realms of
possibility. There is, however, much art in this
unassuming artlessness and Barbara Stockitt is a
skilful gardener. There are good mixed borders with
lavish use of roses, an elegant formal kitchen garden, a
grassy walk of shrubs and roses and, behind the house,
a splendid water garden. It lies at the head of a lawn,
with deep mixed borders leading down towards the
house. A stone-flagged courtyard has box topiary in
pots and more good roses, including the curiously
named but wonderfully blowsy pink climber 'Blairii
Number Two'. The style of the garden transcends
trendiness and is completely in harmony with the
house at its centre. An attractively laid out plant centre
carries a good stock of woody and herbaceous plants,
well worth a visit in its own right.

ROCHE COURT SCULPTURE GARDEN

Wiltshire

Winterslow,
nr Salisbury SP5 1BG
5m E of Salisbury by A30
Tel: 01980 862244
Fax: 01980 862447

Owner: The Earl and
Countess of Bessborough

Open: Daily 11–4

THERE IS a renaissance of the use of sculptures in the garden and this is a splendid place to see them in action. The late Georgian house is in a wonderful position with wide views down a wooded valley and the garden itself is rich in excellent old trees, yew hedges and old walls which make a very good setting in which to display sculpture. Roche Court is partly a private garden and partly a gallery in which sculptures and ceramics are displayed for sale. Some of these are by well known artists such as Barbara Hepworth; others by the new and little known. The exhibits, which change constantly, all benefit from their open air display, and the ensemble of house, garden, views and works of art make it a memorable place to visit.

ROUSHAM HOUSE

Oxfordshire

Steeple Aston OX5 3QX
12m N of Oxford by A4260
and B4030
Tel: 01869 347110

Owner: C. Cottrell-Dormer

Open: Daily 10–4.30.
30 acres. House open

THERE ARE few 18th-century landscape gardens surviving in England where it is still possible to see exactly what the designer intended. Rousham was designed between 1737 and 1741 by William Kent who devised a virtuoso arrangement of statues, buildings, water and a serpentine woodland rill and, above all, made a framework from which to admire the views over the river Cherwell towards the rural landscape beyond. Some of the individual garden buildings are exceptionally beautiful: Praeneste, a wonderful arcaded sweep of golden stone, giving viewpoints of subtly changing aspect; Kent's little covered seat of trellis and boards; and a solemn gothic temple half-shaded by the woods. The statues are of fine quality and almost all of them turn their backs on the garden and gaze out to the countryside. All this is done with the effortless ease of a conjuror pulling rabbits out of a hat. Nearer the house, in the old kitchen garden with its decorative dovecote, there is a charming arrangement of borders and a box-edged rose parterre.

SPECIAL PLANTS

Wiltshire

Illustration:
Mandevilla sanderi

Greenways Lane,
Cold Ashton,
Chippenham SN14 8LA
6m N of Bath by A 46; turn
W opposite turning to Cold
Ashton
Tel: 01225 891686

Open: Mar to Sept, daily
10–3 (also by appointment);
Oct to Feb, best to ring
beforehand

D ERRY WATKINS'S nursery is set in a beautiful secluded valley quite close to the buzz of Bath. She specialises in herbaceous perennials, many of them of borderline hardiness. Some of her greatest rarities were gathered when she spent three months in South Africa on a Winston Churchill Travelling Scholarship. These are marked with an asterisk in her list, mostly names quite unfamiliar to British gardeners. Until you have actually tried borderline plants in an appropriate site in your own garden you cannot judge their hardiness, so it is always worth giving them a judicious try. Apart from the South African collection there are other tender plants and dozens of garden-worthy things of proven hardiness – campanulas, geraniums, linarias, poppies, penstemons, veronicas and much else. A good catalogue is produced (two 2nd-class stamps) and a mail order service is available.

SPINNERS

Hampshire

Boldre,
Lymington SO41 5QE
1m NE of Lymington by
A337
Tel: 01590 673347

Open: Wed to Sat 10–5.
3 acres

ON ACID soil surrounded by woodland, Spinners is both a garden and an outstanding nursery garden selling a diverse selection of woody and herbaceous plants, many rare. The paths that wind downhill are well planted with ornamental shrubs and nearer the house there are excellent borders. Most of the plants displayed in the garden may be bought at the nursery. There are, for example, many different magnolias, at least 50 maples, several dogwoods, rare oaks and witch hazels – and that is only the woody department. There are also choice herbaceous plants – 10 kinds of cyclamen, ferns, decorative grasses, dozens of geraniums and a host of hostas. A catalogue is produced (three 1st-class stamps) but there is no mail order, so a visit is essential.

STOURHEAD

Wiltshire

Stourton,
Warminster BA12 6QH
In Stourton village,
3m NW of Mere by A303
and B3092
Tel: 01747 840348

Owner: The National Trust

Open: Daily 9–7 or sunset if
earlier (23–25 Jul 9–5).
40 acres. House open

ALTHOUGH THIS is probably the most photographed and certainly the best-known landscape garden in England, the experience of visiting it, in different seasons of the year, always provides some new pleasure. It was started in 1741 by the banker Henry Hoare who dammed the river Stour to make a sinuous lake about whose shores he disposed paths, temples, urns, a shivery grotto and, clothing the hillsides, a wealth of trees. Although there has been much subsequent planting, continuing in present times, the character of the original layout is unimpaired. Even at rhododendron time it is possible to escape the crush of visitors, ascend the precipitous paths that wind up away from the lake, and experience the authentic feeling of exhilarating solitude that such gardens inspired in the 18th century. It is, above all, a garden to walk in, following the snaking path that girdles the lake, and exploring every detour that presents itself. By the standards of other great landscape gardens Stourhead is not huge, and one of its most attractive features is that so many of its ingredients may be viewed from different angles or levels, giving the impression of great variety and of a much larger area.

Many of the garden buildings, most of which were designed by the architect Henry Flitcroft, are not only very beautiful but also contain fine works of art. Attempts have been made to link the sequence of buildings and 'events' into some sort of symbolic narrative. Most visitors will forget about symbolism and surrender themselves happily to the enchanting pictures that compose themselves so memorably about the banks of the lake.

STOWE LANDSCAPE GARDENS
Buckinghamshire

Buckingham MK18 5EH
3m NW of Buckingham on
A422
Tel: 01280 822850

Owner: The National Trust

Open: 10–5 (dusk if earlier) during the following periods: 20 Mar to 12 Apr, daily; 13 Apr to 5 Jul, Mon, Wed, Fri, Sun ; 6 Jul to 6 Sept, daily; 7 Sept to 1 Nov, Mon, Wed, Fri and Sun; 27 Dec to 5 Jan 1999, daily. 250 acres. House open

STOWE MAKES all other gardens seem like light snacks – this is the full banquet. It is a giant 18th-century landscape garden in which the greatest garden designers of the day worked – Charles Bridgeman, William Kent and 'Capability' Brown, who was head gardener in 1741. In this vast landscape, grass, trees, water, ornaments and buildings and huge vistas form a series of exquisite pictures. The monuments have all sorts of meanings and are often decorated with literary or political inscriptions. Even without unravelling their significance, visitors can revel in the marvellous shifting scenes – the contrast of immense views and corners of pastoral intimacy, of grazing cattle and classical temples. To walk about Stowe is one of the greatest of all garden experiences. It is especially beautiful on a frosty winter's day.

TUDOR HOUSE GARDEN

Hampshire

Bugle Street,
Southampton SO14 2AD
In the centre of
Southampton; follow signs
to old town and docks
Tel: 01703 332513

Owner:
Southampton City Council

Open: Tue to Fri, 10–12,
1–5, Sat 10–12, 1–4, Sun
2–5

THIS IS a very attractive idea – a dashing recreation of a Tudor period garden, designed by Dr Sylvia Landsberg in 1982 as the annexe to an excellent museum in the old town of Southampton. A knot of box, plants of the period, characteristic columns painted in chevrons and surmounted by heraldic beasts, hives with honey bees, a rose arbour and a tunnel of vines give something of the true character of a garden of the period.

WADDESDON MANOR

Buckinghamshire

THIS IS a Rothschild garden and a splendid one. The house is a fantasy pastiche of a Loire château, finished in 1889 for Baron Ferdinand de Rothschild and built on a wonderful site – the top of a hill commanding views over the Vale of Aylesbury. The slopes of the hill are encircled with walks and clothed in splendid trees and a marvellous collection of statues animates the scene. To the south of the house are

Waddesdon,
nr Aylesbury HP18 0JH
6m NW of Aylesbury by
A41
Tel: 01296 651211
Fax: 01296 651293

Owner: The National Trust

Open: Mar to 20 Dec, Wed
to Sun and Bank Hol Mon
10–5. 160 acres. House
open

terraced gardens which have been restored with
elaborate bedding schemes to their original Edwardian
splendour, as shown in contemporary photographs.
Huge quantities of bedding plants are used – with the
Rothschild racing colours of blue and gold in
prominence. Further work is in progress in a 10-year
programme to restore other parts of the gardens which
were laid out by the French landscape architect Lainé,
who also worked on the estates of the French
Rothschilds. To one side of the house a superb aviary
of delicate tracery and rococo curlicues houses a
splendid collection of exotic birds. The house, now
freshly restored, looks more beautiful than ever.

WEST GREEN HOUSE GARDEN

Hampshire

Thackhams Lane, West
Green, nr Hartley Wintney
RG27 8JB
2 1/4m NE of Jnct 5 of M3
Tel and Fax: 01252 844611

Owner: Marylyn Abbott
(The National Trust)

Open: 20 May to 17 Aug,
Wed to Fri 11–4. 6 acres

WEST GREEN House is a devastatingly attractive
early 18th-century brick house, whose features
repeatedly embellish views from the garden. A formal
walled garden dates from the 19th century and from
1975 onwards Alistair (now Lord) McAlpine
commissioned from the architect Quinlan Terry a
series of richly decorative monuments in the outer
areas. After Lord McAlpine left, the garden fell into
neglect. It has now been taken in hand by an
Australian of formidable energy and foresight. An
excellent gardener, she has already transformed the
formal enclosures about the house where topiary and
patterned hedging echo the sprightly decorativeness of
the house, and has introduced much fine ornamental
planting. The large walled former kitchen garden is

now in shipshape order with good borders, impeccable hedges and topiary, and lively plantings of fruit and vegetables intermingled with ornamental planting. To one side a cool green terraced space affords views of one of the prettiest facades of the house with a series of busts in niches. Miss Abbott is now tackling the areas containing Quinlan Terry's monuments – but already there is much to relish.

GILBERT WHITE'S HOUSE

Hampshire

Selborne,
nr Alton GU34 3JH
In Selborne village, 5m SE
of Alton by B3006
Tel: 01420 511275

Owner:
Oates Memorial Trust

Open: Mid Mar to 24 Dec,
daily 11–5; 27 Dec to mid
Mar, Sat and Sun 11–5.
5 acres

GILBERT WHITE was as passionately observant about gardening as he was about natural history and his writings on the subject, contained in his *Garden Kalendar*, are still well worth reading. This place – his former house and garden – is sacred ground. Behind the house, which is in the village high street, the garden has wonderful views across to the wooded ridge known as the Hanger. Yew hedges and topiary, a laburnum tunnel and herbaceous borders are well cared for. These are relatively modern features but there still remains much from White's time – the ha-ha he made in 1761, part of his fruit wall and a decorative sundial. An ambitious programme, based on White's writings, is now under way to restore the garden to its original state. Already completed are a quincunx, wooden ha-ha, mount, a naturalist's garden and the Six Quarters – beds of plants known to Gilbert White.

SOUTH-WEST ENGLAND

Cornwall
Devon
Dorset
Somerset

Arlington C

Marwood Hill ●

BARNSTAPLE

● Tapele

Docton Mill ●

Gl
C

Rosemoor ●
Garden

○ BUDE

OAKHAMPTON

A30

A386

Tresco Abbey

ISLES OF SCILLY

Pencarrow House ● Rowden Gardens ●

BODMIN ○   Garden House ●   TAVIST

A38   Cotehele ●

Lanhydrock ●

Duchy of Cornwall
● Nursery

Saltra
House

PLYMOUTH ○

Heligan   Antony ● Mount Edg

Barbara Hepworth Museum   Bosvigo House   ● Trewithen   Headland
& Sculpture Garden

TRURO

Burncoose &
Southdown

Caerhays Castle

Trengwainton

A39

A30

A386

Trebah   Penjerrick
Glendurgan

PENZANCE

A394

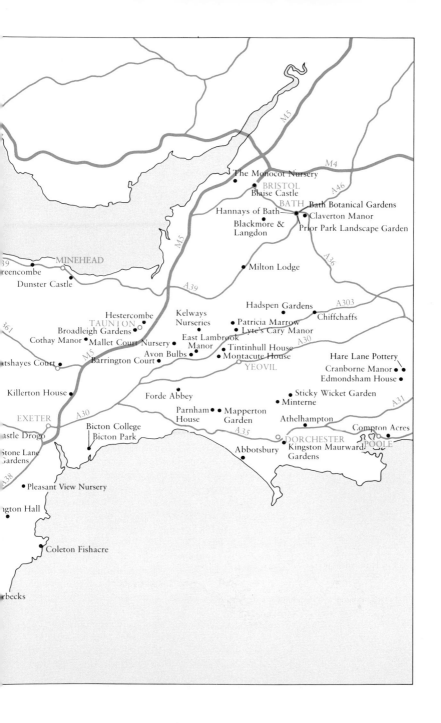

The Monocot Nursery

BRISTOL
Blaise Castle

BATH · Bath Botanical Gardens
Hannays of Bath · Claverton Manor
Blackmore & · Prior Park Landscape Garden
Langdon

Milton Lodge

MINEHEAD
Greencombe
Dunster Castle

A39

Hadspen Gardens
A303
Hestercombe · Kelways · Chiffchaffs
TAUNTON · Nurseries · Patricia Marrow
Broadleigh Gardens · East Lambrook · Lyte's Cary Manor
Cothay Manor · Mallet Court Nursery · Manor
· Tintinhull House · Hare Lane Pottery
Avon Bulbs · Montacute House · Cranborne Manor
Batshayes Court · Barrington Court · YEOVIL · Edmondsham House

Killerton House

Forde Abbey · Sticky Wicket Garden
Parnham · Mapperton · Minterne
EXETER · House · Garden · Athelhampton
Castle Drogo · A30 · A35 · Compton Acres
Bicton College · DORCHESTER · POOLE
Stone Lane · Bicton Park · Abbotsbury · Kingston Maurward
Gardens · Gardens

Pleasant View Nursery

ngton Hall

Coleton Fishacre

rbecks

ABBOTSBURY SUB-TROPICAL GARDENS

Dorset

Abbotsbury,
nr Weymouth DT3 4LA
1/2m W of Abbotsbury,
9m NW of Weymouth
by B3157
Tel: 01305 871412/871344
Fax: 01305 871092

Owner: Ilchester Estates

Open: Daily 10–5 (dusk in
winter); closed 25 Dec.
20 acres

BENEFITING FROM a remarkably mild microclimate, Abbotsbury Gardens have an immense range of plants. The garden was started in the 1760s but the 4th Earl of Ilchester introduced many new plants in the 19th century. From the original walled garden with its beautiful wingnut (*Pterocarya fraxinifolia*), paths lead to the valley garden, a gentle combe with camellias, magnolias and rhododendrons in old woodland. Asiatic primulas enliven the banks of the stream in spring, followed by gunnera, petasites, rodgersias and rheums. It is a garden worth visiting at any time of the year; in winter, for example, it is full of interest. Everywhere there is something to catch the eye in the surrounding jungle-like luxuriance. A plant centre has some good plants for sale.

ANTONY HOUSE

Cornwall

Torpoint PL11 2QA
5m W of Plymouth by
Torpoint car ferry and A374
Tel: 01752 812191

Owner: The National Trust

Open: Apr to 29 Oct, Tue,
Wed, Thur and Bank Hol
Mon 1.30–5.30; Jun to Aug,
also Sun 1.30–5.30.
25 acres. House open

WHEN A house is as beautiful as Antony there is always a danger that any garden will be outfaced. As it is, helped by the genius of Humphry Repton, the two go together in perfect harmony. The house – an early 18th-century dream of silver Pentewan stone – presents its north facade to land which slopes gently towards the distant Tamar estuary. The view from the house, over shallow rose-planted terraces, is towards an immense lawn broken in the middle ground only by a superb old black walnut (*Juglans nigra*). Far beyond this, Repton pierced an opening through a deep belt of woodland to give glimpses of the shimmering water in the distance – a dazzling effect achieved with such simplicity. In the woods there are marvellous trees, including some ancient holm oaks which Repton admired and was careful to preserve. A flower garden, and a distinguished knot of box and germander, are enclosed in yew, and in the old vegetable garden there is an immense collection of daylilies of which Antony holds a National Collection. South of all this is a giant cork oak (*Quercus suber*), a wonder to see.

ANTONY WOODLAND GARDEN AND WOODS

Cornwall

Torpoint PL11 2QA
5m W of Plymouth by
Torpoint car ferry and A374

Owner: Carew Pole Garden
Trust

Open: Apr to 29 Oct, Mon
to Sat 11–5.30, Sun 2–5.30.
100 acres

ADJOINING THE house and garden at Antony, and still owned by the family that built it, is an atmospheric woodland garden. Sir John Carew Pole started to plant it before World War II but was interrupted by active service. He subsequently added an immense number of magnolias and rhododendrons which flourish in the naturalistic setting of a wooded combe protected to the west by windbreaks. The woods fringe the estuary of the river Lynher and an idyllic walk gives glimpses of the mainland and the castellated silhouette of Ince Castle.

ARLINGTON COURT

Devon

Arlington,
nr Barnstaple EX31 4LP
7m NE of Barnstaple by
A39
Tel: 01271 850629

Owner: The National Trust

Open: Apr to 1 Nov, daily
except Sat (open Sat Bank
Hol weekends) 11–5.30.
25 acres. House open

THE PLEASURES of Arlington are not dramatic but they are distinctive. The best thing here is a little Victorian garden with, as its central ornament, a handsome gabled glasshouse crowned with a decorative metal heron, the crest of the Chichester family who owned the estate for many centuries. The garden is backed by a high wall and the ground descends in bold turfed terraces to the entrance steps which are flanked by a pair of cast-iron herons holding wriggling worms in their beaks. On either side of a central pool and fountain, arbours are festooned with roses in summer. The Victorian garden is some distance from the house which is set in lawns with fine specimen trees, including a good collection of species of ash. The lake was made at about the same time as the Victorian garden and a classical urn on a plinth to its north-east is in memory of Miss Rosalie Chichester who gave the estate to the National Trust.

ATHELHAMPTON

Dorset

Athelhampton,
Dorchester DT2 7LG
5m NE of Dorchester on
A35(T)
Tel: 01305 848363
Fax: 01305 848135

Owner: Patrick Cooke

Open: Mar to Oct, daily
except Sat 10.30–5 (closed
Sun in winter). 15 acres.
House open

THE GREAT thing about the garden at Athelhampton is the beauty of its design. This is a medieval manor house of rare character, and the garden, which was designed in the 1890s by F. Inigo Thomas, fits it to perfection. A balustraded terrace ornamented with two elegant summer houses overlooks a narrow canal, and beyond, disposed on a sunken lawn with a pool, are twelve giant pyramids of clipped yew. On the far side a gate leads through to a series of enclosed gardens – cunningly connected to the house by penetrating vistas – which are richly ornamented with statues, fountains, obelisks, beautifully detailed walls and gate piers in golden Ham stone. The whole place is a virtuoso performance – a garden bristling with decorative exuberance that is, at the same time, both harmonious in itself and perfectly related to house and site.

AVON BULBS

Somerset

Illustration: Albuca nelsonii

Burnt House Farm,
Mid Lambrook,
South Petherton TA13 5HE
10m W of Yeovil by A3088
and A303 to South
Petherton
Tel and Fax: 01460 242177

Open: Mid Feb to mid Apr;
end Sept to mid Nov, Thur
to Sat 9–4.30 (check by
telephone); also by
appointment

AVON BULBS regularly wins Gold Medals at Chelsea for the beauty of its displays, and its catalogue is stuffed with good things. There is an emphasis on species or natural forms and many genera are represented in quantity (e.g. 20 species and forms of fritillary and 28 snowdrops). There is an excellent range of cyclamen, camassias, crocosmias, eythroniums, irises, narcissi and tulips. Keep an eye open for all sorts of rare, tender bulbous plants such as albuca, eucomis and tulbaghias, which make superb pot plants The nursery's business is chiefly bulbs but it strays into other desirable areas such as hellebores, of which a choice selection is offered. There are several excellent woodland plants such as corydalis, dicentra, scopiola and smilacina. The list (four 2nd-class stamps) is exceptionally good, beautifully illustrated in colour and full of valuable advice on cultivation. A mail order service is provided.

BARRINGTON COURT

Somerset

nr Ilminster TA19 0NQ
5m NE of Ilminster off
A303
Tel: 01985 847777

Owner: The National Trust

Open: Apr to Oct, daily
except Fri 11–5.30. 9 acres.
House open

THE BEAUTIFUL gabled manor house, of golden Ham stone, was built in 1514. The gardens have a pronounced Arts and Crafts atmosphere with marvellous basket-weave brick paths and fine masonry in walls and outhouses. Much of this is the work of the architects Forbes and Tate in the 1920s, for whose intricately planned enclosures Gertrude Jekyll designed the planting, one of her very last commissions. The lily garden to one side of the stable block shows her touch, with a central pool, raised beds of azaleas and bold clumps of crinums. East of it there is a charming new white garden, designed by Christine Middleton, the present head gardener, in segmental beds radiating from the centre. A gate leads through to the iris garden of Jekyllesque flavour, with a colour scheme of pink and lavender. A beautifully kept walled kitchen garden provides fruit and vegetables which are sold in season.

BATH BOTANICAL GARDENS

Somerset

Royal Victoria Park,
Upper Bristol Road,
Bath BA1 2NQ
W of city centre by Upper
Bristol Road

Owner: City of Bath

Open: Daily 9–sunset.
15 acres

AS BOTANIC gardens go this is on a modest scale but it is very attractively laid out on a fine sloping site and is rich in good plants. Here, it is the trees and larger shrubs, often finely underplanted with bulbs, that are of special distinction. There are excellent specimens, many mature, of the golden *Catalpa bignonioides*, Japanese cherries, an exceptional dogwood (*Cornus kousa chinensis*), superb magnolias and Japanese maples. An atmospheric dell, across the road to the north of the gardens, has a monument to Shakespeare and lovely drifts of anemones and bluebells in season. The whole is excellently cared for by the city parks department.

BICTON COLLEGE OF AGRICULTURE

Devon

Illustration: Agapanthus praecox sbsp. *minimus*

East Budleigh, Budleigh Salterton EX9 7DP
6m NE of Exmouth by A376
Tel: 01395 562300

Owner: Bicton College

Open: Daily 11–4.30.
19 acres

PART OF the same estate as Bicton Park, Bicton College now opens its doors to members of the public, who will find much to interest them. An avenue of monkey puzzles leads towards the house, beyond which are several collections of trees and shrubs – among them camellias, cherries, eucalyptus, magnolias and maples. The college holds the National Collections of agapanthus and pittosporum; the former is a real eye-opener (especially the lovely, and rarely seen, species). In a 2-acre walled garden a nursery has many excellent plants for sale, including several tender rarities.

BICTON PARK GARDENS

Devon

THINGS ARE changing at Bicton Park, which is being restored to its true character as a pleasure garden. At the heart of it is a formal arrangement, the Italian Garden, which in essence dates from the early 18th century but now has a jolly Victorian character with bedded-out parterres, fountains, urns and palm

East Budleigh, Budleigh
Salterton EX9 7DP
6m NE of Exmouth by
A376
Tel: 01395 68465

Owner:
Bicton Park Trust Company

Open: Mar to Oct, daily
10–6 (Mar and Oct 10–4).
50 acres

trees. To the north is a range of glasshouses with
collections of fuchsias and pelargoniums and, to the
west, a stunning curvaceous palm house, like a ship's
prow seen from below. Beautifully restored, this very
early building dates from 1820, and has been planted
with a splendid range of conservatory plants. To one
side of the Italian Garden there is an ornamental shell-
house set in a ferny rock garden and, another relic of
the early 19th century, an American garden in which
plants from North America are grown. A woodland
railway through the grounds gives views of a fine
arboretum and of the brick mansion. There is much to
see and admire in this lively place, not least the high
standards of maintenance.

BLACKMORE & LANGDON LTD
Somerset

Pensford, Bristol BS18 4JL
6 1/2m S of Bristol by A37
Tel and Fax: 01275 332300

Open: Daily 9–5 (Sun 10–4)

O LD-ESTABLISHED FAMILY firms such as this are
becoming very rare. Blackmore & Langdon was
founded in 1901 and has won over 60 Gold Medals at
the Chelsea Flower Show and countless others
elsewhere. It is best known for delphiniums, border
phlox and begonias, and many varieties of these are
available only from Blackmore & Langdon whose
catalogue every year advertises interesting new
cultivars. It also sells gloxinias and polyanthus. The
catalogue (s.a.e.) is particularly informative, and
excellent specialist pamphlets on growing some of the
plants are issued. A mail order service is provided and
various sundries, including special wire supports for
begonias, are available. A visit at delphinium time is a
wonderful treat.

BLAISE CASTLE
Bristol

T HE BLAISE Castle estate, all but engulfed in pretty
horrible suburbia, is an enchanting relic of English
landscape taste. The Great House at Henbury, a Tudor
manor, was acquired in 1762 by Thomas Farr who in
1766 commissioned a splendid Sham Castle from the
architect Robert Mylne. It remains on a lofty eminence
rising above trees – 'The finest place in England; worth
going fifty miles at any time to see' as Jane Austen's

Henbury, Bristol BS10 7QS
5m NW of Bristol by A4108
Tel: 0117 9506789

Owners: Bristol City
Council; National Trust

Open: Daily dawn–dusk.
50 acres

Isabella Thorpe said in *Northanger Abbey*. Later in the century Humphry Repton came to landscape the park and his 'Red Book' is on view at Blaise Castle House. Repton's colleague John Nash was called in in the early 19th century to design Blaise Hamlet, a group of wildly picturesque staff cottages. These are designed in a full-blown fantasy vernacular with thatched roofs and gothic windows. Owned by the National Trust, the hamlet is impeccably kept and of devastating charm. It lies on the other side of the main road from the park – but is an essential part of a visit.

BOSVIGO HOUSE

Cornwall

Bosvigo Lane,
Truro TR1 3NH
In the W suburbs of Truro
by A390; at Highertown
take Dobbs Lane (near
Sainsbury roundabout).
Bosvigo House is 500 yards
on the left
Tel and Fax: 01872 275774

Owners:
Michael and Wendy Perry

Open: Mar to Sept, Wed to
Sat 11–6. 3 acres

BOSVIGO HOUSE is a surprising and very attractive garden to find on the suburban edge of Truro. In the garden, however, all that seems far away. The Perrys are perfectionists, and have made one of the most attractive of recent gardens. To one side of the handsome 18th-century house is a woodland garden, whose 'hot' borders explode into life in late summer with blazing crocosmias, dahlias, roses, nasturtiums and alstroemerias. About the house are several beautifully planted enclosures showing exciting and fastidious colour harmonies. It is rare in Cornwall for a garden to keep up the interest well into September, as Bosvigo certainly does. The Perrys also sell excellent plants, some rare. There is a good catalogue (four 2nd-class stamps) but no mail order.

BROADLEIGH GARDENS

Somerset

Illustration: *Tulipa bakeri*
'Lilac Wonder'

Bishops Hull,
Taunton TA4 1AE
3m SW of Taunton by A38
and minor roads
Tel: 01823 286231
Fax: 01823 323646

Open: Mon to Fri 9–4 to
view only. Mail order and
pre-booked sales only

T HIS IS an outstanding nursery specialising in bulbs but also with many herbaceous plants. Although the business is mail order only, you may visit the garden and view the plants on the spot. Spring is, of course, a good time but Lady Skelmersdale has all sorts of bulbous treats up her sleeve throughout the year – a rare selection of colchicums and autumn-flowering crocuses, for example. This is not a place for instant gardeners but you can go round, notebook in hand, making a list to order from the excellent well-illustrated catalogues (two 1st-class stamps) which are issued in January and June.

BURNCOOSE NURSERIES AND GARDEN

Cornwall

Gwennap,
Redruth TR16 6BJ
3m SE of Redruth on A393
Tel: 01209 861112
Fax: 01209 860011

Open: Mon to Sat 8.30–5,
Sun 11–5. *Garden:* 30 acres

T HE NURSERY is in the ownership of the Williams family, famous plant collectors who also own Caerhays Castle. It carries a varied general stock of over 3,000 varieties, but there are specialities for which it is outstanding, some of which would be considered hopelessly tender anywhere outside the privileged south-west (for example, *Metrosideros*). The emphasis is on woody plants, such as camellias, magnolias and rhododendrons, of which it has especially good selections. Several rarities are stocked (for example, *Sinowilsonia henryi*) which are scarcely to be found anywhere else. A very good catalogue (£1.00) is published, from which mail orders may be placed.

Alongside the nursery is a fine old woodland garden dating back to the 19th century, in which bamboos, camellias, magnolias and, above all, magnificent rhododendrons are attractively displayed among handsome trees.

CAERHAYS CASTLE
Cornwall

nr Gorran FA1 7DE
In Caerhays village,
10m S of St Austell by
minor roads
Tel: 01872 501310
Fax: 01872 501870

Owner: F.J. Williams

Open: 16 Mar to 8 May,
Mon to Fri 11–4; also
25–26 Apr 11–4. 100 acres

THIS IS a special place for lovers of the three greatest groups of ornamental Asiatic shrubs: camellias, magnolias and rhododendrons. The Williams family, who own it, sponsored some of the great plant hunters – such as George Forrest and E.H. Wilson – and their discoveries found a marvellous home in this wild coastal setting. North of the early 19th-century castle designed by John Nash, woodland sweeps up the hill. It is a place for the observant visitor – the garden's chief glories may lie hidden in the jungle and the excitement of discovery is one of the exceptional pleasures here. Apart from the great trio of flowering shrubs there are many others, some of them exceptionally rare and first planted here – such as the exotically scented *Michelia doltsopa* with its flowers of creamy yellow. The lavish feast of spring blossom, in this wildly romantic place, is a marvellous sight.

CASTLE DROGO
Devon

Drewsteignton EX6 6PB
21m W of Exeter by A30
Tel: 01647 433306

Owner: The National Trust

Open: Apr to 1 Nov, daily
10.30–5.30. 12 acres. Castle
open

CASTLE DROGO, the last castle to be built in Britain, was designed by Edwin Lutyens and started before World War I. It has a dramatic position on a rocky bluff near Dartmoor, commanding wide views with the river Teign in the distance. The garden, to the north of the drive, is concealed behind ramparts of yew strongly echoing the bold forms of the castle. Granite steps and a path lead to a rectangular sunken garden of subtly varying levels. Here, in each corner, is a shady arbour of *Parrotia persica* trained over a framework, and around two central lawns are lavishly planted mixed borders, among which scalloped paths of Mughal influence thread their way. In late spring an immense old wisteria snakes along the terrace walls, its

flowers dripping to the beds below. Granite steps rise
to a path lined with flowering shrubs, leading to a
huge circular croquet lawn (which visitors may use)
hedged in yew, devoid of ornament but with powerful
atmosphere.

CHIFFCHAFFS

Dorset

Chaffeymoor, Bourton,
Gillingham SP8 5BY
At W end of Bourton, 3m
E of Wincanton off A303
Tel: 01747 840841

Owner:
Mr and Mrs K.R. Potts

Open: Garden: 5 Apr to 20
Sept, Sun (except 2nd Sun
in month), Wed and Bank
Hol Mon 2–5.30. *Nursery:*
17 Mar to 14 Nov Tue to
Sat 10–1, 2–5, and whenever
garden is open. 11 acres

T HIS GARDEN, in a surprisingly secluded valley just
off the A303, was started from nothing in 1983,
and the owners later incorporated within it their
nursery garden, Abbey Plants. The sloping site has
been skilfully terraced and linked with stone paths and
steps. The soil is acid and a very wide range of plants
is grown in beds separated by curving lawns. The
different levels, and secluded nooks and crannies,
provide a variety of sites in an attractively informal
setting. Across a field is a woodland garden threaded
with streams, where moisture-loving plants such as
primulas, gunnera and rheums thrive in the shade of
rhododendrons and many ornamental trees. All this is
an admirable example of what can be achieved by
skilled gardeners in a remarkably short time. The
nursery has a good range of plants at modest prices
and a visit is essential as there is no mail order.

CLAVERTON MANOR

Somerset

Claverton,
nr Bath BA2 7BD
4m SE of Bath by A36
Tel: 01225 460503
Fax: 01225 480726

Owner: The American
Museum in Britain

Open: end Mar to
beginning Nov, daily except
Mon 1–6 (Sat and Sun
12–6; Bank Hol Sun and
Mon 11–6). 10 acres.
House open

C LAVERTON MANOR, with its wonderful views
across the Avon valley, is an elegant Bath stone
mansion designed by Sir Jeffry Wyatville. The position
of the garden, on south-facing slopes, is beautiful,
with excellent old trees – evergreen oaks, limes and
beeches – providing a backdrop for the gardens made
here since the American Museum came in 1961. A
transatlantic flavour is given by a collection of herbs
used in colonial times disposed in box-edged beds with
a bee skep at the centre. The George Washington
garden to the west of the house is inspired by the great
man's Virginian estate of Mount Vernon. Here are
sweeping beds edged in brick or box, gravel paths and
an elegant octagonal pepper-pot gazebo. Further down
the slopes an arboretum planted with American trees
and shrubs vividly reminds the visitor of the debt owed
by British gardens to American flora. All this is
impeccably maintained.

COLETON FISHACRE GARDEN

Devon

T HIS IS a remote corner of south Devon and to find
a garden here at all seems pretty unlikely; to find
one of such special charm as this is amazing good
fortune. The house, built by Oswald Milne, a follower
of Edwin Lutyens, for the D'Oyly Carte family, looks

Coleton, Kingswear,
Dartmouth TQ6 0EQ
4m S of Brixham off B3205
Tel: 01803 425466

Owner: The National Trust

Open: Mar, Sun 2–5; Apr to
1 Nov, Wed, Thur, Fri, Sun,
and Bank Hol Mon
10.30–5.30 or dusk if
earlier. 20 acres

down a narrow valley that descends to the sea. The
garden has a very warm microclimate and the sea
nearby adds to the humidity. Plants flourish here and
many tender things, tricky if not impossible to grow
elsewhere in Britain, seem luxuriantly at home. A
stream runs the whole length of the garden,
occasionally breaking out into little pools, its banks
finely planted with moisture-loving herbaceous
perennials. The sides of the valley, threaded with
winding paths, are densely planted with trees and
shrubs. There are many camellias and rhododendrons
but also far more exciting things – tender exotics such
as the crape myrtle (*Lagerstroemia indica*), *Mandevilla
suaveolens* and thickets of mimosa (*Acacia dealbata*).

COMPTON ACRES

Dorset

IN SPITE of Compton Acres' popularity, garden snobs
should not turn their backs on it for it has an
immense amount to offer. The precipitous site, with
old pine woods close to the sea, reveals occasional
splendid views to the Isle of Purbeck. The garden is
arranged in a series of thematic episodes, each of
which is beautifully arranged to give surprise: an

Canford Cliffs Road,
Poole BH13 7ES
1 1/2m W of Bournemouth
by A35 and B3065
Tel: 01202 700778
Fax: 01202 707537

Owner:
Pamlion Properties Ltd

Open: Mar to Oct, daily
10–6. 10 acres

Italian garden with a long pool, splashing fountains, clipped hedges and statues; a palm court with a Moorish flavour; an elaborate water garden with conifers and paths winding over rocks; and an immense Japanese garden of great character – shady, richly ornamental and dramatic. There are many excellent plants – in particular rhododendrons in a valley garden and many conifers and heathers in the heather dell. All this is done with panache and maintained to exemplary standards.

COTEHELE

Cornwall

St Dominick,
nr Saltash PL12 6TA
8m SW of Tavistock off
A390
Tel: 01579 350434

Owner: The National Trust

Open: Apr to 1 Nov, daily
11–dusk. 10 acres. House
open

THE GABLED and towered courtyard house, built in late Tudor times of moody grey granite by the Edgcumbe family, is at the centre of a garden that has many different faces. The house itself and its splendid outhouses and courtyards provide sheltered corners for all sorts of tender things such as the yellow-flowered *Jasminum mesnyi*. North-west of the house is a meadow which in spring is bright with daffodils. From here a gate leads through to a garden of more formal atmosphere, with a pool at the centre and a good border running along the northern wall. East of the house a series of terraces is planted with wallflowers in spring, followed in summer by roses, and there are some superb magnolias on the lower lawn. From the bottom terrace a secret passage leads through to a complete change of atmosphere. Here is a woodland garden in a steep valley, with a pool and an ancient dovecote shaped like a giant beehive. In the woods are camellias, magnolias and rhododendrons richly underplanted with ferns and moisture-loving plants; hostas, primulas and the bold foliage of *Gunnera manicata* relish the banks of a rushing stream.

COTHAY MANOR

Somerset

nr Wellington TA21 0JR
5m W of Wellington by A38
and minor roads (follow
signs to Thorne St
Margaret)
Tel: 01823 672283

Owner:
Mr and Mrs A.H.B. Robb

Open: May to Sept, Thur
and 1st Sun in each month
2–6. 5 acres

THE MARVELLOUSLY romantic house at Cothay is the perfect English manor house. It dates from the late middle ages, is built of stone as all old houses in these parts are, and is set in wonderful country. New owners have taken in hand a remarkable and attractive garden which had been laid out between the wars by Colonel Reginald Cooper, a friend of Harold Nicolson at Sissinghurst and of Lawrence Johnston at Hidcote. Behind the house he devised a sequence of garden rooms leading off a long grass-pathed passage, the whole hedged in yew. The Robbs have worked hard to restore the beautiful yew hedges and have already achieved much by way of replanting in the enclosures. A paved terrace runs along this, the western, facade of the house with much lively and appropriate planting. An internal courtyard entered on the far side of the house also presented opportunities for decorative planting which the Robbs have seized. Visitors will follow the evolution of this lovely place with excitement; so far the owners seem to have done all the right things.

CRANBORNE MANOR GARDENS
Dorset

nr Wimborne BH21 5PP
In Cranborne village,
16 1/2m SW of Salisbury by
A354 and B3081
Tel and Fax: 01725 517248

Owner: Viscount and
Viscountess Cranborne

Open: Garden: Mar to
Sept, Wed 9–5; *Garden
Centre:* all year, Mon to Sat
9–5 (Sun 10–5). 10 acres

THE MANOR house, once a medieval hunting lodge, has been in the Cecil family since the 17th century. There are mixed borders, an enclosed herb garden, walks edged with espaliered apple trees, a 17th-century mount and the charm of an ancient place embosomed in even more ancient woods. The garden centre next door to the manor carries a wide general stock but with especially good collections of old and shrub roses and clematises. A mail order service is provided for roses only, and a catalogue of roses is issued (£1.00).

DARTINGTON HALL
Devon

Dartington,
nr Totnes TQ9 6EL
2m NW of Totnes by A384
Tel and Fax: 01803 862367

Owner:
Dartington Hall Trust

Open: Daily dawn–dusk.
30 acres

THE HOUSE is one of the most spectacular medieval mansions in Devon, and the garden which lies chiefly to the south-west of it is designed on a heroic scale. The natural combe has been sculpted into great grassy terraces looking down onto an expanse of turf – according to legend, a medieval jousting lawn. The formal arrangement to the north of the terraces was designed by the American garden designer Beatrix Farrand, her only work in England. On the highest terrace, in the shade of immense old sweet chestnuts, a splendid stone carving by Henry Moore of a reclining woman turns her back on the terraces below. Nearby, a vertiginous flight of steps sweeps down the hill and giant magnolias ornament each side. At the far end of the terraces more steps lead up to an ornamental pond with a fountain of carved swans in the shade of a very large *Elaeagnus umbellata* 'Parvifolia', and further to the west glades open out in old woodland.

DOCTON MILL

Devon

Spekes Valley,
nr Hartland EX39 6EA
Between Lymebridge Cross
and Milford; 3 m S of
Hartland follow signs to
Elmscott and Lymebridge
Cross
Tel and Fax: 01237 441369

Owner:
Mr and Mrs M.G. Bourcier

Open: Mar to Oct, daily
10–5. 8 acres

T HIS GARDEN has been made since 1980 and is a
model of sensitive planting and design in an
exceptionally beautiful site. In a secluded valley near
the sea, it possesses a favourable microclimate. In
spring the garden explodes into life with an immense
collection of daffodils and the upper slopes of the
valley sparkle with the young foliage of many shrubs
and ornamental trees. An excellent bog garden and the
banks of streams are planted with moisture-loving
plants – lysichitons, ligularias, candelabra primulas
and hostas, with bold contrasts of foliage shape and
colour. The intricate planting near the house contrasts
well with a woodland garden that merges with the
surrounding landscape.

DUCHY OF CORNWALL NURSERY

Cornwall

Penlyne, Cott Road,
Lostwithiel PL22 0BW
2m NE of Lostwithiel
off A390
Tel: 01208 872668
Fax: 01208 872835

Open: Daily except Bank
Hol 9–5 (Sun 10–5)

T HIS IS the kind of nursery which, in an ideal
world, every gardener would have just down the
road. Its exceptional qualities are the range of plants –
almost 3,000 both woody and herbaceous – and their
very high quality. Being in Cornwall it stocks many
tender things that flourish in those balmy parts –
corokias, drimys, feijoa, several myrtles and
prostantheras. In every department there is a wide
range and something worth having. It is impeccably
run and prices are more than fair. There is an excellent
catalogue (£2.00) but no mail order.

DUNSTER CASTLE

Somerset

T HE CASTLE occupies a marvellous position on its
great wooded tor. It is partly 13th-century but
much added to, especially in the 19th century by
Anthony Salvin. The microclimate here is very
privileged and the spectacular rocky crag on which the
castle is built provides shelter to tender plants. The
garden, which is informally arranged to spiral up the

Dunster,
nr Minehead TA24 6SL
3m SE of Minehead by
A396
Tel: 01643 821314

Owner: The National Trust

Open: Jan to Mar, Oct to
Dec, daily 11–4 (closed 25
Dec); Apr to Sept, daily
10–5. 17 acres. Castle open

wooded slopes to a secluded plateau at the summit, has many plants from Australasia – such as pittosporums, mimosas and olearias – and the lovely white Banksian rose. On a sunny terrace a large lemon tree, over 150 years old, is given winter protection and fruits handsomely. Camellias and magnolias are brilliant in early spring. The National Trust has been restoring and adding to this garden in recent years – planting a fascinating selection of olive cultivars on the castle's southern slopes, for example.

EAST LAMBROOK MANOR

Somerset

East Lambrook, South
Petherton TA13 5HL
3m N of A303 to South
Petherton
Tel: 01460 240328
Fax: 01460 242344

Owner: Mr and Mrs
Andrew Norton

Open: Garden: Mar to Oct,
daily except Sun (open May
Bank Hol weekend) 10–5;
Nursery: daily except Sun
10–5. 1 1/2 acres

THE GARDEN was made by Margery Fish from 1938 and, publicised by her excellent books, became one of the best known in England. Mrs Fish invented a style of inspired cottage gardening, often using carefully chosen forms of wild plants. The design is informal and, although it is given structure by clipped evergreens and pollarded willows, there is scarcely a straight line in the place. Her garden, restored since 1985 by the present owners, is full of excellent plants very well grown and many rare. It is also full of lessons for all gardeners about the importance of siting plants and the art of choosing plants to perform in each season. The garden holds the National Collection of species and primary hybrids of hardy geraniums. An excellent nursery sells a good range of plants, chiefly herbaceous, at excellent prices. There is a catalogue (four 1st-class stamps) but no mail order service; but it is much better to visit, admire, and buy on the spot.

EDMONDSHAM HOUSE

Dorset

Edmondsham, nr
Wimborne BH21 5RE
17m SW of Salisbury by
A354 and B3081
Tel: 01725 517207

Owner: Mrs J. Smith

Open: Apr to Oct, Wed and
Sun, Bank Hol Mon 2–5.
6 acres

THE HOUSE at Edmondsham is marvellous and splendidly two-faced – ornately Tudor and Jacobean on one side, crisply Georgian on the other – and framed by excellent old trees. The chief garden interest here is an old 1-acre kitchen garden, walled in brick and cob, cultivated entirely organically. Fruit and vegetables are bursting with vigour, and broad double herbaceous borders flank a path. With its impeccable potting shed, its old well and pump and its beautifully restored pit house, this is a fascinating example of the kitchen gardens of the past, upon which households were absolutely dependent.

FORDE ABBEY

Somerset

THE LATE medieval monastic buildings at Forde are spectacular, and near the house old yew hedges with wambly tops and a procession of sentinel clipped yews provide bold ornament in keeping with the splendour of the architecture. At some distance, across undulating turf with many fine specimen trees, a lake

Chard TA20 4LU
7m W of Crewkerne
off B3165
Tel: 01460 220231
Fax: 01460 220296

Owner: M. Roper

Open: Daily 10–4.30.
30 acres. House open

– the Great Pond – is overlooked by a curious summerhouse of pleached beech; beyond, is a fine bog garden with sheets of Asiatic primulas followed by the ornamental foliage of *Gunnera manicata*, *Lysichiton americanum* and the royal fern *Osmunda regalis*. In the old kitchen garden the Abbey Nursery sells a wide range of excellent plants with an emphasis on the tender and the unusual.

GARDEN HOUSE

Devon

Buckland Monachorum,
Yelverton PL20 7LQ
5m S of Tavistock by A386
Tel: 01822 854769

Owner:
The Fortescue Garden Trust

Open: Mar to Oct, daily
10.30–5. 8 acres

O N THE very edge of Dartmoor the Garden House is hidden in a wooded valley. Here, around some romantically decaying 16th-century ruins, on precipitous terraces and surrounded by old walls, Lionel Fortescue from 1945 onwards made a suitably romantic garden, from which there are lovely views over garden and countryside. Clematis and roses scale the stone walls and there are wonderful riches of plants, especially herbaceous, artfully disposed. Here are no cold and calculating vistas – everything depends on the quality of the planting and meticulous upkeep. Fortescue's successor, Keith Wiley, has now expanded the garden within the walls and beyond them, with ambition and skill. He has respected the character of the original garden but immensely enriched the planting. To the west of the walled garden he has made a completely new garden with a sweeping glade of Japanese maples, an alpine bed with creeping thyme, rhodohypoxis and sedums, and a 'ruined cottage' garden with flowers growing in the collapsed masonry. An impeccable nursery sells marvellous plants, none commonplace and all good value.

GLEBE COTTAGE PLANTS

Devon

Illustration: *Geranium
pratense* 'Mrs Kendall
Clark'

Pixie Lane, Warkleigh,
Umberleigh EX37 9DH
6m W of South Molton
by B3226
Tel and Fax: 01769 540554

Open: Apr to Oct, Tue to
Fri 10–1, 2–5; also by
appointment

CAROL KLEIN specialises in herbaceous plants with
a few woody herbs. She sells exactly the kind of
plants that many people want to grow in their gardens
and she has excellent collections of particular groups –
campanulas, pinks, a long and distinguished list of
hardy geraniums, many penstemons, several
pulmonarias and many other good things. Most of
these may be seen growing in her little garden next to
the nursery. A good catalogue (£1.00) is produced and
plants may be supplied by mail order.

GLENDURGAN GARDEN

Cornwall

Helford River,
Mawnan Smith,
nr Falmouth TR11 5JZ
4m SW of Falmouth on
road to Helford Passage
Tel: 01208 74281/01326
250906

Owner: The National Trust

Open: 3 Mar to Oct, Tue to
Sat and Bank Hol Mon
(closed Good Fri)
10.30–5.30. 25 acres

THE FOXES are a great Cornish family and their
garden exploits contributed immensely to the
horticultural life of the county. Glendurgan was
bought by Alfred Fox in 1821 and his family have been
here ever since. The glen is a deep ravine which
tumbles down to the sparkling water of the Helford
estuary. On either side of the steep banks paths follow
the contours but the bottom of the valley is not so
densely planted as to obscure the marvellous views
across to trees and shrubs on the other side of the
ravine. Deftly infiltrated into the informal planting is a
wandering maze of cherry laurel, planted in 1833 by
Alfred Fox, and making a lively evergreen garden
ornament. Like other Cornish gardens Glendurgan is
abundantly rich in camellias, magnolias and

rhododendrons but it also has exceptional trees such as an unforgettable tulip tree with wide spreading branches, one of the largest in the country. It would be wrong to think of Glendurgan as merely a spring garden – the pleasures continue throughout the gardening season. At any time of the year, the view from the house, at the head of the glen, perfectly composed, is one the visitor will not quickly forget.

GREENCOMBE

Somerset

Porlock TA24 8NU
1/2m W of Porlock by road
to Porlock Weir
Tel: 01643 862363

Owner:
Greencombe Garden Trust

Open: Apr to Jul, Sat to
Tue 2–6. 3 1/2 acres

MUCH OF the character of this remarkable garden is determined by its site – on slopes overlooking Porlock Weir, with a very benign microclimate. The garden was started after World War II by Horace Stroud but it is under Miss Joan Loraine, who made the present garden and passed it over to the Trust that now owns it, that it has come to full fruition. Near the house beds and flowing lawns show strong contrasts of shapely plants – mounds of Japanese maple and soaring spires of cypress. Roses pour down slopes and walls, and paths lead into ancient woodland in which huge hollies, oaks and old coppiced sweet chestnuts provide the background to wonderful magnolias, rhododendrons and maples underplanted with all

kinds of shade-loving plants. There is nothing fiddly or fussy; the whole place has an air of marvellous inevitability. The National Collection of erythroniums is kept here – it is worth making a visit in April especially to see them.

HADSPEN GARDENS

Somerset

nr Castle Cary BA7 7NG
2m SE of Castle Cary by
A371
Tel and Fax: 01749 813707

Owner: N. A. Hobhouse

Open: Mar to Oct, Thur to
Sun and Bank Hol Mon
10–5. 5 acres

THE VERY pretty late 18th-century house in its park-like setting is sheltered by wooded slopes rising to the north behind it. The garden beyond the house has 18th-century origins but in the late 1960s it was taken in hand by Penelope Hobhouse and in 1987 a further impetus came from lively new gardeners, Nori and Sandra Pope. In the old walled kitchen garden are brilliant colour borders disposed round the walls, alive with the Popes' new plantings of subtle harmonies. Nearby, above a huge rectangular pool, a high brick wall affords protection to many tender plants. A nursery sells good plants and new introductions are constantly being made. There is a catalogue (three 1st-class stamps) but no mail order.

THE HANNAYS OF BATH

Somerset

THE HANNAYS are mad about plants and a visit to their nursery is always rewarding because you will certainly find excellent and unfamiliar ones. Some may come from the Hannays' own collecting expeditions.

Sydney Wharf Nursery,
Bathwick, Bath BA2 4ES
In Bath, at bottom of
Bathwick Hill via Sydney
Mews
Tel: 01225 462230/317577

Open: 20 Mar to 18 Oct,
Wed to Sun and Bank Hol
Mon 10–5; also by
appointment

They are especially good on herbaceous plants and on their wild forms; centaureas, cimicifugas, dieramas, digitalis and moraeas are well represented. Among woody plants phlomis and sage are outstanding. An informal garden, merging with the nursery, is unassuming but stuffed with good things. A very good catalogue (£1.40) is produced, with much valuable information, but there is no mail order.

HARE LANE POTTERY

Dorset

nr Wimborne BH21 5QT
2m E of Cranborne on
Alderholt road
Tel: 01725 517700

Open: Sat and Sun 9–5 and
mostly during the week;
please phone to check

HANDMADE GARDEN pots, made from local clay and fired in a wood-burning kiln, were once common; today they are extremely rare. Jonathan Garratt makes a wide range of beautifully fashioned pots, alpine pans and unusual kinds of planter. They vary in colour, some having an attractive darker tinge, but all are finely made and available only at the pottery. All the pots are guaranteed against frost damage; pots planted with bulbs have withstood −12°C at the pottery.

HEADLAND

Cornwall

Battery Lane, Polruan-by-
Fowey PL23 1PW
In the centre of Polruan.
Park in main car park and
walk down St Saviour's
Hill, turning left at Coast
Guard Office
Tel: 01726 870243

Owner: Jean and John Hill

Open: 7 May to 13 Aug,
Thur 2–6. 1 3/4 acres

JEAN AND John Hill came to Headland in 1976. On a splendid rocky promontory jutting out into the mouth of the Fowey estuary, they have made a garden of vital interest to all gardeners who battle against wind and salt-laden air. Paths wind along the contours of precipitous slopes with outcrops of natural rock. Hedges of escallonia, euonymus and privet have proved their worth as shelters. A few handsome mature trees, in particular Monterey pine (*Pinus radiata*) and *Cupressus macrocarpa*, although relishing the seaside climate, suffered grievously from storm damage. Many other woody plants – arbutus, cistus, cotoneaster, hebes – provide wind- and salt-proof ornament. Frosts are rarely severe and such herbaceous plants as aeonium, lampranthus and osteospermum flourish. This is a garden that will also be enjoyed by gardeners not seeking practical guidance about coastal gardening; the winding paths, well-kept plantings, and exquisite views across the estuary give rare pleasure.

HELIGAN
Cornwall

nr Mevagissey,
St Austell PL26 6EN
4m S of St Austell by B3273;
turn right after Pentewan
village
Tel: 01726 844157
Fax: 01726 843023

Owner:
The Heligan Gardens Ltd

Open: Daily 10.30–5.
57 acres

THE PRESIDING genius of this extraordinary place, Tim Smit, is a man of such astounding energy that he could probably make a memorable event out of the restoration of a bus shelter. Here at Heligan, however, he has found a subject worthy of his skills. The lost garden of the Tremaynes, famous in its day, became neglected and forgotten. Tim Smit rediscovered it, and with his partner, John Nelson, formed a trust to restore it. Work started in the spring of 1991 – paths were laid bare and resurfaced, immense brambles uprooted, glades cleared, and gradually a garden of great enchantment was revealed. It is rich in rhododendrons (including several Hooker introductions of the 1840s), many rare and grown to exceptional size, and trees of rare beauty. It also possesses a splendid range of garden buildings – a peach house, an ingenious pineapple pit, melon frames, bee boles and beautiful frames with fish-tail glazing. All these, and tool- and potting-sheds, are now restored, together with a magnificent walled flower garden and vast early glasshouses. Already the garden gives pleasure of the most varied kind. There is much to excite the most demanding of plant lovers, but the special quality of Heligan is that its wild and romantic atmosphere has been triumphantly preserved.

BARBARA HEPWORTH MUSEUM AND SCULPTURE GARDEN
Cornwall

Barnoon Hill,
St Ives TR26 1TG
In the centre of St Ives
Tel: 01736 796226
Fax: 01736 794480

Owner: The Tate Gallery

Open: Apr to Sept, daily
11–7 (Sun and Bank Hol
11–5); Oct to Mar, daily
except Mon 11–5 or dusk if
earlier. 1/4 acre

THIS WAS Barbara Hepworth's own studio and garden and is a splendid place in which to imbibe the full, heady St Ives ambience. Here, in the heart of the town, is an enchanting oasis whose interest is not strictly horticultural. The point of it is the potent atmosphere of a personal miniature landscape. The garden is quite small, stuffed with plants of bold foliage – phormiums, cordylines, *Echium pininana* and bamboos – among which are placed many examples of her sculptures. Although far more cramped than they would be in a museum, they look splendid jostling for position in their jungly setting. The studio in which she worked has been left more or less as it was when

she died – overalls hanging on a hook, chippings of white marble on the floor, tools ready to hand. You may peer into it from the garden, an eery and unforgettable experience – a Marie Céleste of a studio, apparently momentarily deserted, into which the artist will stride at any moment.

HESTERCOMBE

Somerset

Cheddon Fitzpaine,
nr Taunton TA2 8LQ
2m NE of Taunton off
A361
Tel: 01823 337222

Owner:
Somerset County Council

Open: Daily 10–6 (in winter
5). 8 acres

THE GARDEN at Hestercombe was designed by Gertrude Jekyll and Edwin Lutyens just before World War I and is one of their great masterpieces. Since 1973 it has been rescued from the brink of irretrievable collapse and restored with authenticity by Somerset County Council. Here is a marvellous distillation of the essence of the Lutyens/Jekyll garden wizardry – an enclosed area of shifting levels with lively stonework, a symmetrical parterre-like 'Great Plat', iris-fringed rills fed by water-spouting masks, and Miss Jekyll's boldly unfussy planting of massed grey-leafed plants, glossy bergenias, ramparts of rosemary and a pergola of roses and clematis. In 1997, for the first time, another part of the garden was opened – the romantic landscape garden dating from

the 18th century, made in the heyday of the
gentlemanly obsession for landscaping. It was made by
Copleston Warre Bampfylde, a friend of Henry Hoare
of Stourhead, and is now undergoing well merited
restoration but is already a delightful place to visit.

KELWAYS LTD

Somerset

Langport TA10 9EZ
In Langport, 10m E of
Taunton by A358 and A378
Tel: 01458 250521
Fax: 01458 253351

Open: Mon to Fri 9–5, Sat
and Sun 10–4

THIS IS one of the best of all nurseries for daylilies,
irises and peonies, and the many cultivars bearing
the 'Langport' or 'Kelway' name are evidence of the
work of this famous place in the raising of garden-
worthy plants. After a fallow period it is looking up
again. Excellent catalogues are issued, from which
orders are fulfilled by post.

KILLERTON

Devon

Broadclyst, Exeter EX5 3LE
5m NE of Exeter by B3181
and B3185; Jnct 28 of M5
Tel: 01392 881345

Owner: The National Trust

Open: Daily 10.30–dusk.
22 acres. House open

THE CHARMS of Killerton reveal themselves
gradually. Near the house a pair of fortissimo
mixed borders is ornamented with elegant Coade
stone urns. Beyond, the lawn unrolls, interrupted by
countless trees and shrubs of an acid-loving type –
magnolias, rhododendrons, stewartias, styrax and
maples. A rustic summerhouse, with a touch of
Grimm's fairy tales, has a wonderful interior of rattan,
wickerwork and pine cones. Behind, a masterly rock
garden in an old quarry sparkles with hellebores,
hostas and geraniums among mossy rocks under a
canopy of old camellias and maples. In late spring the
air is scented with sheets of *Cyclamen repandum*.

KINGSTON MAURWARD GARDENS

Dorset

THE HOUSE at Kingston Maurward is a grand early
18th-century stone mansion, built for the Pitt
family. The estate was eventually acquired by the
Hanbury family, a great horticultural dynasty, owners
of the famous subtropical garden at La Mortola in

Dorchester DT2 8PY
On the E edge of
Dorchester by A35 bypass
Tel: 01305 264738
Fax: 01305 250059

Owner: Kingston
Maurward College

Open: Easter to Oct, daily
10–5.30. 35 acres

Italy, and donors of land to Wisley gardens. It is now a college of agriculture and horticulture which has pulled off the remarkable feat of restoring the gardens on a lavish scale, opening to the public in 1995. It is, thus, still in its youth but it has tremendous promise. Here are burgeoning borders, fine Edwardian terraced gardens, a Japanese garden, a penstemon terrace (the National Collection is held here) and a rose garden. For many gardeners the most interesting thing is the use of tender bedding plants which hit their stride in late summer. Cannas, bananas with leaves as big as elephant's ears, castor-oil plants, sages and other exotic things vividly show the dramatic possibilities of this neglected style of gardening.

KNIGHTSHAYES COURT

Devon

Bolham,
Tiverton EX16 7RQ
2m N of Tiverton by A396
Tel: 01884 254665

Owner: The National Trust

Open: Apr to 1 Nov, daily
11–5.30. 40 acres. House
open

THE GARDENS at Knightshayes have two faces, both of them very handsome. Near the house are generously planted borders and a formal garden with yew hedges, standard wisterias, lead figures and a cool pool overhung by a weeping pear. Looking away from the house are marvellous rural views. East of the formal garden is one of the best small woodland gardens in the country, in which exceptional shrubs and ornamental trees are disposed to brilliant effect. At first sight it seems just a very attractive piece of woodland but the more you look the more you will see rare plants used with rare skill. In spring the display of bulbs is a fabulous sight, with *Erythronium* 'Knightshayes Pink' spreading like a lovely weed. There is a small selection of very good plants for sale.

LANHYDROCK

Cornwall

Bodmin PL30 5AD
2 1/2m SE of Bodmin by
A38 or B3268
Tel: 01208 73320

Owner: The National Trust

Open: Mar to 1 Nov, daily
11–5.30 (Mar and Oct
11–5). 25 acres. House open

THE HOUSE, a romantic mixture of the 17th and 19th centuries, is set in exquisite parkland, and an avenue of sycamores and beeches marches to the castellated entrance lodge. Beyond it a formal courtyard garden has rows of vast clipped Irish yews, beds of modern roses, and ornate bronze urns. Behind the house and church is a yew-hedged circular garden with herbaceous beds containing the National

Collection of crocosmias, which make the garden particularly worth visiting in late summer. Beyond this a woodland garden is stuffed with flowering shrubs and trees, especially rhododendrons and exceptionally fine magnolias, of which there are 120 different kinds.

LYTE'S CARY MANOR

Somerset

Charlton Mackrell,
Somerton TA11 7HU
4m SE of Somerton off
B3151
Tel: 01985 847777

Owner: The National Trust

Open: Apr to Oct, Mon,
Wed and Sat 2–6 or dusk if
earlier. 3 acres. House open

THE ENTRANCE to the late medieval manor house is through a forecourt with a central path flanked by yew topiary clipped into cottage-loaf shapes. This mixture of formality and simplicity characterises the garden. A door leads through to a lavish mixed border of herbaceous plants under old roses, while, on the other side of the path, a yew hedge is clipped into buttresses with decorative finials. Beyond a formal orchard open lawns and statues lead to a shady tunnel of hornbeam and a secret garden. Lytes Cary is no horticultural masterpiece but it provides the perfect setting for a rare house.

MALLET COURT NURSERY

Somerset

Curry Mallet,
nr Taunton TA3 6SY
In Curry Mallet village,
5m SE of Taunton by A358
and A378
Tel: 01823 480748
Fax: 01823 481009

Open: Mon to Fri 9–1, 2–5

JAMES HARRIS is known among tree-lovers as 'Acer' Harris and sells one of the finest selections of maples commercially available – almost certainly the largest in the country. His nursery is primarily devoted to trees and shrubs, with a particular emphasis on those grown from seed collected in the wild. He sells, for example, a vast range of oaks (160 kinds), many birches, rowans and magnolias, as well as shrubs, from China, Korea and Japan. There is a catalogue (s.a.e. 100g) and mail order service but a visit is always worthwhile to discover treasures that have not yet found their way onto the list.

MAPPERTON GARDENS

Dorset

Beaminster DT8 3NR
2m SE of Beaminster by
B3163
Tel: 01308 862645
Fax: 01308 863348

Owner: The Earl and
Countess of Sandwich

Open: Mar to Oct, daily
2–6. 12 acres. House open
by appointment to groups
only

To THE east of the fine 17th-century house, the garden, hidden in a long combe, comes as a surprise – a splendid formal arrangement of descending terraces and cross vistas. At the head of the valley an orangery looks down flagged paths past a rose-festooned pergola and along the central vista, guarded by stone eagles, which ends with two long ornamental pools. All this is copiously ornamented with topiary of yew and box, handsome urns and statues, and plenty of places to sit and admire the garden and the gabled house rising above it. This lively pastiche of a 17th-century garden, with all the trimmings, was laid out as recently as the 1920s. It is beautifully executed and makes an entirely unexpected and wonderful contrast to idyllic views of cattle grazing in the park-like countryside beyond.

PATRICIA MARROW

Somerset

Kingsdon,
nr Somerton TA11 7LE
In the middle of Kingsdon,
2m SE of Somerton off
B3151
Tel: 01935 840232

Open: Daily dawn–dusk
but check by phone

As SO many of the old-established nursery gardens cut back on their stock, much smaller, specialist nurseries have become one of the best sources of the more unusual plants. Mrs Marrow is a gardening institution in the West Country – a demon propagator who chooses her plants with great care. There is nothing commonplace here and much that you will not find easily elsewhere. She stocks a very large number of hardy plants, woody and herbaceous, some of which may not be quite so hardy in the frozen north. She issues no catalogue and provides no mail order service, but part of the essential charm of the place lies in meeting her. She does not bully customers but she talks about her plants so seductively that you will certainly bear away more than you bargained for.

MARWOOD HILL GARDENS

Devon

Barnstaple EX31 4EB
4m N of Barnstaple signed
from A361
Tel: 01271 42528

Owner: Dr J.A. Smart

Open: Garden: daily
dawn–dusk; *Nursery:* daily
11–5. 20 acres

THERE ARE many reasons for visiting Marwood Hill but the chief interest of the garden lies in the very large number of plants grown in appropriate habitats in the attractive valley setting. It was started in 1949 by Dr Jimmy Smart who took over a neglected old garden. Flowering shrubs and ornamental trees clothe the slopes of the upper garden and at the bottom of the valley small lakes are linked together by streams. A bog garden between two of the lakes burgeons with ligularias, candelabra primulas and irises. In high summer the banks are covered by the plumes of an immense number of astilbes – 135 different species and cultivars, a National Collection. In addition, National Collections of *Iris ensata* and tulbaghias are held here. There is also a good nursery. There is a catalogue (70p) but no mail order, so a visit is essential.

MILTON LODGE

Somerset

HERE IS a garden that takes full advantage of its beautiful position – with the city of Wells and its great cathedral below it to the south, and Glastonbury Tor in the distance beyond the Vale of Avalon. From the 18th-century house a terrace overlooks the steeply sloping site, with mixed borders, yew hedges and vertiginous descents giving way to parkland with

nr Wells BA5 3AQ
1/2m N of Wells off A39
Tel: 01749 672168

Owner:
D.C. Tudway Quilter

Open: Good Fri to Oct,
daily except Sat 2–6.
12 acres

ornamental trees. At some distance from the house, on the other side of the Old Bristol Road, is a real rarity – the Combe, an 18th-century gentleman's arboretum now in splendid maturity. This walled and bosky valley, full of fine trees to which the present owner adds, has immense charm and is much appreciated by the citizens of Wells who saunter there of a fine summer's evening.

MINTERNE

Dorset

Minterne Magna,
Dorchester DT2 7AU
In Minterne Magna village,
9m N of Dorchester by
A352
Tel: 01300 341370
Fax: 01300 341747

Owner:
Lord and Lady Digby

Open: Apr to Oct, daily
10–7. 21 acres

AT MINTERNE the rare quality of the garden lies in the gradual revealing of exotic flowering trees and shrubs in a beautiful setting. From the house there are views down a shallow valley to a sinuous lake set in parkland ornamented with superlative old trees. The woodland below is rich in exceptional examples of *Davidia involucrata*, magnolias, maples and rhododendrons. In the valley the banks of a stream are richly planted – vast drifts of primulas as well as exotic shrubs and trees, many of spectacular size. The visitor either follows the lower walk, nose-to-nose with the plants, or takes the upper, with views across the valley. The path arrives at a more open setting, a bridge arches over the stream, and on the bank sheep graze among superb oaks and limes.

THE MONOCOT NURSERY

Somerset

Jacklands, Jacklands
Bridge, Tickenham,
Clevedon BS21 6SG
Near Tickenham village,
on the B3130, 8m W of
Bristol by B3128
Tel: 01275 810394 (before 9
a.m., after 6 p.m.)

Open: Mon to Fri 10–6;
also by appointment

THE DARINGLY botanical name of this little nursery is a good clue to what it is. Mike Salmon sells bulbs, specialising in species and natural forms. If you are looking for overweight daffs and beefy multi-coloured tulips this is *not* the place for you. Instead, here are exquisite narcissi (every species you have ever heard of and some you haven't), rare tulbaghias, thirty species of crocus (not counting forms), a long list of colchicums and all sorts of treasures, many of which are not to be found elsewhere. The nursery is a charming mess but Mr Salmon knows his alliums, and he is one of the finest sources in the country for rare bulbs. There is a mail order service (for seeds as well as for bulbs) and fascinating lists are produced (£1).

MONTACUTE HOUSE
Somerset

Montacute TA15 6XP
In Montacute village,
4m W of Yeovil by A3088
Tel: 01935 823289

Owner: The National Trust

Open: Apr to 1 Nov, daily
except Tue 11–5.30 or dusk
if earlier; 4 Nov to Mar
1999, Wed to Sun 11.30–4.
12 acres. House open

THE LATE Tudor house, built of lovely golden Ham stone, is well situated in a garden to match. To the east of the house a walled forecourt has good herbaceous borders with lively colour schemes. The Tudor walls are ornamented with stone finials and in each corner an airy Elizabethan gazebo gives views to the deer park beyond. North of the house a raised walk overlooks a deep border with shrub roses underplanted with peonies, and a stately lawn surrounded by clipped Irish yews with a circular poool at its centre. All about are venerable yew hedges, some handsomely blowsy with age, and the eye is constantly drawn to the great house. Do not miss the splendid view of the house from the western wrought-iron gate with an avenue of clipped Irish yews.

MOUNT EDGCUMBE
Cornwall

Cremyll,
Torpoint PL10 1HZ
2 1/2m SE of Torpoint
Tel: 01752 822236
Fax: 01752 822199

Owner: City of Plymouth
and Cornwall County
Council

Open: Park and formal
garden: daily dawn–dusk;
Earl's Garden (entrance via
house): Apr to Oct, Wed to
Sun and Bank Hol Mon
11–5. 865 acres. House

IT IS hard to pin down the rare character of this place – but there is certainly nowhere like it. The site, on a sloping headland overlooking Plymouth Sound, is beautiful, and the castellated mansion turns its face to this, down a vast triple avenue of oaks and limes. The Edgcumbe family, also of Cotehele, came here in the mid 16th century and their estate became so famous that Admiral Medina Sidonia vowed that he would live there after his Armada had beaten the English. At the foot of the hill are formal gardens – a French garden, an English garden, an orangery and an Italianate garden with double staircase and flamboyant statuary, a pool, bedding schemes and orange trees in Versailles boxes. All this has recently been undergoing restoration. The parkland, laced with marvellous walks, runs to the very edge of the cliffs – interrupted with picturesque ruins and a columned temple from which there are lovely views of the sea.

OVERBECKS GARDEN

Devon

Sharpitor,
Salcombe TQ8 8LW
1 1/2m SW of Salcombe by
minor roads
Tel: 01548 842893/843238

Owner: The National Trust

Open: Daily 10–8 or sunset
if earlier. 6 acres

OVERBECKS IS a very unusual place, lost on the precipitous heights above the Salcombe estuary. It was the creation of Otto Overbecks who left it to the National Trust in 1937. It enjoys a remarkably mild microclimate and, with views through trees of shimmering water, it is fairly easy to imagine yourself on the *corniches* on the Côte d'Azur. Even the steps leading down into the garden, with their sinuous handrail, have a Mediterranean feel to them. The garden is terraced and its very sharp drainage and abundant sunshine permits many tender plants to flourish as they do in few other places on mainland Britain – callistemons, Chusan palms, mimosa, olearias, olives and tender pittosporums. On the lower slopes, an old *Magnolia campbellii*, planted in 1901, is a famous sight in spring, covered with its hot pink flowers. The earlier part of the year is a wonderful time to visit, when the garden is extraordinarily floriferous and the air laden with sweet scents. In high summer it takes on the character of an exotic jungle.

PARNHAM HOUSE

Dorset

Beaminster DT8 3NA
1m S of Beaminster by
A3066
Tel: 01308 862204

Owner: John Makepeace

Open: Apr to Oct, Sun,
Tue, Wed, Thur and Bank
Hol Mon 10–5. 14 acres.
House open

SWARMING WITH decoration – gables, castellations and bristling chimneys – Parnham House is a Tudor mansion comprehensively done over by John Nash in the early 19th century. The estate was acquired in 1976 by the famous furniture maker John Makepeace who has restored it with energy and imagination. To the south, a deep terrace with stone gazebos at each end overlooks an immense lawn with rows of giant yew cones and water runnels. Beyond, superb woodland is framed by great cedars of Lebanon. On the east side of

the house the entrance forecourt has decorative walls crowned with finials and borders planted with roses. Beyond the house, behind old yew hedges and brick walls, Jennie Makepeace has reinvigorated ambitious herbaceous borders.

PENCARROW HOUSE

Cornwall

Washaway,
Bodmin PL30 3AG
3 1/2m NW of Bodmin by
A389 and B3266
Tel: 01208 841369

Owner: The Molesworth-St
Aubyn Family

Open: Easter to mid Oct,
daily dawn–dusk. 50 acres.
House open

PENCARROW IS set in a broad valley with the very pretty 18th-century house facing south along it. The Italian Gardens, with turfed terraces, urns and a fountain, lie immediately south of the house. Beyond this, a vast meadow opens out, edged on either side by ramparts of magnificent trees and shrubs. From a Victorian rock garden a path leads through the woodland garden to a lake and an American Garden. You should return by the path on the other side, with lovely views of the house framed in great trees and old rhododendrons with, in spring, bluebells splashed with wild garlic. It is a marvellous English scene – fine house, formal gardens, enticing woodland and far views of cattle grazing in rich Cornish pastures.

PENJERRICK

Cornwall

FEW GARDENS have the wonderful atmosphere of Penjerrick – another creation of the Fox family, the great Cornish master gardeners. Penjerrick has a valley site sloping towards the sea. But here there is a character of wildness which provides exactly the right

Budock,
nr Falmouth TR11 5ED
3m SW of Falmouth by
minor roads
Tel: 01872 870105

Owner: Mrs R. Morin

Open: Mar to Sept, Wed,
Fri and Sun 1.30–4.30.
15 acres

contrast to some of the more swaggering rhododendrons which are such a striking feature of the garden. Superlative old beeches, copper and ordinary, date from the early 1800s and provide a stately background to more exotic planting. Here are exceptional tree ferns, many examples of the tender large-leafed rhododendrons, an exceptional *Davidia involucrata* and the most magnificent *Podocarpus salignus* in the country. In early spring many outstanding magnolias flaunt their flowers in the lovely jungle that surrounds them. The garden continues beyond a road, spanned by a bridge, and here in a jungle-like setting thickets of bamboos edge a lake and alluring fern-fringed paths wind up the side of the valley, giving marvellous views.

PLEASANT VIEW NURSERY

Devon

Two Mile Oak, nr Denbury,
Newton Abbot TQ12 6DG
2 1/2m S of Newton Abbot
off A381
Tel and Fax: 01803 813388

Open: Nursery: 18 Mar to
17 Oct, Wed to Sat 10–5;
Garden: May to Sept, Wed
and Fri 2–5. 2 acres

THIS VERY attractive nursery, impeccably kept, possesses two National Collections of plants – of sages (*Salvia*) and of abelias. The first, with 150 species and cultivars, is of greater interest to gardeners but abelias (10 species and cultivars), those pretty, late-flowering shrubs, also have a quiet charm. The catalogue (five 2nd-class stamps) is full of good things, especially southern hemisphere shrubs. But there are often plants at the nursery which are not listed (such as the distinguished *Brachyglottis rotundifolia*) and, furthermore, the garden is well worth visiting. It has a whole section devoted to salvias, which shows what versatile and effective garden plants they are. There is also a separate list of salvias, and of salvia seed (s.a.e), and a mail order service is available.

PRIOR PARK LANDSCAPE GARDEN

Somerset

THE PALLADIAN mansion of Prior Park (now a school) was built in the 1730s for Ralph Allen, probably to the designs of John Wood. In the combe below the house a miniature landscape park was laid out, at first with advice from Allen's friend Alexander

On Combe Down, 1m S of
the centre of Bath
Tel: 01985 843600

Owner: The National Trust

Open: Daily except Tue
12–5.30 or dusk if earlier.
Closed 25–26 Dec and 1
Jan. NOTE: No parking at
the garden; phone for
details of access. 28 acres

Pope. In 1750 an enchanting Palladian Bridge was
added, making an architectural focal point for the
scene and spanning the neck of a miniature lake. Some
buildings (such as a gothic temple) no longer survive
but a handsome classical Sham Bridge does. The
essence of the place, as a visitor wrote in 1746, consist
of 'The natural beauties of wood, water and prospect,
hill and dale, wilderness and cultivation.' The
National Trust has recently taken over the garden and
has done much to restore and preserve the precious
Elysian atmosphere of this miniature landscape park
so close to the heart of Bath.

ROSEMOOR GARDEN

Devon

THERE ARE two gardens at Rosemoor: one was
made in the early 1960s by Lady Anne Palmer, an
intimate woodland garden with more formal planting
nearer the house; the other is a more razzmatazz affair
complete with Visitors' Centre, ambitious formal rose
gardens and giant borders, all of which have been
made by the Royal Horticultural Society since it
became the owner in 1988. The two gardens are
separated by the B3220 under which there is a passage.

Great Torrington
EX38 8PH
1m SE of Great Torrington
by B3220
Tel: 01805 624067
Fax: 01805 624717

Owner: The Royal
Horticultural Society

Open: Apr to Sept, daily
10–6; Oct to Mar, daily
10–5. 40 acres

A lake and a stream garden with good moisture-loving plants make an attractive prelude to the tunnel at the far side of which are splendid ramparts of rocks planted with ferns and other plants suitable to the site. Lady Anne's garden has an excellent collection of trees and shrubs of the kind which relish the acid soil – dogwoods (a National Collection), eucryphias, maples, pieris, rhododendrons and vacciniums. By the house there are lawns, borders and a tennis court that has been transformed into a Mediterranean garden. At the Visitors' Centre a shop sells a wide range of well grown plants and marvellous pots.

ROWDEN GARDENS

Devon

Illustration: Ranunculus ficaria 'Brazen Hussy'

Brentor,
nr Tavistock PL19 0NG
NW of Brentor village, on
road to Liddaton and
Chillaton
Tel: 01822 810275

Open: Apr to Sept, Sat, Sun
and Bank Hol Mon 10–5;
also by appointment

SOMETHING NEW always seems to be happening at Rowden Gardens nursery, which has in the past specialised in aquatic plants but now has a wider range – in all, over 3,000 species and varieties with a strong emphasis on herbaceous perennials, some very rare and some 'Rowden' cultivars. There are particularly good collections of ferns, primulas, water irises and rheums. Behind the nursery rows of slender canal-like pools display the nursery's wares in very decorative fashion. National Collections of polygonums and celandines (*Ranunculus ficaria*) are held here. There is an informative illustrated catalogue (£1.50) and a mail order service. But many plants that are not listed are to be seen at the nursery, and John Carter will probably seduce you into buying them.

SALTRAM HOUSE

Devon

Plympton,
Plymouth PL7 3UH
3m E of Plymouth by A38
Tel: 01752 336546

Owner: The National Trust

Open: 2–23 Mar, Sat and
Sun 11–4; 28 Mar to Sept,
daily except Fri (but open
Good Fri) and Sat
10.30–5.30; Oct, daily
except Fri and Sat
10.30–4.30. 21 acres. House
open

ALTHOUGH WITHIN sight of the urban sprawl of
Plymouth, Saltram still preserves its character of
a gentlemanly house set in parkland. The early 18th-
century house was enriched by spectacular new rooms
by Robert Adam for the Parker family. The parkland –
grazed by deer to the very walls of the house in the
18th-century – is now embellished with ornamental
trees, superb sweet chestnuts and the Spanish plane
(*Platanus* × *hispanica*) among them. From the stately
pedimented orangery, built in 1775, paths lead to a
gothic pavilion. An avenue of limes, with pale narcissi
in spring, forms a boundary. All this is understated
and, of its kind, perfect.

STICKY WICKET

Dorset

Buckland Newton DT2 7BY
In Buckland Newton
village, between the church,
the school and the Gaggle
of Geese pub, 10m N of
Dorchester by B3143
Tel: 01300 345476

Owners:
Peter and Pam Lewis

Open: Mid Jun to mid Sept,
Thur 10.30–8. 2 acres

PETER AND Pam Lewis are interested in colour and
the admirable plants grown here, including a
profusion of roses, are disposed with a sharp eye for
harmony. In the Round Garden, for example, plants
are arranged in segments ebbing and flowing from
pastels to richer red, purple and magenta. The Lewises
are also keen to garden with nature rather than against
it, so they provide water for frogs, berries for birds, a
dovecote and a haven for ducks and poultry. You may
have no interest in such things but they will not intrude
on the pleasure of a beautifully kept garden brimming
with good plants admirably used.

STONE LANE GARDENS

Devon

THE NATIONAL Collections of plants are not
necessarily in places of beauty nor is their aim to
be attractively laid out. Stone Lane Gardens, however,
has National Collections of birches (*Betula*) and alder
(*Alnus*) disposed in a marvellous rural setting on the
edge of Dartmoor. The trees are most beautifully
arranged, in groves of a single species which preserve
the identity of those propagated from seed gathered in

Stone Farm,
Chagford TQ13 8JU
Off A382, 14m W of Exeter
by A30 and Whiddon Down
exit
Tel and Fax: 01647 231311

Owner: Kenneth and June
Ashburner

Open: 30 May to 19 Sept,
daily 2–6. 5 1/2 acres

a particular site in the wild. Many of the birches, especially the Himalayan kinds, have dazzlingly beautiful bark displaying startling variations. The alders also have a beauty of a quieter kind. The Ashburners use excellent association plants of an appropriately wild sort – bold species roses, thickets of grey-stemmed *Rubus cockburnianus*, rowans, vacciniums and the attractive Korean evergreen *Ilex crenata*. In summer it becomes the setting for 'The Mythic Garden Sculpture Exhibition' in which contemporary artists display their wares, finely arranged among the trees. The effect is enchanting, original and full of inspiration.

TAPELEY PARK

Devon

Instow EX39 4NT
2m N of Bideford by A39
Tel: 01271 42371/860528

Owner: N.D.C.I. Ltd

Open: Easter to Oct, daily
except Sat 10–5. 10 acres.
House open

TAPELEY PARK deserves to be much better known. The mid 18th-century tycoon's mansion of pink brick occupies an unforgettable position in parkland, with wonderful views down to the river Taw. South of the house is a dazzling Italian garden designed by the neo-classical architect John Belcher in the early 20th century. Terraces gently descend the hill, with a sundial at the centre, and a row of sentinel Irish yews

guards the lowest terrace to the west. Handsome statues decorate the walls, and others, on the far side of the lawn, gaze out towards the countryside. Borders have recently been replanted to the lively designs of Mary Keen and Carol Klein. In the woods on one side are a gothic pavilion and an ice house with a walled kitchen garden beyond.

TINTINHULL HOUSE

Somerset

Tintinhull,
nr Yeovil BA22 8PZ
In Tintinhull village,
5m SW of Yeovil off A303
Tel: 01935 822545

Owner: The National Trust

Open: Apr to 30 Sept,
daily except Mon and Tue
(open Bank Hol Mon)
12–6. 3/4 acre. House open

THE DESIGN of this small garden, created by Phyllis Reiss between the wars, is so clever that it provides an inexhaustible model for gardeners. The very pretty 17th-century Ham stone house lies at the centre of the garden and its beautiful early 17th-century pedimented facade dominates one of the chief garden views. The garden is divided into separate 'rooms' by walls or hedges, each area with a distinctive atmosphere. The Eagle Court west of the house has a central flagged path edged with clipped mounds of box and richly planted borders. The path leads to a little white garden, hedged in yew, in which white anemones, roses and lilies glow under miniature silvery willows. An opening leads through to a decorative kitchen garden where the useful and ornamental happily intermingle. The pool garden above it, with its summerhouse at one end, has a pair of masterly borders – one with hot colours of red and yellow, and the other with cool silvers and mauves. The whole garden area is less than one acre – yet it manages to include, with no sense of claustrophobia, a great range of planting styles.

TREBAH

Cornwall

Mawnan Smith, nr
Falmouth TR11 5JZ
4m SW of Falmouth, signed
from A394 and A39
approaches to Falmouth
Tel: 01326 250448
Fax: 01326 250781

Owner:
Trebah Garden Trust

Open: Daily 10.30–5.
25 acres

TREBAH IS the creation of Charles Fox, of the great Cornish dynasty of garden makers, who came here in 1831. When Major and Mrs Hibbert bought the estate in 1981 the garden had suffered years of neglect of which today there is no sign. They were pioneers in the restoration of Cornish plantsmen's gardens. Set in a long, slender ravine, the garden sweeps down south to the Helford river with paths running along each side of the valley, giving vertiginous views over great rhododendrons, magnolias, groves of the tree fern *Dicksonia antarctica*, and palms. A stream runs along the bottom of the ravine, with a waterfall and pools and thickets of hydrangeas and *Gunnera manicata*. The contrast of exotic foliage, viewed from above or below, and the dramatic view down the ravine are the most memorable things at Trebah.

TRENGWAINTON GARDEN

Cornwall

Madron,
nr Penzance TR20 8RZ
2m NW of Penzance by
B3312
Tel: 01736 63021

Owner: The National Trust

Open: Mar to 29 Oct, Sun
to Thur and Good Fri
10.30–5.30 (Mar and Oct
10.30–5). 15 acres

SIR EDWARD Bolitho was the chief creator of this garden in the 1920s, when he added to it some of the spectacular new discoveries of the plant hunters, especially those of Frank Kingdon-Ward. Some rhododendrons from Kingdon-Ward's 1927–8 expedition to north-east Assam first flowered out of their native habitat at Trengwainton. From the entrance lodge a very long drive, densely lined with ornamental trees and shrubs, provides the main axis of the garden. On one side an extraordinary walled kitchen garden now protects especially tender exotics. These flourish among rare magnolias and other ornamental trees and shrubs such as eucryphias, michelias, stewartias and *Styrax japonica*. Beyond the drive, an excellent stream garden created by Sir Edward Bolitho is beautifully planted with candelabra primulas, meconopsis, ligularias and skunk cabbage. In the woodland behind are immense rhododendrons – with spectacular examples of some of the large-leafed species such as *R. sinogrande*, *R. macabeanum* and *R. falconeri*. At the end of the drive the house looks out across a lawn to far views of St Michael's Mount, a splendid eyecatcher.

Illustration opposite:
Trengwainton

TRESCO ABBEY

Cornwall

Tresco,
Isles of Scilly TR24 0QQ
By helicopter or ferry from
Penzance
Tel: 01720 422849
Fax: 01720 422868

Owner: R. Dorrien Smith

Open: Daily 10–4. 16 acres

THERE IS no other garden like this in the world. The island has a most benign microclimate, with moderate rainfall but high humidity from the sea. It was started in 1834 by Augustus Smith who planted windbreaks and built up terraces on which to cultivate a huge range of plants, especially those of the Southern Hemisphere. This, greatly added to by his descendants who still live here, is the garden that visitors may see today. It is primarily a collection of plants, but it is craftily designed with gravel paths leading along terraces and cross vistas giving thrilling views through the sub-tropical luxuriance. There are, however, emphatic repeat plantings – of different kinds of palms, of sweetly scented *Euphorbia mellifera*, of the splendidly architectural *Echium pininana* with its soaring spires of flowers, and of the giant purple-flowered *Geranium maderense* – giving structure to the abundance. It gives unique and exhilarating pleasure and on any day of the year there will be some rare and lovely plant performing.

TREWITHEN

Cornwall

Grampound Road,
nr Truro TR2 4DD
7m W of St Austell by A390
Tel: 01726 883647
Fax: 01726 882301

Owner: A.M.J. Galsworthy

Open: Mar to Sept, Mon to
Sat 10–4.30 (walled garden
closed Apr and May).
25 acres. House open

BEHIND THE elegant 1723 house there is an immense lawn, 200 yards long, with trees and shrubs crowding in on either side. From the far end, this is seen to provide a marvellous setting for the house, like a deep stage framed in wonderful plants. The garden was made by George Johnstone who came here in 1903 and cleared existing woodland, enriching the planting with many of the Asiatic plants newly introduced in the 1920s. Paths wind through this woodland and at every turn there is something wonderful to see. It is at its most spectacular in early to late spring but has many pleasures to offer later in the year. Nor is it only a woodland garden. The formal walled garden should not be overlooked: with its wisteria-draped pergola, Irish yews and beautifully planted borders it is an admirable piece of work. There is an excellent plant shop selling many of the plants particularly associated with the garden (e.g. the beautiful *Ceanothus arboreus* 'Trewithen Blue').

WALES AND WEST-CENTRAL ENGLAND

Cheshire
Gloucestershire
Hereford and
Worcester
Shropshire

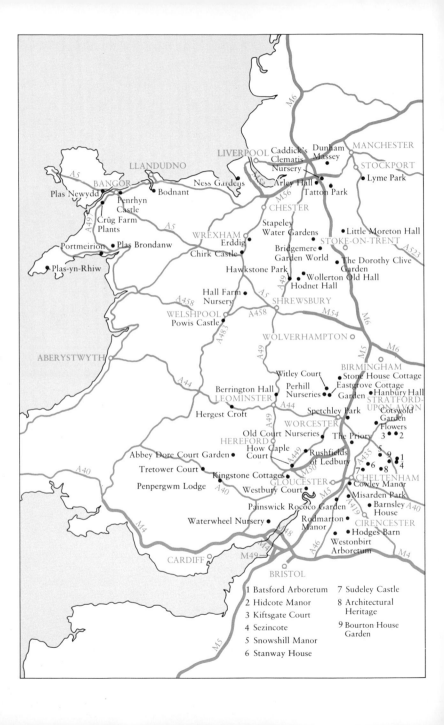

MANCHESTER

LIVERPOOL
Caddick's   Dunham
Clematis   Massey
Nursery   STOCKPORT

LLANDUDNO   • Lyme Park
                        Ness Gardens   • Arley Hall
BANGOR   Tatton Park
Plas Newydd   • Bodnant
Penrhyn   CHESTER
Castle
Crûg Farm   Stapeley
Plants   Water Gardens   • Little Moreton Hall
                        WREXHAM   STOKE-ON-TRENT
Portmeirion   • Plas Brondanw   Erddig   Bridgemere
                        Chirk Castle   Garden World   The Dorothy Clive
• Plas-yn-Rhiw   Garden
                        Hawkstone Park   Wollerton Old Hall
                                        Hodnet Hall
                        Hall Farm
                        Nursery   SHREWSBURY
                WELSHPOOL   A458
                        Powis Castle
                                                WOLVERHAMPTON

ABERYSTWYTH
                                                BIRMINGHAM
                                        Witley Court   Stone House Cottage
                        Berrington Hall   Perhill   Eastgrove Cottage
                        LEOMINSTER   Nurseries   Garden   Hanbury Hall
                                                        STRATFORD-
                        Hergest Croft   Spetchley Park   UPON-AVON
                                        WORCESTER   Cotswold
                                                        Garden
                        Old Court Nurseries   The Priory   Flowers
                        HEREFORD   How Caple   3 • • 2
                        Abbey Dore Court Garden •   Court   Rushfields
                                                of Ledbury   5
                        Tretower Court   Kingstone Cottages   9   1
                                                        6   8   4
                        Penpergwm Lodge   Westbury Court   7
                                        GLOUCESTER   CHELTENHAM
                        Waterwheel Nursery   Painswick Rococo Garden   Cowley Manor
                                        Rodmarton   Misarden Park
                                        Manor   Barnsley
                                                House
                                                CIRENCESTER
                                        Westonbirt   • Hodges Barn
                                        Arboretum
                        CARDIFF
                                        BRISTOL

1 Batsford Arboretum   7 Sudeley Castle
2 Hidcote Manor   8 Architectural
3 Kiftsgate Court   Heritage
4 Sezincote   9 Bourton House
5 Snowshill Manor   Garden
6 Stanway House

ABBEY DORE COURT GARDEN
Hereford and Worcester

Abbey Dore,
nr Hereford HR2 0AD
11m SW of Hereford by
A465 and B4347
Tel: 01981 240419
Fax: 01981 240279

Owner: Mrs C.L. Ward

Open: Mar to 3rd Sun in
Oct, daily except Wed 11–6
(also open before March for
hellebores; telephone for
dates). 6 acres

ABBEY DORE Court on the banks of the river Dore in one of the prettiest parts of England has both an attractive garden and a nursery with a good range of the herbaceous perennials that may be seen growing in the garden. There is no catalogue and no mail order service, so a visit is essential. Abbey Dore makes much use of euphorbias, those fashionable and valuable greenery-yallery plants. Throughout the garden the planting is of a very high standard; especially beautiful is a pair of mixed borders planted predominantly in yellow- and white-flowered plants, with gold and variegated foliage and the occasional sombre note of rich purple. Claris Ward, who owns the garden, keeps adding to it, so every visit reveals something new.

ARCHITECTURAL HERITAGE
Gloucestershire

Taddington Manor,
nr Cutsdean,
Cheltenham GL54 5RY
14m NE of Cheltenham by
B4632, B4077 and minor
roads; 15m E of Jnct 9 of
M5
Tel: 01386 584414
Fax: 01386 584236

Open: Mon to Fri 9.30–5.30
(closed Bank Hol); Sat
10.30–4.30

IN AND around the handsome outhouses of a Cotswold manor house, Architectural Heritage displays an alluring collection of garden urns, seats, fountains and statues – from frolicking dolphins to coy maidens. You will need a long purse to take away any of these lovely treasures but you may then possess a potently decorative garden antique of high quality. The very large and varied stock changes all the time and it is worth visiting to see what there is and bear away some ornamental treasure.

ARLEY HALL

Cheshire

Arley,
nr Northwich CW9 6NA
5m W of Knutsford by
minor roads; Jncts 19 and
20 of M6; Jnct 10 of M56
Tel: 01565 777353
Fax: 01565 777465

Owner: Viscount and
Viscountess Ashbrook

Open: Apr to Sept, Tue to
Sun and Bank Hol Mon
12–5. 12 acres

A PAIR OF herbaceous borders was laid out at Arley Hall in 1846, a great novelty, and they survive to this day, beautifully maintained. From June to the end of the gardening season they are one of the great garden sights of England. Pairs of topiary yew 'dumb waiters' form entrances at each end, and a broad grass path separates the borders which have a series of yew buttresses on each side, breaking up an otherwise uncomfortably long stretch of planting. A path leads from the borders to a procession of giant columns of clipped holm oak and views over parkland There are also borders of shrub roses, old walled gardens with good mixed borders, a simple terraced walk above a ha-ha, and much else to see. Still in private ownership, Arley Hall preserves the agreeable atmosphere of a garden kept for its own delight.

BARNSLEY HOUSE GARDEN

Gloucestershire

THIS IS a famous garden, made by David and Rosemary Verey since 1951. Influenced by her knowledge of garden history, Mrs Verey contrived a heady mixture of ingredients – a pleached lime walk, knot gardens, an ornamental *potager*, temples and statuary. The real distinction, however, lies in the planting, especially in the use of herbaceous plants and in subtle associations of form and colour. Barnsley

Barnsley,
nr Cirencester GL7 5EE
In Barnsley village, 4m N of
Cirencester by B4425
Tel and Fax: 01285 740281

Owner: Charles Verey

Open: Mon, Wed, Thur and
Sat 10–6 or dusk if earlier.
4 acres

House is well known through Mrs Verey's own
excellent books – but there is no substitute for a visit
to the garden itself which is in a constant state of
gentle but stimulating change as new discoveries are
made. Unusually, the garden is open throughout the
year and a winter visit, with the structural bones laid
bare, is especially rewarding. A nursery sells an
excellent stock of choice and often rare plants of the
sort grown in the garden.

BATSFORD ARBORETUM

Gloucestershire

Moreton-in-Marsh
GL56 9QF
1m NW of Moreton-in-
Marsh by A44
Tel: 01608 650722
Fax: 01608 650290

Owner:
The Batsford Foundation

Open: Mar to 5 Nov, daily
10–5. 50 acres

THIS ARBORETUM, started in the 1880s, has recently
been revitalised with an enormous amount of new
planting. It is now well worth visiting at any time of
the year and even demon dendrologists will find
marvellous things – over 80 kinds of oak, for example,
and many wonderful individual specimens. But for less
rarified tastes the place is full of interest, with all trees
well labelled and the landscape enlivened by statues
(including a fine bronze Buddha) and ornamental
buildings. It is a marvellous place in which to walk and
learn about trees. There is also a large plant centre
which carries a good general stock.

BERRINGTON HALL

Hereford and Worcester

nr Leominster HR6 0DW
3m N of Leominster by A49
Tel: 01568 615721

Owner: The National Trust

Open: Apr, Fri, Sat, Sun
(open Bank Hol Mon but
closed Good Fri) 1.30–5.30;
May to Jun, and Sept, Wed
to Sun and Bank Hol Mon
1.30–5.30; Jul and Aug,
daily 1.30–5.30; Oct to 1
Nov, Fri, Sat, Sun 1.30–4.30.
10 acres. House open

THE BROWN stone mansion was designed by Henry Holland and completed in 1781, and the unspoilt landscape park was laid out by his partner and father-in-law 'Capability' Brown. There was no house or garden here before, so this is an unusual period piece. From the vast Arch of Triumph at the entrance, an avenue of clipped mounds of golden yew leads towards the front door of the house. On one side a magnificent brick-walled 18th-century kitchen garden has a fascinating collection of historic varieties of apple and, leading up to the wrought-iron entrance gate, a pair of good mixed borders. The walls provide protection for some unusual tender plants including the grandest of all buddlejas, *B. colvillei*, with huge panicles of red flowers in May or June.

BODNANT

Clwyd

Tal-y-Cafn,
Colwyn Bay LL28 5RE
8m S of Llandudno by A470
Tel: 01492 650460

Owner: The National Trust

Open: 14 Mar to Oct, daily
10–5. 80 acres

BODNANT WAS started in the late 19th century at the height of the rhododendron craze. The steep slopes of the Conwy valley provided a wonderfully romantic site for their cultivation, and with the rushing waters of the River Hraethlyn at his feet, the visitor today may convincingly imagine himself in a dream-like valley of the Himalayas. Rhododendrons and camellias flourish under a high canopy of conifers. Nearer the house there is a completely different garden – formal terraces descend in stately progression to a vast lily pool and the crispest yew hedges you will ever see. At the upper level is one of the most photographed garden sights in Britain – a curved tunnel of laburnum which in May and June drips gold and still has the power to take your breath away. This is an old-fashioned garden, almost a period piece, if only in terms of the superlative maintenance – even the yew hedges are still clipped by hand. The Head Gardener has been a Puddle for three generations and what the Puddles don't know about running a garden is probably not worth knowing. A large nursery, especially good for acid-loving shrubs, also sells plants by mail order.

BOURTON HOUSE GARDEN

Gloucestershire

Bourton-on-the-Hill,
Moreton-in-Marsh
GL56 9AE
2m W of Moreton-in-
Marsh by A44
Tel: 01386 700121
Fax: 01386 701081

Owner:
Mr and Mrs R. Paice

Open: end May to third Fri
in Oct, Thur and Fri and
Bank Hol Sun and Mon
12–5. 3 acres

THIS BEAUTIFULLY kept private garden fizzes with decorative exuberance. Surrounding an exceptionally pretty 18th-century house is a feast of ornamental planting and well designed spaces. Here are fine borders, lawns like Wilton carpet, stately walks, lively topiary and a dashing little walled *potager* with beds edged in silver or common box. By most people's standards this is a large garden but it contains many valuable lessons for owners of smaller plots. Many tender plants, some rare, are grown in containers and there are always good plants for sale.

BRIDGEMERE GARDEN WORLD

Cheshire

Bridgemere,
nr Nantwich CW5 7QB
6m SE of Nantwich on A51
Tel: 01270 520381
Fax: 01270 520215

Open: Mon to Sat 9–8, Sun
10–8; closes 5 in winter

NO OTHER garden centre has the sense of horticultural excitement that you will find here. It is a huge place – 25 acres in all – and there are enormous numbers of plants of every kind; it probably carries the greatest commercially available range in the country. They are grouped in a way that is useful to the gardener – both under type of plants (herbaceous, roses, etc) or by use (ground-cover, shade-loving, etc). A separate 6-acre display garden, 'The Garden Kingdom', shows the plants in action. There is no mail order, but all gardeners will enjoy a visit to see excellent and unfamiliar plants.

CADDICK'S CLEMATIS NURSERIES

Cheshire

Lymm Road, Thelwall,
Warrington WA13 0UF
In Thelwall village, off A56;
Jnct 20 of M6 and Jnct 9 of
M56
Tel: 01925 757196

Open: Feb to Oct, Tue to
Sun 10–5; Nov, Tue to Sat
10–4

CADDICKS WAS started only in 1984, by Harry Caddick, a lockmaster on the Manchester Ship Canal. He now sells a wonderful collection of clematis beautifully displayed in new premises. Caddick's sells nothing but these essential garden plants, and its catalogue (£1.00) of over 300 varieties is one of the best – informative and very well illustrated in colour. A mail order service is provided.

CHIRK CASTLE

Clwyd

Chirk LL14 5AF
1/2m W of Chirk village by
A5
Tel: 01691 777701

Owner: The National Trust

Open: Apr to 2 Oct, daily
except Mon and Tue (open
Bank Hol Mon) 11–6;
3 Oct to 1 Nov, Sat and Sun
11–6. 5 acres. Castle open

CHIRK IS a 13th-century border castle and its massive defensive towers are echoed in the billowing old topiary cones of yew that march down its east side. The castle was built for defensive purposes and commands lovely views. The garden as it is today is almost entirely 20th-century but there are much older features – in the sunken rose garden, for example, is a sundial made for the garden in the 17th century. From the castle forecourt an opening cut into a yew hedge guarded by a pair of bronze nymphs leads through to the upper lawn and a deep mixed border punctuated by groups of flowering cherries. On this windy site woodland provides protection for magnolias, rhododendrons and unusual plants such as the Chilean firebush (*Embothrium coccineum*) with its scarlet flowers, and *Eucryphia glutinosa*.

THE DOROTHY CLIVE GARDEN

Shropshire

Willoughbridge, nr Market
Drayton TF9 4EU
9m SE of Nantwich by A51
Tel: 01630647237
Fax: 01630 647902

Owner: Willoughbridge
Garden Trust

Open: Apr to Oct, daily
10–5.30. 8 acres

FEW GARDENS have such diversity of interest as this. The garden was started in 1940 by Col. Harry Clive who realised the attractions of the site: a former gravel pit with acid soil on a fine south-facing, well watered slope which provides many habitats for a very wide range of plants. At the very top of the hill, in the old quarry, Col. Clive's original woodland garden is now fully mature; it is rich with azaleas, maples, rhododendrons and other ornamental trees and shrubs. A rushing multi-tiered waterfall is a brilliant sight in high summer, fringed with the coloured plumes of astilbes and ligularias. On the slopes below the old quarry a garden of a completely different character, planned by the garden designer John Codrington, was developed after Col. Clive's death. In the upper reaches broad grassy paths running along the contours of the hill divide lavishly planted mixed borders. Paths then run downhill at a brisker pace, between informal and scree beds, with a lily pond at the bottom.

COTSWOLD GARDEN FLOWERS

Hereford and Worcester

Sands Lane, Badsey,
Evesham (nursery);
1, Waterside, Evesham
WR11 6BS (office)
On the E edge of Badsey
village, 2m E of Evesham by
minor roads
Tel and Fax: 01386 47337
(office); 01386 833849
(nursery, phone only)

Open: 9 Mar to 12 Oct,
Mon to Fri 8–4.30, Sat and
Sun 10–6; 13 Oct to 8 Mar
1999, Mon to Fri 8–4.30.
Open at other times by
appointment

BOB BROWN has one of the most alluring lists of plants imaginable, chiefly of herbaceous perennials. You could easily fill your borders with dazzling things by stocking up from him alone. He has excellent ranges of achilleas, aquilegias, arums, dozens of asters, five different forms of *Corydalis flexuosa*, euphorbias – and so, irresistibly, on and on through the alphabet. The emphasis is on species and absolutely the best cultivars. An admirable catalogue is produced (free) and a mail order service is available. The nursery is delightful, with profusely filled deep borders spreading out beyond the glasshouses. Bob Brown is in semi-detached cahoots with another nurseryman, Martin Tustin (01386 832124), just round the corner, who sells only lavenders. His marvellous selection is listed in the Cotswold Garden Flowers catalogue and includes all the finest cultivars (over 50!) of *Lavandula angustifolia*.

COWLEY MANOR

Gloucestershire

Cowley,
nr Cheltenham GL53 9NL
5m S of Cheltenham off
A435
Tel: 01242 870540

Owner: The Cowley Manor
Partnership

Open: Mar to Oct, daily
except Mon and Fri 2–6.
50 acres

COWLEY MANOR is an ancient estate which was much altered in the 19th century when it was owned by James Horlick. Apart from making a famous bedtime malted drink, the Horlicks were great gardeners, and also owned the famous woodland garden on Gigha (see page 279). At Cowley it is the wooded valley of the river Churn, and its ornamental pools, that constitute the landscape's trump card. The Horlicks made a spectacular baroque cascade and formal pool which survive, gloomy and mysterious but impressive. Since 1994, under the direction of Noel Kingsbury, new planting has been made on the valley slopes. He is influenced by recent German and Dutch ideas about bold, naturalistic use of herbaceous perennials on the grand scale. As the planting becomes wilder and woollier it will make a powerful contribution to the fine existing landscape.

CRÛG FARM PLANTS

Gwynedd

Griffith's Crossing,
nr Caernarfon LL55 1TU
2m NE of Caernarfon off
A487
Tel and Fax: 01248 670232

Open: 28 Feb to 27 Sept,
Thur to Sun and Bank Hol
Mon 10–6

BLEDDYN WYNN-JONES was bitten by the love of plants and gave up farming to start this dazzling nursery five years ago with his wife, Sue. The climate here on the edge of Snowdonia is balmy and wet, providing good conditions for the cultivation of the woodland plants they love. Here are many anemones, asarums, daphnes, dicentras, hellebores, hostas, pulmonarias and trilliums. An exceptional list of hardy geraniums includes some new introductions. The Wynn-Joneses have formed the habit of going on plant-collecting jaunts to the Far East, whence new plants flow to the nursery, many of which may be seen displayed in the owners' garden alongside. There is no mail order service but a useful catalogue is produced (s.a.e. and one 2nd-class stamp).

DUNHAM MASSEY

Cheshire

Altrincham WA14 4SJ
3m W of Altrincham by
A56
Tel: 0161 941 1025

Owner: The National Trust

Open: 4 Apr to 1 Nov, daily
11–5.30. 250 acres. House
open

THE NATIONAL Trust is often very skilful at the art of breathing new life into old gardens. At Dunham Massey, with its grand early 18th-century house, a pattern of formal avenues of the same period, charges towards the horizon. Replanting of beeches, limes and oaks has given this new focus. From the house a double staircase leads to a sprightly Edwardian parterre, bedded in summer with zonal pelargoniums mixed with verbena and edged with rich blue lobelia. Clipped mounds of holm oak and hedges of golden yew give permanent ornament. Informal lawns spread out, overlooked by an 18th-century orangery with, half-concealed in the woods behind, a well house disguised as a rustic retreat. Grassy walks lead along a moat where the banks are densely planted with astilbes, ferns, hostas, irises and rodgersias. The walk continues to a simple lawn, from which views are revealed of the house reflected in the tranquil waters of the moat.

EASTGROVE COTTAGE GARDEN

Hereford and Worcester

Sankyns Green,
Little Witley WR6 6LQ
8m NW of Worcester on
road between Shrawley
(B4196) and Great Witley
(A443)
Tel: 01299 896389

Open: Apr to Jul, Thur to
Mon 2–5; Sept to 10 Oct,
Thur to Sat 2–5 (closed
Aug). 1 acre

IF YOU did not know what a cottage garden should look like this would be a good place to learn. The cottage itself, tiled and ancient, is set in lovely countryside and the garden, flawlessly kept, is full of lively planting and cunning design. There are formal ingredients – a splendid zigzagging hedge of the neatest possible *Lonicera nitida*, carefully placed benches in enclosures, and a romantic rose arbour; the garden itself is chiefly composed of curving borders and sweeps of lawn. A very wide range of plants, some extremely unusual, is grown. Malcolm and Carol Skinner, who made the garden, also run an outstanding nursery which concentrates on herbaceous perennials, hardy and half-hardy, in which even the keenest gardeners will make discoveries. A very good list is produced (five 2nd-class stamps) but there is no mail order service.

ERDDIG

Clwyd

nr Wrexham LL13 0YT
2m S of Wrexham by A525
Tel: 01978 313333

Owner: The National Trust

Open: 21 Mar to 2 Oct, daily except Thur and Fri (open Good Fri) 11–6 (Jul and Aug 10–6); 3 Oct to 1 Nov, daily except Thur and Fri 11–5. 13 acres. House open

THE FORMAL garden to the east of the long low early 18th-century house is one of the very few in Britain to survive the craze for landscape gardens in the second part of the 18th century. It has now been sensitively restored by the National Trust and is full of delights. It is enclosed by brick walls on which are espaliered old varieties of fruit trees. These are underplanted with many varieties of daffodil, and the central area has formal orchards of apple trees. A gravel path leads from the Edwardian parterre under the east windows of the house, by tubs of Portugal laurels clipped into mushroom shapes, towards a slender canal flanked with old limes. At its end, exquisite wrought-iron gates give views of the country beyond. A flowery Victorian parterre has variegated maple, agapanthus, clematis and cheerful bedding, and nearby, on the north-facing wall, is the National Collection of ivy. A path continues to a pair of stone urns and a memorably gloomy moss walk in the woods of shady laurel and holly.

HALL FARM NURSERY

Shropshire

Vicarage Lane, Kinnerley, nr Oswestry SY10 8DH
In Kinnerley village, 2m W of the A5 midway between Shrewsbury and Oswestry
Tel: 01691 682135

Open: Mar to mid Oct, Tue to Sat 10–5

CHRISTINE FFOULKES-JONES has been building up the reputation of her nursery with a fine crop of medals at RHS shows and a burgeoning catalogue of herbaceous perennials. She is interested in garden-worthy plants rather than botanical curiosities, although there are certainly some rarities in her list. She has fine collections of hardy geraniums (over 80 kinds listed), foliage plants, penstemons and

Illustration: Salvia sclarea var. *turkestanica*

pulmonarias. In addition, there are distinguished ornamental grasses and a selection of rockery/scree plants. There is no mail order but a good catalogue is produced (four 1st-class stamps).

HANBURY HALL

Hereford and Worcester

Hanbury,
Droitwich WR9 7EA
4 1/2m E of Droitwich by
B4090 and minor road; Jnct
5 of M5
Tel: 01527 821214

Owner: The National Trust

Open: 29 Mar to 28 Oct,
Sun to Wed 2–6. 15 acres.
House open

HANBURY HALL, built of brick and stone in 1701, is one of the prettiest houses in England and the view of it as you approach it across fields will take the breath away. The Vernon family who built it also commissioned a great garden from George London, the leading designer of the day, which was destroyed in the 1780s at the height of the landscaping craze. The National Trust has now reinstated London's formal gardens to the west of the house to dazzling effect. A four-square giant sunken parterre edged in box is planted with bold blocks of plants and a topiary shape at the centre of each bed. Beyond this is a formal 'wilderness' and to one side a formal orchard. It all suits the house to perfection.

HAWKSTONE PARK

Shropshire

THIS WILD and woolly landscape garden has recently been brought spectacularly back to life and now offers the most complete experience of a high-style 'picturesque' garden. It was created by the Hill family from the 1740s onwards. Their trump card was the splendid lie of the land, with marvellous red

Weston-under-Redcastle,
Shrewsbury SY4 5UY
14m NE of Shrewsbury by
A49 or A53 and minor
roads
Tel: 01939 200611
Fax: 01939 200311

Owner: Hawkstone Estate

Open: Apr to Oct, daily
9–5. 300 acres

sandstone crags erupting from wooded slopes. They made tunnels through the rock, and a labyrinthine grotto, and embellished the heights with splendid ornaments and buildings. A 100ft-tall column is crowned by a giant figure of a 16th-century Hill, and inside a vertiginous spiral staircase takes the intrepid visitor to a gusty viewing platform from which the views are remarkable. Dr Johnson visited in 1774 and was thrilled by 'striking scenes and terrifick grandeur' – and you will be, too.

HERGEST CROFT GARDENS
Hereford and Worcester

Kington HR5 3EG
1/2m W of Kington
signposted off A44
Tel: 01544 230160

Owner: W.L. Banks

Open: 10 Apr to 1 Nov,
daily 1.30–6.30. 50 acres

THIS IS one of the best private collections of woody plants in Britain, and has an exceptionally attractive atmosphere. The house was built in 1896 by William Hartland Banks who also started the collection of plants, many of which were raised from seed gathered in the wild. The garden falls into two chief parts – that near the house, and Park Wood which lies across fields and contains a fine collection of rhododendrons. It is useless to attempt to list the great riches of this place. There are marvellous plants everywhere, and of particular interest are the National Collections of maples (excluding *Acer japonicum* and *A. palmatum* cultivars), birches and zelkovas. An exceptionally pretty kitchen garden has good borders.

HIDCOTE MANOR GARDEN
Gloucestershire

Hidcote Bartrim, nr
Chipping Campden
GL55 6LR
4m NE of Chipping
Campden by B4632
Tel: 01386 438333

Owner: The National Trust

Open: Apr to Sept, daily
except Tue and Fri 1–7 (Jun
and Jul also open Tue
11–7); Oct to 1 Nov, daily
except Tue and Fri 11–6.
10 acres

ALTHOUGH AMONG the best known gardens in Britain, Hidcote still has the power to startle. It was begun before World War I by an American, Major Lawrence Johnston, who devised a type of garden that many think of as quintessentially English. First, it is a garden built up of separate 'rooms', each connected to the next but often with dramatic contrasts. For example, a pair of blazing red borders leads through to a cool green alley of pleached hornbeams. Second, the firm layout provides a disciplined setting for an immense range of plants of which Johnston was a pioneer rediscoverer – especially of old roses – and

which he used in a swashbuckling manner in contrast with the crisp authority of his layout. Everywhere something enticing is glimpsed through an opening, across a pool, down steps or framed by a distant gate.

HODGES BARN

Gloucestershire

Shipton Moyne,
Tetbury GL8 8PR
E of Shipton Moyne village,
2 1/2m S of Tetbury by
A433 and minor road
Tel: 01666 880202
Fax: 01666 880373

Owner:
Mrs Charles Hornby

Open: Apr to mid Aug,
Mon, Tue and Fri 2–5.
8 acres

HODGES BARN is an exceptionally pretty house – a pair of lovely ancient domed dovecotes converted into an elegant house. The garden was started by the grandmother of the present owner's late husband, who planted many trees and laid out a bold design which has been enriched in recent times. Enclosed areas about the house, hedged or walled, are skilfully planted and make the most of lovely views of the house or of the rural countryside beyond. Everywhere there are excellent roses – climbers and shrubs near the house and the species and wilder types among trees. A naturalistic woodland garden is marvellous in spring and in a more formal woodland glade the former stew pond is edged with moisture-loving plants. Deft touches of formality – a procession of Irish yews, well placed ornaments or lively topiary – give crisp contrast to the lavish planting. All is impeccably kept and sparkles with the excitement of gardening.

HODNET HALL GARDENS
Shropshire

Hodnet, nr Market Drayton
TF9 3NN
5 1/2m SW of Market
Drayton by A53; 12m NE of
Shrewsbury by A53
Tel: 01630 685202
Fax: 01630 685853

Owner: Mr and the Hon.
Mrs A.E.H. Heber-Percy

Open: Apr to Sept, Tue to
Sat 2–5, Sun and Bank Hol
Mon 12–5.30. 70 acres

HEBERS HAVE been at Hodnet for an immense time but the garden can never have been in a better state than it is today. The main house was built in 1870 by Anthony Salvin on an eminence with views south over a lake; a decorative Tudor dovecote forms an eyecatcher in the distance. Immediately below the south terrace of the house are good mixed borders, and steps lead down towards the lake which is part of a chain of pools planted with moisture-loving plants – astilbes, ferns, *Gunnera manicata*, hostas, primulas and rodgersias. By the east end of the lake is a circular bed with a figure of Father Time surrounded by concentric beds of hydrangeas, peonies and roses.

HOW CAPLE COURT GARDENS
Hereford and Worcester

nr Ross-on-Wye HR1 4SX
4m N of Ross-on-Wye by
A449 and B4224
Tel: 01989 740626
Fax: 01989 740611

Owner: Mrs Peter Lee

Open: Apr to Oct, Mon to
Sat 9–5.30, Sun 10–5.
11 acres

THIS MARVELLOUS place is undergoing restoration but already so much has been done that it is well worth visiting. The grandfather of the present owner's late husband was mad about gardens and laid out an ambitious scheme appropriate to the spectacular site. On one side of the house a series of dramatic terraces linked by steps looks across the Wye valley towards the Brecon Beacons to the south. The bottom terrace has a pool, Italianate statues, sentinel Irish yews and cascades of old roses. In the wooded valley alongside the house the dell garden has a vast circular pool, a Florentine garden with a pattern of canals, the remains of a huge pergola and a loggia. A nursery in the stable yard sells some good plants, particularly shrub roses.

KIFTSGATE COURT
Gloucestershire

THE NAME Kiftsgate means to many gardeners that beautiful and embarrassingly vigorous rambling rose *R. filipes* 'Kiftsgate', and although the garden, started in the 1920s by Heather Muir, is certainly full of roses there is much else to admire. The house has a splendid setting, teetering on the edge of a precipitous

Chipping Campden
GL55 6LW
3m NE of Chipping
Campden by B4632
Tel and Fax: 01386 438777

Owner: Mr and Mrs A.H.
Chambers

Open: Apr to May, Wed,
Thur and Sun 2–6; Jun to
Jul, Wed, Thur, Sat and Sun
12–6; Aug to Sept, Wed,
Thur and Sun 2–6; Bank
Hol Mon 2–6. 6 acres

valley across which, through the woods, are views of
the Vale of Evesham. About the house is a series of
enclosed gardens in which formality is blurred by
generous planting. Four Squares has peonies,
rodgersias and penstemons among indigofera, berberis
and kolkwitzia. The rose borders have a central path
hedged in *Rosa versicolor,* behind which rise ramparts
of shrub roses, and the 'Kiftsgate' rose zips 50 feet into
the branches of a copper beech. Below all this, paths
wind steeply down the valley side where, under the
canopy of trees, cistuses, hebes, phlomis and senecio
relish the dry conditions. At the foot of the slope is a
pool overlooked by a classical temple. A small but
choice selection of plants is for sale.

KINGSTONE COTTAGES

Hereford and Worcester

Weston-under-Penyard,
Ross-on-Wye HR9 7NX
2m E of Ross-on-Wye by
A40 and minor roads
Tel: 01989 565267

Owner:
Mr and Mrs M. Hughes

Open: May to beginning
Jul, Mon to Fri 9–4 or by
appointment

SOPHIE HUGHES is an expert on pinks and at
Kingstone Cottages she holds the National
Collection of old garden cultivars – over 140 species
and cultivars. These are among the oldest and most
irresistible garden plants, already treasured by
gardeners in Tudor times and, by the 18th century, one
of the most collected of the florist's flowers. Some
surviving cultivars go back to this period. At
Kingstone Cottages plants from the collection are
displayed in a little parterre but many more are
scattered in the mixed plantings of the charming
cottage garden. There are good plants for sale; pinks,
of course but others too. There is a catalogue of (s.a.e.
and one 2nd-class stamp) and a mail order service.

LITTLE MORETON HALL

Cheshire

Congleton SW1 4SD
4m SW of Congleton by
A34
Tel: 01260 272018

Owner: The National Trust

Open: 21 Mar to 1 Nov,
Wed to Sun 12–5.30 (25 Jul
to 6 Sept and Bank Hol
Mon 11–5.30); 7 Nov to 20
Dec, Sat and Sun 12–4 or
dusk if earlier. 1 acre.
House open

THE HALF-TIMBERED, famously wambly 15th-century house is surrounded by a moat. Little is known about what sort of garden the house had in its heyday but there are the remains of an artificial mount of the sort that might have been used for viewing a formal knot or parterre. With this in mind, Graham Stuart Thomas laid out a charming little knot garden of box hedges, gravel and topiary yew obelisks based on a 17th-century pattern. At each side a pattern of square beds hedged in box contains a standard gooseberry bush underplanted with blocks of a single herbaceous plant – germander, strawberries, woodruff or London pride. All this is perfectly appropriate to the setting and a model of what may be done in a small space.

LYME PARK

Cheshire

Disley,
Stockport SK12 2NX
6 1/2m SE of Stockport by
A6
Tel: 01663 762023/766492
Fax: 01663 765035

Owner: The National Trust

Open: 29 Mar to 29 Oct,
daily 11–5; for winter
opening times phone for
details. 15 acres. House
open

AT LYME Park the best parts of the garden have an exciting Victorian flavour that contrasts strikingly with the grand Frenchified house of the early 18th century. To one side of the house a well planted orangery of 1862 overlooks a parterre with Irish yews and urns, its beds planted in spring and summer with bright bedding schemes. On a terrace above, a rose garden with flagged paths and a central pool is enclosed in yew hedges and partly shaded by a pair of beautiful old limes. To one side a path sweeps uphill between deep herbaceous borders whose colour scheme modulates from oranges and yellows to blues and violets as it recedes from the house. North-west of the house, suddenly revealed below a high terrace, is an eye-stopping sight: the so-called Dutch garden, a dazzling arrangment of a fountain, statues of the four seasons, and a geometric pattern of beds edged in tightly clipped ivy and planted with single blocks of begonias, yellow or orange marigolds, santolina or purple verbena. For those who scoff at bedding, this comes as a revelation.

MISARDEN PARK

Gloucestershire

Miserden, Stroud GL6 7JA
7m SE of Gloucester
Tel: 01285 821303

Owner:
Major M.T.N.H. Wills

Open: Apr to Sept, Tue to Thur 9.30–4.30. 12 1/2 acres

T̶HE HOUSE is of the early 17th century with additions in 1920 by Sir Edwin Lutyens who also influenced the style of the terrace garden and forecourt alongside the house. The site is marvellous, on the edge of a valley with long views over wooded country. South and east of the house are excellent ornamental trees, with pleasure gardens disposed on the slopes above. At their heart is a long walk of yew hedges whose tops are decorated by a series of undulating topiary humps. On one side a pair of great mixed borders is separated by a broad grass walk, and on the other a formal rose garden is backed with elegant trellis fencing. The garden is extremely well kept and is full of interest. A nursery sells the kinds of plants seen in the garden.

NESS GARDENS

Cheshire

NESS GARDENS were founded by A.K. Bulley, who sponsored the first expeditions of two of the greatest plant hunters of the 20th century – George Forrest to western China in 1904 and Frank Kingdon-Ward to Yunnan in 1911. Other expeditions followed and the plants introduced are among the best specimens in the gardens today. The site of the garden was good – with undulating land, acid soil and natural outcrops of stone. Bulley planted windbreaks of holly,

Ness, Neston,
South Wirral L64 4AY
11m NW of Chester off
A540
Tel: 0151 3530123
Fax: 0151 3531004

Owner:
The University of Liverpool

Open: Mar to Oct, daily
9.30–sunset; Nov to Feb,
daily (except 25 Dec)
9.30–4. 63 acres

evergreen oak, pines and poplars, and built up an outstanding range of plants. From the gardener's point of view, however, there are other valuable features: a heather garden, herbaceous borders, a large rock garden, many roses, immense numbers of flowering trees and shrubs, and a woodland garden.

OLD COURT NURSERIES LTD

Hereford and Worcester

Colwall,
nr Malvern WR13 6QE
3m SW of Malvern by A449
and B4218
Tel: 01684 540416
Fax: 01684 565314

Open: Apr to Oct, Wed to
Sun 10–1, 2.15–5.30

T HE GREAT glory of Old Court Nurseries is the collection of Michaelmas daisies, one of the National Collections and a wonderful sight in September and October. But the nursery also sells an excellent range of herbaceous perennials and rock garden plants. These are handsomely displayed in the adjoining Picton Garden which is open at the same times as the nursery. Paul Picton has an excellent eye for a good plant and any gardener will find something desirable. Michaelmas daisies only are sold by mail order and a list of them is issued.

PAINSWICK ROCOCO GARDEN

Gloucestershire

T HIS IS one of the most ambitious restorations of a private historic garden ever undertaken. The garden had all but disappeared but its restoration – based on a painting of it by Thomas Robins of 1748 – is now almost complete. In a secret combe behind the

Painswick,
nr Stroud GL6 6TH
1/2m N of Painswick by
B4073
Tel and Fax: 01452 813204

Owner: Painswick Rococo
Garden Trust

Open: 2nd Wed in Jan to
Jun, Wed to Sun and Bank
Hol Mon 11–5; Jul to Aug,
daily 11–5; Sept to Nov,
Wed to Sun 11–5. 10 acres

house are wonderful garden buildings, woodland
walks, pools and a snowdrop grove to take your breath
away. A mysteriously two-faced gothic gazebo looks
down a yew alley towards a distant pond. Paths snake
up and down the wooded slopes of the combe, giving
glimpses of alcoves, temples and pools. Work
continues – the Eagle House, filigree gothic exedra and
vegetable garden have been reconstructed with great
success. More recently the Red House is red once
again, and a fine laburnum tunnel has been made.

PENPERGWM LODGE

Gwent

Abergavenny NP7 9AS
3m E of Abergavenny by
B4598; turn N opposite
King of Prussia pub
Tel: 01873 840208

Owner:
Mr and Mrs Simon Boyle

Open: Mid Apr to mid Oct,
Thur to Sat 2–6; May to
Jun, also Sun 2–6. 3 acres

CATRIONA BOYLE inherited a good garden when
she took over at Penpergwm Lodge, and has
added much fine planting. Lawns by the house have
excellent trees, and a south-facing paved terrace
burgeons with *Carpenteria californica*, cistus, diascias,
indigofera, myrtle and penstemons – this is a mild part
of the country. On the far side of the house a stately
procession of 'rooms' is hedged in yew. The former
vegetable garden has arches of roses and vines with
ebullient herbaceous planting below, an apple tunnel, a
pair of rose borders backed with purple beech and a
vine walk. Some good specialist plants are sold, chiefly
herbaceous. This is the home, too, of Catriona Boyle's
Garden School which gives lively one-day courses with
distinguished gardeners.

PENRHYN CASTLE

Gwynedd

Bangor LL57 4HN
1m E of Bangor by A5122
Tel: 01248 353084

Owner: The National Trust

Open: 25 Mar to 1 Nov,
daily except Tue 11–5.30
(Jul and Aug 10–5.30).
47 acres. Castle open

THE GIANT castle built in 1827 in neo-Norman style,
rises on a bluff with marvellous views north to
Beaumaris Bay and south towards Snowdon. Parkland
surrounds the castle but the chief interest is the old
kitchen garden on a steep slope with a formal terrace,
parterres of roses and penstemons, and a rose arbour
at the top; at a lower level are ornamental trees and
shrubs – eucryphias, magnolias, sophora and styrax; at
the lowest level a pergola has clematis intertwined with
fuchsias. In the stream garden below the huge leaves of
Gunnera manicata are splendidly placed against groves
of purple-leafed maples.

PERHILL NURSERIES

Hereford and Worcester

Worcester Road,
Great Witley WR6 6JT
1/4m SE of Great Witley
village on A443
Tel: 01299 896329
Fax: 01299 896990

Open: Daily 9–5, Sun
10.30–4.30

ALPINES AND herbaceous perennials are the speciality of this nursery, which carries a stock of over 2,500 different species and varieties. There are particularly good collections of campanulas, penstemons, phlox, pinks, salvias, silenes and sisyrinchiums. There are always too many plants to be listed, so a visit and a rummage is sure to reveal something desirable. There is now a mail order service and a plant list is produced (six 2nd-class stamps).

PLAS BRONDANW GARDENS

Gwynedd

Llanfrothen,
Penrhyndeudraeth
LL48 6SW
3m N of Penrhyndeudraeth
by A4085
Tel: 01766 770484/770814

Owner: Trustees of the
Second Portmeirion
Foundation

Open: Daily 9–5. 4 acres

PLAS BRONDANW belonged to the architect of Portmeirion, Sir Clough Williams-Ellis, who lived here from 1902 into the 1960s. On wooded slopes on the edge of Snowdonia, it has one of the most magnificent natural settings of any garden in Britain. Williams-Ellis laid out an inventive formal garden enlivened by the cheerful panache that makes him so attractive (who else could make such a delightful pavilion out of *corrugated iron*, exquisitely shaped and painted, as that which lurks in the woodland here?). Yew hedges connect house and garden, and 'borrowed landscapes' are given full emphasis, including a breathtaking view of Snowdon and of Cnicht neatly framed through a *claire voie*. The place swarms with architectural trimmings – an orangery, terraces, balustrades, urns, statues and *jeux d'esprit*. Do not miss the walk up through the woods behind the house to the spectacular rocky ravine with its watchtower and the look-out point high on the hill above.

PLAS NEWYDD

Gwynedd

Illustration opposite:
Plas Brondanw Gardens

THE HOUSE of Plas Newydd is a famously decorative piece of gothic fantasy built in 1793 by James Wyatt and overlooking the waters of the Menai Strait. This is a mild but windy place and one of the striking things about the garden is the decorative use of unfamiliar hedging plants – fuchsia, griselinia and

Llanfairpwll,
Anglesey LL61 6EQ
1m S of Llanfairpwll by A5
Tel: 01248 714795

Owner: The National Trust

Open: Apr to 1 Nov, daily
except Fri and Sat 11–5.30.
31 acres. House open

potentilla. There is a pretty little formal terraced
garden between the house and the strait but the real
garden excitement comes with the parkland to the
west, known as 'West Indies', in the design of which
Humphry Repton had a hand. Here countless good
ornamental trees and shrubs – camellias, magnolias,
maples and the Chilean firebush – flourish among
older cedars, an exceptional sycamore and Monterey
cypresses. A rhododendron garden, three-quarters of a
mile to the north of the house, has recently been
restored and is open only during flowering time from
the beginning of April to early June.

PLAS-YN-RHIW

Gwynedd

Rhiw, Pwllheli LL53 8AB
12m from Pwllheli on S
coast road to Aberdaron
Tel: 01758 780219

Owner: The National Trust

Open: Apr to 30 Sept, daily
except Tue and Wed (20
May to 30 Sept also open
Wed) 12–5. 1 acre. House
open

THE LLEYN peninsula is the most westerly part of
Wales, and this enchanting little garden is one of
the most remote on the mainland of Britain. The
elegant stone house is built on precipitous wooded
slopes giving beautiful views over Hell's Mouth Bay.
Cobbled paths and box hedges divide the densely
planted garden, and old plants of sweet bay, a fig,
myrtles and artemisias give a Mediterranean air. The
microclimate is very benign here, so plants like
Euphorbia mellifera grow to great size, and the tender
climber *Lapageria rosea* flourishes. Few gardens of this
size have such pungent and memorable atmosphere.

PORTMEIRION

Gwynedd

Penrhyndeudraeth
LL48 6ET
2m SE of Porthmadog
Tel: 01766 770228
Fax: 01766 771331

Open: Daily 9.30–5.30

IN A wooded combe overlooking the estuary of
Traeth Bach towards the Harlech hills the architect
Sir Clough Williams-Ellis let rip with a fantasy
Italianate village. He incorporated old architectural
fragments into his buildings – cupolas, colonnades,
statues and enough balconies to meet the needs of the
world's population of Romeos and Juliets. Among
these buildings there is interesting planting with a
Mediterranean feeling – Chusan palms and Italian
cypresses punctuate the scene, and cistus and
artemisias flourish on the rocky slopes. There is a hotel
in the village and the houses are available for rent.

POWIS CASTLE

Powys

Welshpool SY21 8RF
1m S of Welshpool by A483
Tel: 01938 554336

Owner: The National Trust

Open: Apr to 1 Nov, daily
except Mon and Tue (open
Bank Hol Mon) 11–6 (Jul to
Aug, daily except Mon
1–5). 24 acres. Castle open

THERE ARE few historic gardens that have so much
to offer the gardener as Powis Castle. Here are the
splendid remains of a great formal garden of the 17th
century – with grand terraces and immense old yews.
On these terraces the National Trust has laid out a
brilliant series of borders, with wall plants and
climbers forming a background to fortissimo displays
of border perennials designed to provide interest
throughout the summer into early autumn. Here, also,
is an exceptional collection of pots, beautifully planted
with carefully judged combinations. A woodland
garden below the castle has great atmosphere, with
views through trees of the castle on its promontory.

THE PRIORY

Gloucestershire

THE HOUSE at Kemerton is an elegant Georgian box
of Cotswold stone but the priory ruins are visible
among the densely planted borders. The garden has a
protected site on the south-facing slopes of Bredon
Hill. Here Mrs Healing and her late husband laid out
a series of brilliant borders in which colour harmony,

Kemerton GL20 7JN
6m S of Pershore by B4080
Tel: 01386 725258

Owner: The Hon. Mrs
Peter Healing

Open: Jun to Sept, Thur
2–6; also Sun 24 May, 21
Jun, 12 Jul, 2 Aug, 23 Aug,
6 Sept 2–6. 4 acres

some of it refreshingly bold, and contrasts of foliage
were the essential principles. Unusual plants chosen
with an artist's eye fill these borders and they flower
over an extended period. Providing contrast are broad
sweeps of lawn with beautiful ornamental trees
(especially maples), yew hedges, and a pergola of roses
and vines. A nursery sells some excellent plants but
there is no mail order.

RODMARTON MANOR
Gloucestershire

Rodmarton,
nr Cirencester GL7 6PF
In Rodmarton village,
6m SW of Cirencester by
A433
Tel: 01285 841253
Fax: 01285 841298

Owner: Mr and Mrs Simon
Biddulph

Open: 15 May to 26 Aug,
Wed 2–5; 16 May to 29 Aug,
also open Sat 2–5; also by
appointment. 8 acres

THE ARCHITECT Ernest Barnsley started
Rodmarton in 1909 and it became a shrine of the
Cotswolds crafts movement. The grey, gabled house
has an intricate garden, also designed by Barnsley,
divided into 'rooms' and of a lively atmosphere. It is
formal in spirit but the planting has a cottage-garden
informality. A flagged path separates double borders
overflowing with old roses, peonies and campanulas,
backed with stone walls and a yew hedge and
enlivened with topiary of yew and box. Behind the
house a pattern of enclosures is divided by yew hedges
and a lime walk frames views of the rural landscape.

RUSHFIELDS OF LEDBURY
Hereford and Worcester

Ross Road,
Ledbury HR8 2LP
1 1/2m SW of Ledbury by
A449
Tel: 01531 632004

Open: Wed to Sat 11–5;
also by appointment

RUSHFIELDS OF Ledbury describe themselves,
accurately, as sellers of 'choice garden plants'.
They regularly garner gold medals at the regional
shows. Brian and Jenny Homewood's stock has an
emphasis on herbaceous perennials. There are good
collections of aruncus, euphorbias, hardy geraniums,
hostas, penstemons (over 40 kinds), pulmonarias and
interesting grasses. The very rare double-flowered
sweet rocket is stocked, and there is a splendid
selection of the beautiful hellebores cultivated by the
legendary Helen Ballard. The latter are cultivars of
Helleborus orientalis in rare and lovely colours – the
deepest plum, pale pink or white freckled with maroon
spots. An informative catalogue is produced (s.a.e. A5
29p plus £1.00); although there is no mail order
substantial orders (over £50 worth) may be delivered
by special arrangement.

SEZINCOTE

Gloucestershire

nr Moreton-in-Marsh
GL56 9AW
1 1/2m W of Moreton-in-
Marsh by A44

Owner:
Mr and Mrs D. Peake

Open: Jan to Nov, Thur, Fri
and Bank Hol Mon 2–6 or
sunset if earlier. 10 acres.
House open

THE HOUSE at Sezincote was built in around 1810 by Sir Charles Cockerell and has a wonderful Indian character. Sir Charles was one of three brothers all of whom had connections with India – his brother S.P. Cockerell designed the house at Sezincote. At first the scene is quintessentially English; a sweeping drive and lovely parkland ornamented with exceptional cedars of Lebanon scarcely prepares the visitor for the exotic experience in store. Soon the drive runs over an Indian bridge surmounted by statues of bulls; below, a stream flows from a pool with an island bearing a curious column entwined with a three-headed snake. The banks of the stream are richly planted with hostas, rodgersias and skunk cabbage, relishing the moisture. On the far side of the bridge a figure of Souriya overlooks the temple pool. Old woodland spreads all around, studded with ornamental trees. Near the house a formal garden with a canal flanked by soaring Irish yews is overlooked by a grand curving conservatory with minarets, ending in an octagonal domed pavilion. This heady mixture of subtle layout, excellent plants and orientalist decoration deep in the Cotswolds is a unique experience.

SNOWSHILL MANOR

Gloucestershire

Snowshill,
nr Broadway WR12 7JU
In Snowshill village,
3m S of Broadway
Tel: 01386 852410

Owner: The National Trust

Open: Apr to 1 Nov, daily
except Tue 1–5 (closed
Good Fri); May to Sept
same days 12–5.30.
2 acres. House open

CHARLES WADE, antiquarian and architect, was responsible for this extraordinary place where the garden was partly designed by the Arts and Crafts architect M.H. Baillie Scott. The house is a pretty stone-tiled Cotswold manor and the garden lies on steep west-facing slopes to one side. Wade terraced the slope and linked the separate spaces with stone steps and a bold descending avenue of Irish yews. Within the various garden enclosures he deployed a rich repertoire of garden ornaments – sundials, an armillary sphere, a gilt figure of St George and the Dragon, pools, and benches painted in the distinctive 'Wade blue'. Flower beds and climbing roses look wonderful against the honey-coloured stone. The charm of this modestly sized garden lies in its lively decorative sense, different levels and endlessly shifting viewpoints.

SPETCHLEY PARK

Hereford and Worcester

nr Worcester WR5 1RS
3m E of Worcester by A422
Tel: 01905 345224/345213

Owner: Spetchley Garden
Charitable Trust

Open: Apr to Sept, Tue to
Fri and Bank Hol Mon
11–5, Sun 2–5. 25 acres

THE HEART of the garden is a maze of walks, borders and hedged enclosures which are so full of excellent plants that one's attention is repeatedly drawn by some lovely specimen, making it easy to lose one's orientation. The Berkeleys have been here a long time but from the gardening point of view the most important event was the marriage in 1891 of Robert Berkeley to Rose Willmott, the older sister of the famous gardener Ellen Willmott of Warley Place, who designed the fountain garden at Spetchley. Here a fountain lies at the centre of four large squares, enclosed in yew hedges and densely planted. Running along one side is an immense border in which roses, philadelphus and other shrubs are generously underplanted with herbaceous perennials – campanulas, delphiniums, geraniums and peonies. The suave stone Georgian mansion overlooks a park with a lake and clumped trees. In July the woods on one side are filled with martagon lilies, plum-coloured and white, a fabulous sight. I know tidier and less weedy gardens but I know few of more irresistible character.

STANWAY HOUSE

Gloucestershire

Stanway,
nr Cheltenham GL54 5PQ
In Stanway hamlet, 11m NE
of Cheltenham by B4632
and B4077
Tel: 01386 584469
Fax: 01386 584688

Owner: Lord Neidpath

Open: Jun to Sept, Tue and
Thur 2–5. 20 acres

IN STRAIGHTFORWARD gardening terms it would be hard to justify including this beautiful place. But the setting for the Elizabethan and Jacobean house is unforgettably lovely. Behind it, well-wooded land slopes up towards a pyramid-like folly which in the 18th century was at the head of a spectacular cascade. Its remains have recently been excavated and it is hoped that it will be restored. Do walk up to the pyramid; the view is breathtaking and, on the way, an exhilarating cross vista through the woods is revealed. Everywhere there are exceptional trees: old cedars of Lebanon and sweet chestnuts by the pyramid; a lovely tulip tree by the house; and a pair of ancient spreading oriental planes past the medieval tithe barn as you enter. It's not a place for fiddly borders but any gardener will love it.

STAPELEY WATER GARDENS

Cheshire

London Road, Stapeley,
Nantwich CW5 7LH
1m SE of Nantwich by A51
Tel: 01270 623868
Fax: 01270 624919

Open: Mon to Fri 9–6, Sat,
Sun and Bank Hol Mon
10–6 (in winter 2–5).
53 acres

THERE IS nothing else like this anywhere in Britain. It is a tremendous celebration of water gardens and their plants. Although there is plenty of razzmatazz there is also nurserymanship of a high order and the gardens display the largest collection of hardy and tender water-lily varieties in the world – over 350 varieties are grown. There are also many other water-loving plants displayed in immense glasshouses and out-of-doors. A mail order service is provided and the well-illustrated catalogue (£1.00) tells you probably all you need to know about making, stocking and maintaining a water garden.

STONE HOUSE COTTAGE

Hereford and Worcester

Stone, nr Kidderminster
DY10 4BG
2m SE of Kidderminster by
A448
Tel: 01562 69902
Fax: 01562 69960

Owner: Major and the
Hon. Mrs Arbuthnott

Open: Mar to Sept, Wed to
Sat 10–5.30 (also some Suns
for National Gardens
Scheme); Oct to Feb, by
appointment only. 3/4 acre

JAMES ARBUTHNOTT is a demon bricklayer and his wife Louisa a brilliant propagator. The garden, an old walled kitchen garden, now bristles with look-out towers, gazebos, arcades and other charming architectural geegaws which make ornaments as well as supports for the countless climbing, twining and ramping plants that are a speciality of the garden. Hedges of yew and purple plum divide the space and at the centre a pair of burgeoning borders culminates in a sundial. Ornamental trees and shrubs are planted in grass, and near the house raised beds contain alpines and smaller plants. An excellent nursery specialises in wall plants, some very unusual, and some with reputations for dubious hardiness that have proved remarkably tough in this not particularly mild climate. A good catalogue (s.a.e.) is produced but there is no mail order service.

SUDELEY CASTLE
Gloucestershire

Winchcombe, nr
Cheltenham GL54 5JD
8m NE of Cheltenham by
A46
Tel: 01242 602308
Fax: 01242 602959

Owner: Lord and Lady
Ashcombe

Open: Apr to Oct, daily
10.30–5.30. 10 acres. Castle
open

THIS SPECTACULAR place has a grand late medieval castle with later additions and a garden that takes full advantage of the architectural setting. Roses are the great thing at Sudeley, and they look wonderful against the old stone walls. At the entrance a long lily pool runs in front of the ruins of a 15th-century great barn, its roofless walls draped with climbing roses and clematis. Beyond the castle a recently replanted formal Victorian garden has a pool surrounded by L-shaped beds of old shrub roses underplanted with herbs. On either side are immense old tunnels of yew, and the surrounding lawns are studded with topiary shapes of golden and common yew. Old trees – walnuts, limes and a vast cedar of Lebanon – stand out superbly against the castle walls. In 1995 a knot garden was created to commemorate Queen Elizabeth I. A good nursery sells herbs, topiary and an especially distinguished collection of roses.

TATTON PARK
Cheshire

Knutsford WA16 6QN
3 1/2m N of Knutsford,
signposted from the centre
of the town
Tel: 01565 654822
Fax: 01565 650179

Owner: The National Trust

Open: Apr to Sept, daily
except Mon (open Bank
Hol Mon) 10.30–6; Oct to
Mar, daily except Mon
11–4. 60 acres. House open

THE HOUSE was designed in the early 19th century for the Egerton family by Lewis Wyatt; he also had a hand in the gardens which have an exuberant 19th-century flavour. South of the house, on a terrace, a dapper parterre designed by Joseph Paxton is brilliantly bedded out in summer. Her Ladyship's Garden, by the house, is a sunken garden with a pergola and rosebeds. Fine mixed borders with buttresses of yew are backed by the formerly heated walls of the kitchen garden. Nearby, a unique fernery designed by Wyatt houses tender ferns spiked with brilliant blue agapanthus, and an orangery protects citrus plants and sub-tropical climbers. Both are newly restored, a splendid sight. On sloping land south of the house a long walk pierces well-wooded lawns, with glimpses to the west of a serpentine network of lakes. Here is an exceptional Japanese garden, built in 1910 by Japanese gardeners, in which maples, moss-covered stones, an arched bridge and a Shinto temple make a convincing picture under a canopy of old trees. It is one of the finest Japanese gardens in the country.

TRETOWER COURT

Powys

Tretower, nr Crickhowell
In Tretower village, 3m NW
of Crickhowell by A479
Tel: 01874 730279

Owner: Cadw: Welsh
Historic Monuments

Open: end Mar to end Oct,
daily 9.30–6. 1 acre. House
open

O F THE various attempts to recreate a medieval garden, Tretower is quite one of the most attractive. The setting is a lovely one, beneath the windows and grey stone walls of the 15th-century manor house of the Vaughan family. Nothing is known about the garden that existed here in the late middle ages but what has been recreated is based on historical knowledge of gardens of that period. In 'Sir Roger Vaughan's Pleasure Garden' lattice-work fences enclose beds planted with correct plants of the period – primulas, violas, peonies, periwinkles and pinks. A remarkably wide range of ornamental plants was used in gardens of the period. A shady tunnel arbour is richly festooned with clematis, honeysuckle, roses and vines, with shade-loving herbaceous plants at their feet – hellebores, lily-of-the-valley, Solomon's seal and violas. Old varieties of fruit with evocative names – the apples 'Court Pendu Plat', 'Gennet Moyle' and 'Catshead', for example – are all of Sir Roger's time. A memorably atmospheric view of the garden is to be had through the old glass of the leaded windows of the first-floor rooms.

WATERWHEEL NURSERY

Monmouthshire

Bully Hole Bottom, Usk
Road, nr Shirenewton,
Chepstow NP6 6SA
5m NW of Chepstow by
B4235; Jnct 2 of M48;
signed Bully Hole Bottom
Tel: 01291 641577

Open: Daily except Sun and
Mon (open Bank Hol Mon)
9–6 (phone before making a
long journey)

DESMOND AND Charlotte Evans's nursery always has for sale some mouthwatering plant which you certainly do not have in your garden. They carry a large stock but, as Desmond puts it, they 'specialise in not specialising'. Their range is wide, woody and herbaceous, within which are some exceptional groups – many euonymus (some you will find nowhere else), several mahonias (including the new *M. pallida*), unusual kinds of *Skimmia japonica* and several viburnums. Among herbaceous plants are many euphorbias, the best geraniums, ornamental grasses and some very pretty cultivars of periwinkle. There is a list, and mail order is available in autumn, but this is pre-eminently a place to nose around in.

WESTBURY COURT

Gloucestershire

Westbury-on-Severn
GL14 1PD
9m SW of Gloucester by
A48
Tel: 01452 760461

Owner: The National Trust

Open: Apr to 1 Nov, Wed to
Sun and Bank Hol Mon
11–6 (closed Good Fri); also
by appointment. 4 acres

THIS LATE 17th-century formal water garden, made for a house that was destroyed, survived by the skin of its teeth and has now been beautifully restored. On low-lying land on the banks of the Severn, formality is given by two parallel canals edged with yew hedges whose crests are decorated with yew and holly topiary. An elegant Dutch-style pavilion overlooks the head of one canal and a boundary wall is covered in pre-1700 varieties of espaliered fruit. In one corner is a secret walled garden, overlooked by a charming little summerhouse, in which box-edged beds burgeon with plants in cultivation before 1700 and the paths are shaded by an arbour of honeysuckle and clematis. Nearby, a parterre of box topiary and annuals has been recreated from an 18th-century print. On the way out, keep an eye open for an unexpected and unforgettable sight behind the pavilion – an immense holm oak (*Quercus ilex*), probably the oldest in the country.

WESTONBIRT ARBORETUM
Gloucestershire

Westonbirt,
nr Tetbury GL8 8QS
3m SW of Tetbury by A433
Tel: 01666 880220
Fax: 01666 880559

Owner: The Forestry
Commission

Open: Daily 10–8 or sunset
if earlier. 600 acres

THIS IS one of the greatest collections of trees in the country but it is far more than just a collection. It was started in 1829 by Robert Holford who had a brilliant eye for arranging the huge quantities of trees which he so energetically collected. Planting has been continued by subsequent members of his family and, since 1956, under the ownership of the Forestry Commission. Westonbirt is not only a marvellous place to learn about and admire trees and shrubs but is also a landscape of rare beauty. The arboretum has National Collections of *Acer japonicum, A. palmatum* cultivars and lowland species of willow (260 species and cultivars) but in most of the major groups it has wonderful trees, some of them fine old specimens. There is something rare and lovely to see every day of the year.

WITLEY COURT
Hereford and Worcester

Great Witley
10m NW of Worcester by
A443
Tel: 01299 896636

Owner: English Heritage

Open: Apr to Oct, daily
10–6; Nov to Mar, Wed to
Sun 10–1, 2–4. 55 acres

EVEN IN their state of romantic decay the gardens at Witley Court are spectacularly memorable. The great house is but a shell – but what a shell! Here in the 1850s W.A. Nesfield laid out a garden of Versailles-like ambitions for the Earl of Dudley. Nesfield called this great enterprise his 'monster work' and its remains will delight visitors today. A vast pool on the south parterre has as its centrepiece a heroic fountain with Perseus snatching Andromeda from the jaws of a scaly monster with lashing tail. Further up the hill two little pavilions look down towards the palace. To its east, Flora besports herself in another fountain surrounded by Tritons. English Heritage is restoring these great

works and soon the water will flow again. There are no pretty borders here, nor any plants of note – it is the scale of the landscape and the quality of the surviving monuments that stick in the mind.

WOLLERTON OLD HALL

Shropshire

Wollerton,
Market Drayton TF9 3NA
1 1/2m NE of Hodnet by
A53; turn right immediately
after Wollerton sign; garden
300 yards on left
Tel: 01630 685760
Fax: 01630 685583

Owner:
John and Lesley Jenkins

Open: May to Aug, Fri and
Sun 12–5. 3 acres

THE JENKINSES' garden was started in 1984 and is a marvellous example of what can be done in a short space of time. It is a garden of compartments and crafty vistas, carried off with rare skill. Different parts show strikingly contrasting moods: a sunken garden of Arts and Crafts character has the calming sound of running water and a quiet colour scheme; 'Lanhydrock' is an explosion of purple cordyline, rich red poppies, inky black aeoniums, and flaming red hot pokers. The parts are harmoniously linked and the planting everywhere shows rare judgement. Many of the effects are dazzlingly simple – a shady walk of limes underplanted with a sea of purple sage, or the opening of a path marked by a pair of staddle stones emerging from clumps of hosta. This is a garden to be enjoyed – and to be plundered for inspiration.

THE
HEART
OF
ENGLAND

Derbyshire
Northamptonshire
Staffordshire
Warwickshire
West Midlands

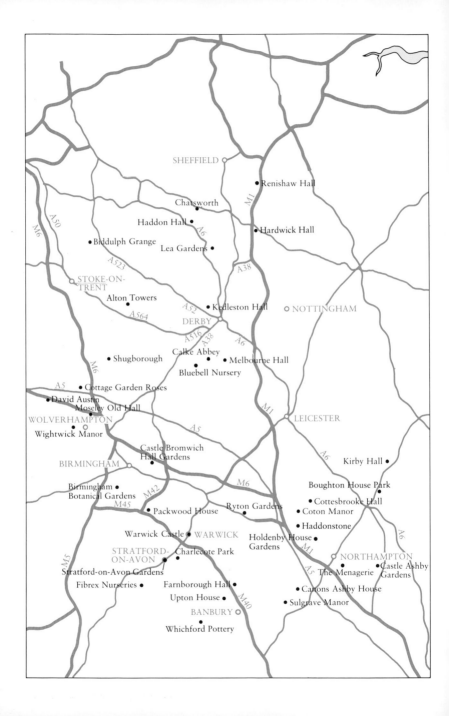

SHEFFIELD

Renishaw Hall

Chatsworth

Haddon Hall

Hardwick Hall

Biddulph Grange

Lea Gardens

STOKE-ON-TRENT

Alton Towers

Kedleston Hall

NOTTINGHAM

DERBY

Shugborough

Calke Abbey

Melbourne Hall

Bluebell Nursery

Cottage Garden Roses

David Austin

Moseley Old Hall

WOLVERHAMPTON

LEICESTER

Wightwick Manor

Castle Bromwich

Hall Gardens

Kirby Hall

BIRMINGHAM

Boughton House Park

Birmingham

Botanical Gardens

Cottesbrooke Hall

Packwood House

Ryton Gardens

Coton Manor

Haddonstone

Warwick Castle

WARWICK

Holdenby House

Gardens

STRATFORD-

ON-AVON

Charlecote Park

NORTHAMPTON

Stratford-on-Avon Gardens

The Menagerie

Castle Ashby

Gardens

Fibrex Nurseries

Farnborough Hall

Canons Ashby House

Upton House

Sulgrave Manor

BANBURY

Whichford Pottery

ALTON TOWERS

Staffordshire

Alton ST10 4DB
18m E of Stoke-on-Trent
Tel: 0990 204060
Fax: 01538 704097

Owner:
The Tussauds Group

Open: Mar to Nov, daily,
9–6 (9–8 on some summer
evenings; check by phone).
500 acres

A RING-A-DING family leisure park, the busiest in Britain, is not a place where you would expect much by way of a garden. The gigantic house was designed for the Earl of Shrewsbury in the first half of the 19th century by a bevy of architects of which the chief was A.W.N. Pugin whose wild gothic palace was said to sacrifice 'domestic comfort to showmanship'. The gardens were made on a similarly lavish scale. In a precipitous dell north of the house huge numbers of conifers clothe the slopes which are animated by exotic buildings, most of which were designed by Robert Abraham: a palatial mosque-like conservatory with many domes and beautiful stonework; a gothic prospect tower on the heights; a memorial to the 15th Earl; and, best of all, a fountain in a lake disguised as a Chinese pagoda. A shady terrace runs in front of the conservatory, with urns and a topiary tunnel of yew. J.C. Loudon thought the whole place was 'in excessively bad taste' – exactly what many people will love. The gardens are splendidly well cared for.

DAVID AUSTIN

West Midlands

A LTHOUGH DAVID Austin grows other things (irises, peonies and daylilies, for example) he is overwhelmingly a rose specialist and one of the very best in the country. He is known above all for old roses

Illustration:
Rosa 'Mary Rose'

Bowling Green Lane,
Albrighton,
Wolverhampton WV7 3HB
7m NW of Wolverhampton
by A41 and A464; Jnct 3 of
M54
Tel: 01902 373931
Fax: 01902 372142

Open: Mon to Fri 9–5, Sat,
Sun and Bank Hol Mon
10–6 or dusk in winter

and his own 'English Roses' which combine the beauty
of flower and form of the old varieties with the repeat
flowering of the modern ones. In fact he does not
disdain modern roses and has a carefully chosen
selection of Hybrid Teas, some of which are now hard
to find. Go, of course, in late June or July and be
bowled over by the beauty and scent. He produces an
excellent, beautifully illustrated and informative
catalogue and sells by mail order.

BIDDULPH GRANGE GARDEN

Staffordshire

Biddulph,
nr Stoke-on-Trent ST8 7SD
5m SE of Congleton by
A527
Tel: 01782 517999

Owner: The National Trust

Open: Apr to 1 Nov, Wed to
Fri 12–6 (closed Good Fri),
Sat, Sun and Bank Hol
Mon 11– 6; 7 Nov to 20
Dec, Sat and Sun 12–4 or
dusk if earlier.
15 acres

GARDENS THAT are snatched from the brink of
extinction always have a special attraction, and
Biddulph is an exceptionally fine example. It was made
by James Bateman and Edward Cooke over a long
period from 1842, when tastes in garden design turned
to the exotic and a flood of newly introduced conifers
inspired the gardening imagination. A frightening
rocky tunnel lit by a glimmer of candle-light leads
suddenly into the glittering gold, scarlet and white
interior of a Chinese pagoda overlooking a pool
fringed with maples. Stone sphinxes and monumental
clipped yews guard the mysterious entrance to Egypt.
A sprightly dahlia walk marches up to a sombre
avenue of deodars piercing deeply into the woodland.
This has been superbly restored by the National Trust;

more work is still being done but the results already make Biddulph an exceptional place. It gives immensely varied pleasures and no other garden in Britain gives such a vivid impression of the excitement of 19th-century gardening.

BIRMINGHAM BOTANICAL GARDENS AND GLASSHOUSES

Birmingham

Westbourne Road, Edgbaston B15 3TR 2m SW of city centre *Tel:* 0121 454 1860

Owner: Birmingham Botanical and Horticultural Society Ltd

Open: Daily 9–7 (Sun 10–7) or dusk if earlier (closed 25 Dec). 15 acres

THERE IS a zip about the Birmingham Botanical gardens. First, they are beautifully gardened – even the bedding schemes manage brilliantly to avoid municipal plodding. Second, although they call themselves botanical gardens, they are treated by locals, and those from further afield, as a public park and there are plenty of horticultural diversions. They were founded in 1829 on an attractively undulating site which was landscaped by J.C. Loudon. Glasshouses of several different climates protect a very wide range of tender plants which includes a collection of warm climate 'economic' plants. Collections of particular groups of plants – introductions by the great plant hunter E. H. 'Chinese' Wilson (who had been a student here), rhododendrons, rock and water plants, and modern roses, are all well displayed.

BLUEBELL NURSERY

Derbyshire

Illustration: Itea ilicifolia

Annwell Lane, Smisby, nr
Ashby-de-la-Zouch
LE65 2TA
1m NW of Ashby-de-la-
Zouch on A50
Tel: 01530 413700
Fax: 01530 417600

Open: Mon to Sat 9–4
(closed 25 Dec–2 Jan)

FOR SOME reason most enterprising young nurseries have specialised in herbaceous plants. Robert and Suzette Vernon sell a few but their hearts and souls are in woody plants of which they offer one of the most mouth-watering selections in the country. From the very desirable but inexplicably overlooked (such as the lovely *Itea ilicifolia*) to rare cultivars of many shrubs and trees (*Quercus cerris* 'Argenteovariegata'!) it is a list bursting with a passion for plants. I defy any gardener to visit the Bluebell Nursery without finding some unfamiliar plant which *must* be bought. There is a mail order service and an admirable catalogue is produced (£1 and two 1st-class stamps).

BOUGHTON HOUSE PARK

Northamptonshire

nr Kettering NN14 1BJ
By Geddington village, 3m
NE of Kettering on A43
Tel: 01536 515731
Fax: 01536 417255

Owner: The Duke and
Duchess of Buccleuch and
Queensberry

Open: May to Sept, daily
except Fri 1–5. 350 acres

THE GREAT house at Boughton has something decidedly French about it. It was started in the 1680s, an addition to a much older house, by the first Duke of Montagu who had been ambassador to Louis XIV. To his great palace the Duke added a formal garden of appropriate scale and splendour, designed by a Dutch gardener, Van der Meulen. In the 18th century the estate became a secondary residence of the Buccleuch family, and the formal garden was not kept up. Today visitors may wander in this vast park of wonderful trees, lakes, canals and exhilarating views.

Sheep graze on the terraces of the old formal garden, now covered in turf, and there are marvellous glimpses of the distant house framed in trees. The character of the place today is essentially that of a landscaped park, but always visible, like the underpainting of an old master, are the smudged but distinguished traces of the earlier garden.

CALKE ABBEY

Derbyshire

Ticknall DE7 1LE
9m S of Derby by A514
Tel: 01332 863822/864444

Owner: The National Trust

Open: Garden: Apr to 1 Nov, Sat to Wed 11–5.30. 10 acres; *Park:* all year dawn–dusk. House open

THE EARLY 18th-century grey stone mansion seems almost like an after-thought when the visitor has traversed the many acres of wonderfully unspoilt ancient parkland that surrounds it. The garden, at some distance from the house, as was often the case in the 18th century, consists of a walled formal garden which has been restored with a pattern of borders with bedding schemes of Victorian appearance. In one corner is a rare 'auricula theatre' – shelves to display auriculas in pots – which is used for pelargoniums in summer. In the restored kitchen garden many old kinds of vegetables and fruit are grown and a fine 18th-century domed orangery has recently been restored.

CANONS ASHBY HOUSE

Northamptonshire

Canons Ashby,
Daventry NN11 6SD
11m NE of Banbury by
A361, A422 and B4525
Tel: 01327 860044

Owner: The National Trust

Open: 11 Apr to 1 Nov, Sat
to Wed 1–5.30 or dusk if
earlier. 3 1/3 acres. House
open

THE BEGUILING brick and stone house, the home of
the Dryden family, was started in the 1550s and
substantially rebuilt in the early 18th century. The
essential layout of the garden as it is today is a rare
survival from the same period. The Green Court by the
west facade, with its decorative stone walls and gates,
is ornamented with giant cones of clipped yew and a
lead statue of a fluting shepherd boy which is probably
by John Van Nost. A door leads under a vast cedar of
Lebanon to the garden proper in which terraces
descend towards decorative gates. Here there has been
much replanting with formal rows of Portugal laurels
and ancient varieties of fruit trees. The Drydens were
an old-fashioned family and rejected the late 18th-
century craze for landscaping, so preserving the
gentlemanly formality that may be seen today.

CASTLE ASHBY GARDENS

Northamptonshire

CASTLE ASHBY was built for the Compton family
between 1574 and 1640 and it is still in their
hands, surrounded by thousands of acres of land. The
Marquess of Northampton has recently undertaken a
strikingly successful restoration of house and garden.
A Victorian terraced garden below the house has been
brilliantly restored with scalloped fountains, ribbon

Castle Ashby
5m E of Northampton by
A428
Tel: 01604 696696
Fax: 01604 696516

Owner: The Marquess of
Northampton

Open: Daily 10–to one hour
before sunset. Terrace
garden by appointment
only. 25 acres

carpet bedding and elaborate arabesques of gravel cut
into the turf. Marvellous parkland to the south-west
was laid out by 'Capability' Brown in 1761 and much
replanting of trees has been carried out. The Italian
garden has a glamorous conservatory designed by
Matthew Digby Wyatt, overlooking formal gardens
with a pond, yew topiary and terracotta urns. A path
leads downhill to an arboretum with some fine trees,
especially the specimens of weeping beech.

CASTLE BROMWICH HALL GARDENS

Birmingham

Old Chester Road, Castle
Bromwich B36 9BT
6m NE of city centre by
A47; Jnct 5 of M6 (exit
northbound only; entry
southbound only)
Tel: 0121 749 4100

Owner: Castle Bromwich
Hall Gardens Trust

Open: Easter to Sept, Mon
to Thur 1.30–4.30, Sat, Sun
and Bank Hol Mon 2–6.
10 acres

CASTLE BROMWICH Hall is a fine brick mansion
built in the 17th century for the Bridgeman
family. The gardens are an exciting survival from the
heyday of English formal garden design of the late
17th and early 18th century and are in the process of
restoration by a privately formed trust. Already much
has been done and this is a very rare opportunity to
see an authentic restoration of a garden of this period
in a marvellous setting of old brick walls and fine
garden buildings. The site is a west-facing slope
divided down the centre by a holly walk – a broad turf
path lined with regularly spaced variegated hollies – a
replanting of the 'Gilded ever Green' mentioned in
surviving records. One end of the walk is punctuated
by an elegant pedimented brick orangery and the other
by the corresponding restored music room. Above the
walk is an area of 'wilderness', formal shrubberies with
winding walks, and below, kitchen gardens and a holly
maze. Work on other features is forging ahead and it
will be fascinating to follow the restoration of this rare
period piece as it progresses.

CHARLECOTE PARK

Warwickshire

THE APPROACH to Charlecote – across an ancient
park with grazing fallow deer – has wonderful
atmosphere. The house, originally an Elizabethan
mansion, was comprehensively done over in the 19th
century. The garden has been revitalised in recent years

Wellesbourne,
Warwick CV35 9ER
5m E of Stratford-on-Avon
by B4086
Tel: 01789 470277

Owner: The National Trust

Open: 3 Apr to 1 Nov, Fri to
Tue 12–5 (closed Good Fri).
30 acres. House open

by the National Trust, with lively mixed borders in the
walled forecourt with its ornate turreted gate-tower.
Charlecote has associations with Shakespeare – he is
supposed to have poached here as a lad – and a border
of flowers mentioned in his plays commemorates him.
Behind the house the river Avon curves across flat
parkland with avenues radiating into the distance. An
admirable park walk of about one mile runs along the
banks of the river, girdling the estate, and gives
wonderful views of the house and its lovely setting.

CHATSWORTH

Derbyshire

Bakewell DE4 1PP
4m E of Bakewell by A6 or
A619 and minor roads
Tel: 01246 582204
Fax: 01246 583536

Owner:
Chatsworth House Trust

Open: Easter to Oct, daily
11–5. 100 acres. House
open

THE CAVENDISHES first made a garden at
Chatsworth in the 16th century and it was
subsequently added to by many of the greatest garden
designers and architects of the day. In the late 17th
century London and Wise were called in; in the 18th
century, 'Capability' Brown landscaped the garden,
undoing one of the greatest of all formal gardens; in
the 19th century Joseph Paxton was head gardener,
adding great conservatories and rockeries. Today, the
garden is full of reminders of the past – a handsome
formal scheme of lime walks and pools to the south;
Paxton's 'conservative' wall; an exquisite orangery of
1698; the dazzling cascade house of 1703 over whose
domed roof water pours as though off an umbrella.
But this is not a museum and there are lively new
borders in front of the orangery shop and the

charming caprice of a miniature ornamental *potager*.
The 1 1/2-acre working kitchen garden is now visitable
and the great yew maze planted in 1961 is once again
open. Above all, views across the valley beyond the
great house to exquisite pastoral scenery provide an
incomparable setting. Good plants are sold at the plant
centre, and Chatsworth makes its own garden
furniture which is of very high quality.

COTON MANOR

Northamptonshire

nr Guilsborough NN6 8RQ
10m NW of Northampton
by A5199 or A428
Tel: 01604 740219
Fax: 01604 740838

Owner: Mr and Mrs Ian
Pasley-Tyler

Open: Easter to Sept, Wed
to Sun and Bank Hol Mon
2–5.30. 10 acres

THE GARDENS at Coton Manor are better than ever,
with sparkling evidence of horticultural
enterprise. The land sloping away from the gabled
stone house is divided into areas of strikingly varied
character – from sun-baked bed to woodland rill edged
with moisture-loving plants. The paved terrace south
of the house, full of plant interest and overhung with
the rose 'Seven Sisters', leads to a fortissimo
herbaceous border hedged in holly. At a distance from
the house an entirely new development is a pretty,
formal herb parterre with gravel paths. Everywhere
there are roses, and other excellent and unusual plants,
and the garden is maintained to very high standards.
An attractive plant-sales area is arranged in the shade
of a fine black walnut.

COTTAGE GARDEN ROSES

Staffordshire

Illustration: Rosa 'Souvenir du Docteur Jamain'

Woodland House, Stretton, nr Stafford ST19 9LG
9m SW of Stafford by A449; 2m from Jnct 12 of M6
Tel: 01785 840217
Fax: 01902 850193

Open: Daily 9–6

Illustration opposite:
Cottesbrooke Hall

T HIS NURSERY specialises in the very best old and wild roses to which have been added modern roses of high quality which possess the virtues of beautiful flowers and lovely scent found in the older kinds. John Scarman, who runs the nursery, knows an immense amount about these plants and has produced one of the best catalogues of roses ever assembled, beautifully illustrated in colour and with a great deal of background information about the plants and their cultivation. He describes it as a selective guide to the most interesting and reliable of the old roses. Roses may be bought in containers at the nursery or supplied bare-rooted by post. John Scarman's own garden alongside the nursery has a splendid display of roses in action. The Rose Garden School, based at the nursery, runs attractive residential courses on practical rose gardening, with visits to other gardens.

COTTESBROOKE HALL

Northamptonshire

nr Northampton NN6 8PF
9m NW of Northampton by A50
Tel: 01604 505808
Fax: 01604 505619

Owner: Captain John Macdonald-Buchanan

Open: Easter to Sept, Wed, Thur, Fri and Bank Hol Mon, also Sun in Sept 2–5. 30 acres. House open

S OME GARDENS deserve to be better known and Cottesbrooke is a prime example. The beautiful early 18th-century brick and stone house has a garden which matches it for beauty and interest. It looks out over wonderful 18th-century parkland and a central vista is aligned on the distant spire of Brixworth church. The garden today is the result of many different influences – the present owner's mother, Lady Macdonald-Buchanan, the Arts and Crafts designer Edward Schultz, Dame Sylvia Crowe and Sir Geoffrey Jellicoe. Around the house there is a cornucopia of

formal gardens: a pair of fortissimo herbaceous borders; a stately walk with yew hedges and wrought-iron gates with fine piers; enclosed gardens with pools and a pergola; and a south-facing terrace with statues and plantings of roses and agapanthus. All about is splendid parkland with countless good trees. At a distance from the house, the wild garden has a beautifully planted stream with arched bridges spanning the water and many Japanese maples giving an eastern atmosphere. There are few gardens anywhere with so much to admire as Cottesbrooke.

COUGHTON COURT

Warwickshire

Alcester B49 5JA
2m N of Alcester on A435
Tel: 01789 400777
Fax: 01789 765544

Owner:
Mrs Clare Throckmorton

Open: 14 Mar to Apr, Sat and Sun 11–5.30 (also open Easter Mon to Wed 11–5.30); May to Sept, daily except Thur and Fri 11–5.30 (also Fri in Jul and Aug); 3 to 18 Oct, Sat and Sun 11–5.30. House open. 20 acres

COUGHTON COURT is an idiosyncratic and most attractive house of different periods, ranging from the early 16th century to the 18th century. The Throckmorton family has lived in these parts for almost 600 years. The gardens, however, are entirely modern, having been made to the designs of Christina Birch, a daughter of the house, since 1991. This ambitious scheme, although of a thoroughly conventional kind, is well thought out and gives much pleasure. The best parts are to be found south of the house where, in a large walled garden, a delightful labyrinth of roses (mostly old shrub roses) is lavishly underplanted with herbaceous perennials. A long walk at right angles links a sequence of enclosures some of which contain colour borders – white, red, cool or hot – all done with panache, with skilful passages of planting. A formal orchard contains hazels and cobnuts, cherries and plums espaliered against a wall and many old varieties of apples and pears. A riverside walk sparkles with bulbs in spring and leads to an admirable new bog garden.

FARNBOROUGH HALL

Warwickshire

nr Banbury OX17 1DU
6m N of Banbury off A423
Tel: 01295 89 202

Owner: The National Trust

Open: Apr to Sept, Wed and Sat, (also 3 and 4 May) 2-6; terrace walk only also open Thur and Fri 2-6.
16 acres

FARNBOROUGH IS a very unusual intimate landscape garden laid out in the 18th century – delicate chamber music rather than resounding symphony. William Holbech inherited the property with its handsome late 17th-century house in 1717 and, with the help of the elusive Sanderson Miller, laid out the grounds in the new landscape taste. Behind the house a half-mile long terrace of grass curves up a slope. Woodland presses in on one side and, on the other, there are occasional views of the countryside and of parkland. The terrace was made in about 1750 at a time when the taste for landscaping included taking advantage of the beauties of surrounding nature and focusing attention on them. Here, the idyllic views of the Warmington valley and of its water-meadows presented exactly the kind of rural scene that was so much treasured. The terrace is embellished with two pavilions, one of which is an unusual oval in section, with an open loggia, and the other in the form of a columned temple. Hidden in the woods a game-larder is built in the form of an exquisite temple and the very end of the terrace is marked by a slender obelisk. It is one of the most original and memorable landscape gardens in the country.

FIBREX NURSERIES LTD
Warwickshire

Illustration: Polystichum setiferum plumoso-divisilobum 'Baldwinnii'

Honeybourne Road, Pebworth, nr Stratford-upon-Avon CV37 8XT 5m NW of Chipping Camden by B4081 and minor roads
Tel: 01789 720788
Fax: 01789 721162

Open: Jan to Mar, Sept to Nov, Mon to Fri 12–5; Apr to Aug, Tue to Sun 12–5; closed Dec

T HE NURSERY has four specialities, in each of which it offers marvellous collections. First, its pelargonium list is enormous, essential browsing for anyone with an interest in those plants. Second, there is a rich selection of ivies with, for example, over 200 varieties of *Hedera helix* varieties. Third, a particularly attractive collection of hardy ferns for which a good catalogue is issued with much valuable information. Lastly, there is a unique selection of very rare cultivars of *Helleborus orientalis*, known as the Raithby hybrids, with lovely and unusual colouring. Mail order is provided and lists (two 2nd-class stamps) of each speciality are published.

HADDON HALL
Derbyshire

Bakewell DE4 1LA 2m SE of Bakewell by A6
Tel: 01629 812855
Fax: 01629 814379

Owner: The Duke of Rutland

Open: Apr to Sept, daily 11–5. 6 acres. House open

H ADDON HALL is an intensely romantic place: a vast castle, built between the 12th and 17th centuries, with turrets, crenellations and tracery windows. It is set in hilly wooded countryside and the garden still has some of the character of the formal gardens of the 17th century. The south garden, a series of terraces with balustrades, dates from the very early 17th century. Buttresses at the lowest level make an attractive and protected setting for roses and other flowering shrubs and climbers. There is a fountain and an immense collection of roses but the eye is constantly drawn to marvellous views of the old stone walls of the castle and to the river looping across the rural landscape below.

HADDONSTONE LTD

Northamptonshire

The Forge House, Church Lane, East Haddon, Northampton NN6 8DB 8m NW of Northampton off A428
Tel: 01604 770711
Fax: 01604 770027

Open: Mon to Fri 9–5.30 (closed Bank Hol Mon and Christmas week)

GARDEN ORNAMENTS and buildings made of reconstructed stone have a long and honourable history. Haddonstone is one of the leading manufacturers and produces a very wide range of statues, urns, columns, garden buildings and architectural detailing. They also undertake to make individual pieces to customers' specifications. Many of the designs are faithful copies of surviving examples in historic gardens and, when weathered, have all the charm of the past. A beautifully kept show garden displays many of the products in a setting planned to display their ornamental use. An elegant catalogue is produced and ornaments may be supplied by Haddonstone's own delivery service.

HARDWICK HALL

Derbyshire

Doe Lea, Chesterfield S44 5QJ
6 1/2m NW of Mansfield by A617 and minor roads; Jnct 29 of M1
Tel: 01246 850430

Owner: The National Trust

Open: Apr to 1 Nov, Wed, Thur, Sat, Sun and Bank Hol Mon 12–5.30 or sunset if earlier. 7 acres. House open

BESS OF Hardwick married successfully (four times) and this is her final architectural flourish, built in the late 16th century when she was in her seventies and Countess of Shrewsbury. She ornamented the parapet of her great house with her initials, ES, carved in fretted stone against the sky. The gardens are disposed in the Elizabethan stone courts to the west and south of the house. The entrance court, with a fine old cedar of Lebanon on the lawn, has splendid mixed borders in which colour and foliage have been cunningly chosen. Repeated plantings of the sprawling, elegant

Aralia elata 'Aureovariegata', and in late summer of
the arching fronds of miscanthus give structure to a
colour scheme – hot reds, oranges and yellow near the
house, and blues, whites and yellow further away. The
south court is divided into four by yew and hornbeam
hedges. One of the divisions is a virtuoso herb garden
in which columns of golden and ordinary hop rise
magnificently from a sea of angelica, artemisia,
lavender, sage, sweet cicely and thyme.

HOLDENBY HOUSE GARDENS

Northamptonshire

Holdenby,
nr Northampton NN8 8DJ
6 1/2m NW of
Northampton by A428 and
minor roads; signposted off
A428 and A50
Tel: 01604 770074
Fax: 01604 770962

Owner: Mr and Mrs James
Lowther

Open: Easter to Sept, Mon
to Fri 1–5, Sun 2–6 (Bank
Hol Sun and Mon 1–6).
10 acres

HOLDENBY WAS built in the 16th century by Sir
Christopher Hatton whose family also owned
Kirby Hall. In its day it was one of the great houses of
England and had a spectacular garden of which
tantalising traces remain today – two magnificent
Elizabethan stone arches and grandiose terracing in the
fields. Aerial photographs reveal the pattern, and vast
scale, of the original garden. The present house is
Victorian and by far the best feature of the garden
today is the dazzling little evocation of a 16th-century
garden designed by Rosemary Verey. It is enclosed in
yew hedges, with a sundial at the centre, and
surrounding beds are decorated with lollipops of box
or holly, mounds of santolina and hedges of lavender
and artemisia. In summer there are drifts of white,
mauve or purple *Salvia viridis* and the surrounding
beds are filled with culinary herbs filling the air with
their savoury scent. The whole is overlooked by a
shady gazebo of clipped yew.

KEDLESTON HALL

Derbyshire

Derby DE6 4JN
3m NW of Derby by A52
and minor roads
Tel: 0132 842191

Owner: The National Trust

Open: Gardens: 28 Mar to 1
Nov, Sat to Wed 11–6; *Park:*
daily 11–6. 7 acres of
gardens. House open

KEDLESTON IS the grandest and possibly the prettiest of Robert Adam's houses, built for Nathaniel Curzon in the 1760s. Adam also had a hand in the park, which forms a lovely approach for the house. To the north, a long serpentine lake is spanned by a three-arched bridge with a rocky cascade below it, and nearby, on the banks, a charming Fishing Room is flanked by a pair of pedimented boathouses. Behind the house, in the well-wooded old pleasure grounds, a circular garden of beds of roses radiating from a central pool is hedged in laurel and overlooked by a domed hexagonal temple. Shrubberies of dogwoods, rhododendrons and roses are embellished by a fine stone urn and, round a corner, the Medicean Lion rises up with a roguish grin.

KIRBY HALL

Northamptonshire

4m NE of Corby by minor
roads
Tel: 01536 203230

Owner: English Heritage

Open: Daily 10–6. 5 acres

THIS IS a ghostly place on the edge of the industrial sprawl of Corby – the uninhabited remains of an exquisite late 16th-century palace built for one of Queen Elizabeth's favourite courtiers, Sir Christopher Hatton. In the late 17th century Charles Hatton made a great garden here. This was restored after excavations in the 1930s but was highly inauthentic – full of HT roses and with a jolly Victorian flavour. Hatton's garden is in fact particularly well documented, including detailed lists of plants. English Heritage is in the process of redoing it, agonizingly slowly, and we must wait to see what they can do. Turf

plats and gravel paths are now in place in front of the house and old varieties of fruit trees have been planted. Few sites are more worthy of restoration and we must hope that things may proceed more quickly.

LEA GARDENS

Derbyshire

Lea, Matlock DE4 5GH
5m SE of Matlock by A6
and minor roads
Tel: 01629 534380
Fax: 01629 534260

Owner: Mr and Mrs J. Tye

Open: 20 Mar to 6 Jul,
daily 10–7. 4 acres

THIS GARDEN, inspired by Bodnant and Exbury but quite small by comparison, was started in 1935 by John Marsden-Smedley. It is a marvellous site, high up on south-facing wooded slopes that run down to the valley of the river Derwent. It makes a splendid setting for the excellent collection of rhododendrons which Marsden-Smedley built up. Subsequent owners have doubled the size of the garden and added alpine screes, many new trees and herbaceous plants. The nursery sells a good range of alpines, azaleas, rhododendrons and kalmias. A list is issued (s.a.e. and 30p) and there is a mail order service.

MELBOURNE HALL

Derbyshire

MELBOURNE IS a fascinating place. The grey stone house presents its most glamorous facade, of 1744, to the garden which was laid out in the early 18th century. Giant steps of turf descend to the Great Basin, a curved pool that crisply reflects the house. On one side is the 'Birdcage', Robert Bakewell's airy

Melbourne DE7 1EN
9m S of Derby by A453
Tel: 01332 862502
Fax: 01332 862263

Owner: Lord Ralph Kerr

Open: Apr to Sept, Wed,
Sat, Sun and Bank Hol
Mon 2–6. 16 acres. House
open Aug only

arbour of wrought iron of sublime delicacy. To the
south lies a pattern of lime alleys, unchanged in
almost 300 years, with grassy walks punctuated by
urns and statues of marvellous quality, some of them
by John Van Nost, the greatest maker of garden
ornaments of the early 18th century. Of the same
period, leading to the west, is an immense tunnel of
yew between whose gnarled trunks the visitor may
walk. On its south side are some very good new mixed
borders, showing that the spirit of gardening at
Melbourne is still very much alive and kicking.

THE MENAGERIE

Northamptonshire

Horton,
Northampton NN7 2BX
5m SE of Northampton off
B526; entrance just S of
Horton village
Tel: 01604 870957

Open: Apr to Sept, Thur
10–4, last Sun of each
month 2–6. Groups by
appointment. 3 acres

THE MENAGERIE is an enchanting classical building
of the 1750s designed by the mysterious architect
and garden designer Thomas Wright, 'the wizard of
Durham'. Gervase Jackson-Stops rescued it from
dereliction, restored it impeccably and made it into a
house. More recently he turned his mind to the garden
and transformed it into a delicious *jeu d'esprit*. An
avenue of limes runs away from the south front,
flanked by radiating hornbeam alleys. Overlooking a
round pool on each side is a thatched building – one
suavely gothic, the other crisply classical. But in each
case the facade that confronts the wilder part of the
garden is faced with rustic woodwork, encrusted with
tormented oak boles. The interiors of these buildings
are as fastidious as their exteriors. The borders by the
south-facing terrace are finely planted with striking

foliage – artichokes, delphiniums, eremurus, thalictrum – and subtle colours. At the entrance the admirable Drywood Nursery sells a small but very choice range of plants. Gervase Jackson-Stops died shortly after the garden was finished – The Menagerie, reflecting his dual interest in rare houses and fine gardens, is a wonderful memorial to him.

MOSELEY OLD HALL
Staffordshire

Moseley Old Hall Lane, Fordhouses, Wolverhampton WV10 7HY
3 1/2m N of Wolverhampton, between A460 and A449, S of M54
Tel: 01902 782808

Owner: The National Trust

Open: 28 Mar to Oct, Sat and Sun, Bank Hol Mon and following Tue (except 5 May) 1.30–5.30 (Bank Hol Mon 11–5); Jun to Oct, also Wed 1.30–5.30; Jul to Aug, also Tue 1.30–5.30 (Bank Hol Mon 11–5); Nov to 21 Dec, Sun 1.30–4.30. 1 acre. House open

AROUND AN unassuming Elizabethan and 17th–century house the National Trust has made a little formal garden rich in the features of the 17th century. The old windows overlook a parterre with a geometric pattern of box hedges, coloured pebbles and lollipops of clipped box – all this taken from a design of 1640. A nut walk leads to a paved path flanked by pairs of medlars, mulberries and quinces. Running down one side of the parterre is a 'carpenter's work' tunnel, festooned with purple-leafed vines and Virgin's Bower clematis (*C. flammula*) and underplanted with aquilegias, geraniums and lavender. The enclosed front garden has box topiary clipped into cones and spirals, and borders of period plants.

PACKWOOD HOUSE
Warwickshire

Lapworth, Solihull B94 6AT
11m SE of Birmingham by A34
Tel: 01564 782 024

Owner: The National Trust

Open: 25 Mar to Sept, Wed to Sun and Bank Hol Mon (closed Good Fri) 1.30–6; Oct to 1 Nov, Wed to Sun 12.30–4.30. 5 acres. House open

A SOLEMN GROUP of immensely tall clipped yews, known as the Multitude and the Apostles, surrounds a mount covered in box. A mysterious spiral path leads to the top which is crowned by a clipped parasol shape of yew. Some of these yews date back to the 17th century and have an unforgettable atmosphere. Nearer the house, a stately gabled brick mansion of the late 16th century, there is a completely different mood, with a pronounced Arts and Crafts feel. A fine wrought-iron gate leads down into a handsomely walled garden overlooked by a long terrace edged with flowery borders and with a gazebo at each end. Below it, overlooked by the windows of the house, a decorative sunk garden with a pool is hedged in yew and has lively summer bedding.

RENISHAW HALL

Derbyshire

Renishaw,
Sheffield S31 9WB
On the edge of Renisha
villagew, 1m NW of Jnct 30
of the M1
Tel: 01246 432042/01777
860755

Owner:
Sir Reresby Sitwell Bt

Open: Easter to mid Sept,
Fri, Sat, Sun and Bank Hol
Mon 10.30–4.30. 10 acres

THIS IS one of the greatest, and most attractive, gardens in England. It is the creation of Sir George Sitwell who in the 1890s studied Italian renaissance gardens (visiting over 200 of them), digested what he saw and came back to the family estate in Derbyshire determined to make an Italianate garden. On south-facing slopes, in an industrial area of England not much resembling Tuscany, he laid out a series of yew-hedged terraces sparkling with statues, urns and fountains. Sir George regarded flowers with some contempt – 'such flowers as might be permitted . . . [should not] call attention to themselves by hue or scent.' The garden he made is beautifully cared for by the family today. However, there are now admirable borders, well judged colour associations and many floriferous fripperies which will delight modern visitors. There is an outstanding collection of shrub roses which reaches its climax in the lower terrace where in late June their scent, intermingled with that of *Buddleja alternifolia* and philadelphus, provides a delicious experience. Although 'hue and scent' are rather prominent here, it does not in the slightest detract from Sir George's renaissance vision.

RYTON GARDENS

Warwickshire

Ryton-on-Dunsmore,
Coventry CV8 3LG
5m SE of Coventry by A45
Tel: 01203 303517
Fax: 01203 639229

Owner: The Henry
Doubleday Research
Association

Open: Daily 10–5.30
(except Christmas holiday).
10 acres

THIS IS the home of the Henry Doubleday Research Association. As well as being the leading centre of organic gardening, it is a fascinating display garden, showing the techniques of ecologically friendly gardening. Regarded by some until recently as the province of cranks, this is now seen to be the best way to garden, working with nature rather than zapping it with chemicals. At Ryton, demonstration areas show techniques of vegetable growing, how to make compost, how to control weeds and pests, and many other things. A wildflower meadow is rich in native plants; a rose garden has varieties that are resistant to disease. This is not only muck and magic – there are also some attractively laid out pleasure gardens. Any gardener will learn from the insights of this unique and enjoyable place.

SHUGBOROUGH

Staffordshire

SHUGBOROUGH IS a dream-like picturesque landscape garden in which marvellous ornaments and garden buildings float into view at every turn. From the house, largely built by Samuel Wyatt for Viscount Anson in the 1790s, a series of shallow terraces descend to the river Sow, decorated with

Milford,
nr Stafford ST17 0XB
6m E of Stafford by A513
Tel: 01889 88 1388

Owner: The National Trust

Open: 28 Mar to Sept, daily
11–5; 1 to 25 Oct Sun only
11–5. 18 acres. House open

golden yew topiary and rose beds. A wild picturesque
ruin designed in 1750 by Thomas Wright crouches on
the water's edge. To one side a rose garden with an
Edwardian flavour has roses trained on arches and
pillars. A path now winds away into the informal heart
of the garden where an arched scarlet Chinoiserie
bridge leads to the pagoda-like Chinese House (1747).
In the woods there is a mysterious Cat's Monument;
the riddling Shepherd's Monument; a dapper Doric
temple; and, in front of the house, handsome parkland
with James 'Athenian' Stuart's beautiful 'Tower of the
Winds' built in 1764.

STRATFORD-UPON-AVON GARDENS

Warwickshire

Illustration: The garden at
Hall's Croft

S TRATFORD IS, of course, thoroughly given over to
the celebration of Shakespeare's life and work.
Some of the various old houses associated with him in
and around the town have gardens of considerable
charm. **Shakespeare's Birthplace** (Henley Street. *Open:*
Mar to Oct, daily 9–5.30 (Sun 10–5.30); Nov to Feb,
daily 9.30–4 (Sun 10.30–4)). A lawn at the back is
ornamented with trees such as a fig, hawthorn, medlar
and quince, all of which are mentioned in the plays. A
pair of pretty, mixed borders is planted to give interest
throughout the year. **Hall's Croft** (Old Town. *Open:*
Mar to Oct, daily 9.30–5 (Sun 10.30–5); Nov to Feb,
daily 10–4 (Sun 1.30–4)). The garden is walled and has
a splendid old mulberry and borders running from a

sundial to the back of the half-timbered house. **New Place** (Chapel Lane. *Open:* Mar to Oct, daily 9.30–5 (Sun 10.30–5); Nov to Feb, daily 10–4 (Sun 1.30–4)). A knot garden follows Elizabethan patterns in its layout of low hedges of box, hyssop and santolina and its surrounding apple tunnels, but is planted in thoroughly 20th-century summer bedding. The Great Garden behind has topiary of box and yew and burgeoning herbaceous borders. **Anne Hathaway's Cottage** (in Shottery village, 1 1/4m NW of Stratford by A422. *Open:* Mar to Oct, daily 9–5.30 (Sun 10–5.30); Nov to Feb, daily 9.30–4 (Sun 10.30–4)). At the front a profusion of planting gives a vision of the English cottage garden.

SULGRAVE MANOR

Northamptonshire

Sulgrave,
nr Banbury OX17 2SD
7m NE of Banbury by
B4525
Tel: 01295 760205

Owner: Colonial Dames of
America

Open: Apr to Oct, daily
except Wed 2–5.30 (Sat and
Sun 10.30–1, 2–5.30); Nov,
Dec and Mar, Sat and Sun
10.30–1, 2–4.30 (closed
25–26 Dec). 2 acres. House
open

G EORGE WASHINGTON'S ancestors lived here and the American connection is proudly emphasised, with the stars and stripes flying splendidly above the roof. The house is a much altered 16th-century stone-tiled manor, added to in 1921 by Sir Reginald Blomfield. He also laid out part of the garden – an architectural design for a crisply formal approach of yew hedges. The entrance to the house lies across an orchard with gravel walks and the forecourt has lawns decorated with topiary yew birds and herbaceous borders flanking the porch. A little herb parterre on a terrace above is shaded by an old walnut tree. A rose garden is edged in box and a sundial stands in the middle, fringed with lavender. There is no attempt at historical planting here but the garden makes an attractive setting for the old house.

UPTON HOUSE
Warwickshire

Banbury,
Oxfordshire OX15 6HT
7m NW of Banbury by
A422
Tel: 0129 670266

Owner: The National Trust

Open: 4 Apr to 1 Nov, daily
except Thur and Fri 2– 6.
19 acres. House open

THE HOUSE, finished in 1695 and built of golden
Hornton stone, lies on the edge of a steep combe;
on its slopes the garden is spread like a patchwork
quilt. Formal steps and a balustrade entwined with
wisteria lead downwards towards areas enclosed in
wavy old yew hedges – among them a marvellous
kitchen garden. Sweeping down the hill are a pair of
herbaceous borders with accents of hot red, and a cool
turf path running down between them to the pool at
the bottom. A mile from the house is a delightful piece
of landscape gardening dating from the 1760s – a lake
and Doric temple (possibly by Robert Adam) deftly
slipped into the countryside, the very essence of 18th-
century elegance.

WARWICK CASTLE
Warwickshire

Warwick CV34 4QU
In the centre of Warwick
Tel: 01926 406600
Fax: 01926 401692

Owner: Pearsons plc

Open: Daily 10–6 (in winter
10–5); closed 25 Dec.
60 acres. Castle open

THIS SPECTACULAR castle was until 1978 the home
of the Earls of Warwick. In front of the orangery
a Victorian parterre is laid out with vivid contrasts of
golden and common yew and blood-red roses.
Peacocks preen and fit well with the mood of the
place. The land falls away abruptly with, framed by
18th-century cedars of Lebanon, a fabulous view –
'Capability' Brown's breathtaking park sweeping down
to a curve in the river Avon 200 feet below. The
Victorian rose garden has been beautifully restored;
old roses with irresistible names like 'Adélaïde
d'Orléans' and 'Variegata di Bologna' are draped in
festoons and rise in columns to produce deliciously
swoony scents in late June and July.

WHICHFORD POTTERY
Warwickshire

JIM KEELING, trained in the traditional craft of
hand-throwing terracotta pots, now leads a team of
potters making a very wide range of different styles.
From plain flower pots to giant Florentine vases
dripping with swags and foliage, all are beautifully

Whichford, nr Shipston-on-Stour CV36 5PG
22m NW of Oxford, E of A34
Tel: 01608 684416
Fax: 01608 684833

Open: Mon to Fri 9–5, Sat and Bank Hol Mon 10–4

made in local clay and are guaranteed frostproof. There is nowhere in Britain quite like this and it is very well worth visiting. Outside the pottery are displayed immense numbers of pots and planters, some beautifully planted up to show their effectiveness in the garden. An excellent catalogue is produced and pots may be ordered to be delivered by carrier.

WIGHTWICK MANOR

West Midlands

Wightwick Bank,
Wolverhampton WV6 8EE
3m W of Wolverhampton by A454
Tel: 01902 761108

Owner: The National Trust

Open: Mar to Dec, Wed to Thur 11–6, Sat, Bank Hol Mon and preceding Sun 1–6. 10 acres. House open

WIGHTWICK MANOR is a piece of ripe High Victoriana – a decorative Pre-Raphaelite mansion made for a paint millionaire – with a garden in keeping. It was laid out in 1887, partly by the watercolourist Alfred Parsons and partly by the architect and garden designer T.H. Mawson, who was responsible for the south terrace and the dramatic procession of great clipped drums of yew that marches purposefully away from it. On one side a 'writers' bed' is filled with plants from the gardens of Dickens, William Morris, Shelley and Tennyson. A formal garden of zig-zag yew hedges, yew topiary and rose beds leads to a walk of variegated holly.

THE
EAST
OF
ENGLAND

Bedfordshire
Cambridgeshire
Essex
Hertfordshire
Lincolnshire
Norfolk
Suffolk

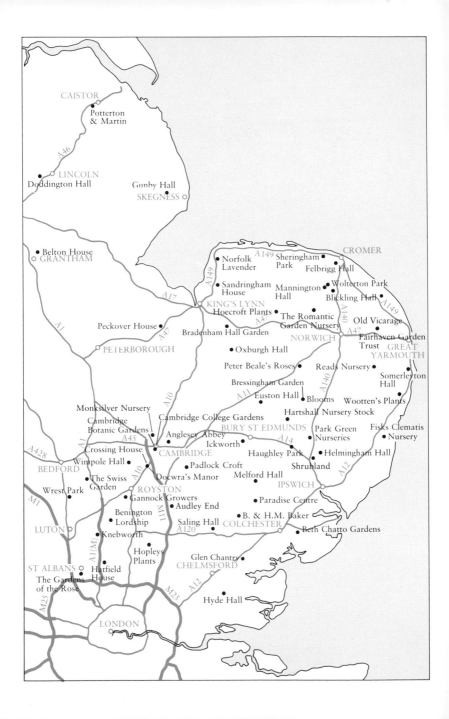

CAISTOR

Potterton
& Martin

A46

LINCOLN
Doddington Hall

Gunby Hall
SKEGNESS

Belton House
GRANTHAM

A17

A1

Peckover House

A47

PETERBOROUGH

A149

Norfolk
Lavender

A149 Sheringham
Park

Felbrigg Hall

Sandringham
House

Mannington
Hall

Wolterton Park

Blickling Hall

A149

KING'S LYNN

Hoecroft Plants

A47

The Romantic
Garden Nursery

A140

Old Vicarage

A47

Bradenham Hall Garden

NORWICH

Fairhaven Garden
Trust

GREAT
YARMOUTH

Oxburgh Hall

Peter Beale's Roses

Reads Nursery

Somerleyton
Hall

A10

Bressingham Garden

A11

Euston Hall

Blooms

Hartshall Nursery Stock

A140

Wootten's Plants

Monksilver Nursery

Cambridge
Botanic Gardens

A45

Cambridge College Gardens

Anglesey Abbey

Ickworth

BURY ST EDMUNDS

A14

Park Green
Nurseries

Fisks Clematis
Nursery

A428

A11

Crossing House

A10

CAMBRIDGE

Haughley Park

Helmingham Hall

A12

BEDFORD

Wimpole Hall

Padlock Croft

Shrubland

A10

Docwra's Manor

Melford Hall

IPSWICH

Wrest Park

The Swiss
Garden

ROYSTON

M11

Gannock Growers

Paradise Centre

Benington
Lordship

Audley End

B. & H.M. Baker

M1

A1(M)

Knebworth

Saling Hall

A120

COLCHESTER

Beth Chatto Gardens

LUTON

Hopleys
Plants

Glen Chantry

CHELMSFORD

ST ALBANS

The Gardens
of the Rose

Hatfield
House

M25

A12

M25

Hyde Hall

M1

M25

LONDON

ANGLESEY ABBEY AND GARDEN

Cambridgeshire

Lode, Cambridge CB5 9EJ
In Lode village, 6m NE of
Cambridge by B1102
Tel: 01223 811200

Owner: The National Trust

Open: Mar to 1 Nov, Wed
to Sun and Bank Hol Mon
11–5 (6 Jul to 6 Sept also
open Mon and Tue 11–5).
100 acres. House open

Anglesey Abbey was an Augustinian priory and its buildings, with many additions, form an alluring ornament at the heart of gardens that Lord Fairhaven started to lay out in 1930. He deployed a marvellous collection of statues and garden ornaments, giving them full decorative presence in subtly contrived settings of alleys, vistas, hedged enclosures and distant prospects. Handsome parkland and some exceptional old trees – particularly limes – give his scheme a rich background. The statues and bold formal designs are what makes Anglesey famous, and walking among them is indeed an exciting experience. But contrasting with these grand formal schemes are more intimate areas – gardens devoted to dahlias and hyacinths, some admirable borders in the herbaceous garden enclosed in a great horseshoe hedge of beech, and a peaceful river walk with grassy banks and a mill-house of rural atmosphere.

AUDLEY END

Essex

Audley End is a much fiddled with Jacobean mansion set in splendid parkland designed by 'Capability Brown' from 1762 onwards. Shortly after this, Robert Adam added various splendid buildings to the estate – a three-arched bridge over the Cam, a

nr Saffron Walden
1m W of Saffron Walden by
B1383
Tel: 01799 522842

Owner: English Heritage

Open: Apr to Sept, Wed to
Sun and Bank Hol Mon
12–5. 50 acres. House open

Temple of Victory and Lady Portsmouth's Column.
Newly restored is a great flower parterre east of the
house, which was designed in 1832 by William Gilpin.
A vast geometric pattern of beds spreads out below the
windows of the house. The planting is a mixture of
old shrub roses, herbaceous perennials and annuals; all
the plants are known to have been available when the
parterre was originally laid out.

B. & H.M. BAKER

Essex

Greenstead Green,
Halstead CO9 1RJ
6m NE of Braintree by
A131 and minor roads
Tel: 01787 476369/472900

Open: Mon to Fri 8–4.30,
Sat to Sun 9–12, 2–4.30

THE BAKERS' speciality is fuchsias and their
fuchsia-red list is a connoisseur's delight. There
has been an explosion of new fuchsia cultivars in
recent years and some of the best old varieties have
been trampled to death in the rush to buy new ones.
Baker's fascinating catalogue (20p plus stamp) lists
varieties going back to the early 19th century and gives
the dates of introduction and the names of their
breeders. Many of these represent the best varieties of
the past   very few are the latest. Most are, of course,
the tender varieties but there is also a section devoted
to hardy kinds, as well as a very unusual list of species.
No mail order service is available.

PETER BEALES ROSES

Norfolk

London Road,
Attleborough NR17 1AY
15m SW of Norwich by
A11
Tel: 01953 454707
Fax: 01953 456845

Open: Mon to Fri 9–1, 2–5
(2–4.30 in winter), Sat
9–4.30, Sun 10–4 (Jan,
closed Sun); closed 24 Dec
to 6 Jan

PETER BEALES is the author of one of the best rose
books of recent times, *Roses,* and here at
Attleborough may be seen one of the best rose
nurseries in Britain. It sells all kinds of roses but the
heart of the business is old-fashioned, species and

modern shrubs, of which it sells a staggering range. If you are searching for an old rose this is probably the best place to start with and a visit in late June will provide an unforgettable sight. A wonderful catalogue is produced, a model of such things, full of valuable information about the history and cultivation of roses. Plants may be supplied by post.

BELTON HOUSE

Lincolnshire

Grantham NG32 2LS
3m NE of Grantham by
A607
Tel: 01476 66116

Owner: The National Trust

Open: Apr to 1 Nov, Wed to
Sun and Bank Hol Mon
(closed Good Fri) 11–5.30
(Jul and Aug 10–5.30). Park
open to pedestrians, from
Lion Lodge gates, at all
times. 100 acres. House
open

BELTON HOUSE is an exquisite mansion dating from the 1690s. The park was landscaped in the late 18th century by William Emes in the style of 'Capability' Brown, but traces of an earlier formal garden survive – including a slender canal at the head of which is a pretty pedimented temple of pale stone. Between the house and the church a grand conservatory designed by Sir Jeffry Wyatville in 1811 overlooks a formal garden with a circular pool and fountain surrounded by a low hedge of purple plum and pale pink roses. Columns of Irish yew, mounds of clipped box and stone urns give vertical emphasis. To the north of the house a walk of golden and common yew columns and mounds is backed by borders with a ghostly planting of white roses, cream petunias and lavender edging. This might have been a pompous and overbearing setting for a very grand house but cheerfulness keeps breaking through.

BENINGTON LORDSHIP

Hertfordshire

Benington, nr Stevenage
4m E of Stevenage by minor
roads; signposted from
Watton-at-Stone
Tel: 01438 869668
Fax: 01438 869622

Owner: Mr and Mrs
C.H.A. Bott

Open: Apr to Aug, Wed
12–5 and Sun 2–5; Bank
Hol Mon 12–5; Sept, Wed
12–5; 3rd Sun in Oct 2–5.
7 acres

A T BENINGTON the remains of a Norman castle, a neo-Norman gatehouse and a 1700 brick mansion give character that is in every way matched by the garden. The house looks across a gentle valley to lakes below, fed by a stream edged with acanthus, astilbes, ferns, geraniums and primulas. To one side, descending the slope, a pair of dazzling herbaceous borders has a colour scheme of cream, white, yellow and blue, with touches of orange and red. Beyond it, the walled kitchen garden has more borders, vegetables and a small nursery. On the other side of the house a formal garden has cream and yellow roses underplanted with irises, aquilegias and catmint.

BLICKLING HALL

Norfolk

Blickling,
Norwich NR11 6NF
15m N of Norwich
Tel: 01263 733084

Owner: The National Trust

Open: 4 Apr to Jul, Wed to
Sun and Bank Hol Mon
10.30–5.30; Aug, daily
10.30–5.30; 2 Nov to Mar
1999, Sun 11–4. 46 acres.
House open

B LICKLING HALL – turreted, gabled and irresistible – was built in around 1620 by Robert Lyminge. The chief part of the garden lies to the east of the house, where a parterre of four square herbaceous beds is brilliantly contrived: the planting rises towards the centre, giving, in late July, the shape of a pyramid. Colours are subtly graded – the beds near the house in yellow and cream, those farther away in blue, pink and red. Rounded cones and curious 'grand-piano' shapes of clipped yew, fine urns and a central fountain decorate the parterre. A pair of sphinxes starts a long gravel walk, backed by azaleas and woodland, leading to a classical temple, from which on either side oak avenues plunge into the woods.

BLOOMS OF BRESSINGHAM
Norfolk

Bressingham,
nr Diss IP22 2AB
3m W of Diss by A1066
Tel: 01379 687464
Fax: 01379 688034

Open: Daily 10–5.30

F EW FAMILIES chose their occupation to suit their name so happily as the Blooms of Bressingham. Although best known for a very wide range of herbaceous plants (more, probably, than any other nursery in the country) they also sell choice collections of alpines, bamboos, conifers, hardy ferns, grasses, heathers, rhododendrons and shrubs. Many varieties, especially of herbaceous plants, bear the name 'Bressingham' and give some idea of the liveliness and enterprise of this influential nursery, which is now opening branches in other parts of the country. Apart from the two gardens created by Alan and Adrian Bloom (see page 218) there is an astonishing collection of plants to be seen at the nursery: over 4,000 species and varieties. A last possible attraction – Alan Bloom receives bed and breakfast guests in his Georgian house, Bressingham Hall.

BRADENHAM HALL GARDEN
Norfolk

West Bradenham,
Thetford IP25 7PQ
18m N of Thetford, 6m E
of Swaffham by A47
Tel: 01362 687279
Fax: 01362 687669

Owner: Lt. Col. and Mrs
R.C. Allhusen

Open: Apr to Sept, 2nd, 4th
and 5th Sun in each month
2–5.30. 27 acres

T HE ALLHUSENS came to this very pretty 1740 brick house in 1951 and embarked on a startlingly unfashionable venture – they began to plant an arboretum which has now grown to splendid maturity. It lies chiefly to the south of the house, pressing in on either side of a broad expanse of lawn, part of a splendid vista leading from the pedimented facade of the house to the rural landscape beyond the garden. Here are many rarities and many beautiful specimens, all accurately labelled. There can be few places where visitors may study and admire so distinguished a collection in such sympathetic surroundings. To the east of the house formal gardens, divided into yew-hedged enclosures, are beautifully gardened and full of interest. A long, deep herbaceous border is cut by a

cross axis leading into a pleached lime walk flanked by two formal gardens: a rose garden and a paved secret garden of Mediterranean character with pots of lemon verbena, *Melianthus major*, daturas and oleanders. The formal gardens are enlivened with statues and girdled by a shady walk of walnuts. Both for its botanical rarities and for the fine ornamental gardening, Bradenham Hall is outstanding.

BRESSINGHAM GARDENS

Norfolk

Bressingham, Diss IP22 2AB
3m W of Diss by A1066
Tel: 01379 687386
Fax: 01379 688085

Owner: Alan Bloom

Open: Bressingham: Apr to early Nov, daily 10–5.30. 6 acres; *Foggy Bottom:* Apr to Nov, Mon and Thur and 1st Sun in month 10.30–4.30. 6 acres

ALAN BLOOM has had a great influence on garden taste through his nursery and his books. In his own Dell garden, alongside the nursery, visitors may see these ideas put into practice. There is, of course, a huge range of herbaceous perennials grown in his famous sweeping island beds. Over 5,000 species and cultivars of herbaceous plants, including 200 or so new plants introduced by the nursery, are displayed in an informal setting. Alan Bloom's son, Adrian, also opens his garden at Foggy Bottom nearby. Here is an admirable collection, cunningly laid out, of trees, shrubs, perennials and grasses.

CAMBRIDGE COLLEGE GARDENS

Cambridgeshire

Illustration: New Court, St John's College

CAMBRIDGE IS strikingly rich in planted space and the Backs running along the west bank of the Cam, provide an exquisite setting for the great college buildings. Within the colleges there is some excellent gardening, and in many instances these more intimate enclosures connect harmoniously with the larger landscape of the Backs. The garden at **St John's College** (St John's St; *Open:* Daily 10.30–5.30 but closed May and Jun) is approached through marvellous 16th-century courts, across the Wren Bridge which has the best view of the most glamorous Cambridge bridge, the Bridge of Sighs. Bold borders run along the gothic screen of New Court, and, in the distance, fine trees mark the Scholars' Garden hedged in yew with an old weeping ash, ornamental trees and mixed borders. **Clare College** (Trinity Lane; *Open:* 2–4) has large and varied gardens of which the best part is the Fellows' Garden, redesigned in 1947 by Professor Willmer. It lies off the Avenue, which has wonderful 18th-century wrought-iron gates, and its most spectacular feature is a dazzling pair of beautifully kept herbaceous borders in blue and yellow, with daylilies, delphiniums, thalictrum and verbascums. **Newnham College** (Sidgwick Avenue; *Open:* 9–4) has fine late-Victorian buildings by Basil Champneys and preserves gardens, made between 1890 and 1914 that are touched with the same atmosphere – yew hedges, lively borders and some excellent trees, among them several *Ailanthus altissima* and a fine *Sorbus latifolia*. This fine garden is chiefly due to the first Principal, Anne Jemima Clough.

CAMBRIDGE UNIVERSITY BOTANIC GARDENS

Cambridgeshire

Cambridge CB2 1JF
3/4m S of city centre by
Trumpington Road (A10)
Tel: 01223 336265
Fax: 01223 336278

Owner: The University of
Cambridge

Open: Daily 10–dusk (6 in
summer, 4 in winter); closed
25–26 Dec. 35 acres

ALTHOUGH THE primary purpose of botanic gardens is to provide material for study, many of them are both beautiful and instructive places for gardeners to visit. This is no exception, and at any time of the year there is much to be seen. Of special interest to gardeners are a particularly good rock garden in which plants are grouped according to country of origin; comprehensive collections of tulips and cranesbills; a huge collection of European species of saxifrage (of which the garden holds the National Collection); and glasshouses protecting different types of plant, from alpines to tropical food plants. There are beds of herbaceous plants and of shrubs, and everywhere there are fine trees, well displayed in the attractively laid out grounds.

BETH CHATTO GARDENS

Essex

Elmstead Market,
Colchester CO7 7DB
1/4 mile E of Elmstead
Market by A133
Tel: 01206 822007
Fax: 01206 825933

Owner: Mrs Beth Chatto

Open: Mar to Oct, Mon to
Sat 9–5; Nov to Feb, Mon
to Fri 9–4

BETH CHATTO'S garden and nursery make a fascinating place to visit. Her nursery is particularly strong on herbaceous plants and she has a special interest in plants with ornamental foliage. She also stresses the importance of habitat, as she shows in her excellent books on the dry and the damp garden. The former car park has been transformed into a quite dazzling gravel garden where no watering is done. Beyond the nursery a series of pools runs along a hollow edged with moisture-loving plants. Further up the slopes sweeping beds contain immense numbers of bulbs and herbaceous perennials backed with shrubs and trees. Beth Chatto is now opening her private woodland garden, a splendour in spring and always worth seeing. An informative catalogue (£2.50) is produced and plants are sold by mail order.

CROSSING HOUSE
Cambridgeshire

78 Meldreth Road,
Shepreth, Royston SG8 6PS
In Shepreth village, 8m S of
Cambridge off A10
Tel: 01763 261071

Owner: Mr and Mrs
Douglas Fuller, and Mr
John Marlar

Open: Daily dawn–dusk.
1/4 acre

THE URGE to make a garden can often be so overwhelming that the small matter of a railway line running through one's plot may easily be brushed aside. Mr Fuller was in charge of the railway crossing and Mrs Fuller made a garden in a diminutive plot alongside the line. Although in general appearance a cottage garden, signs of serious plant collecting are soon detected. Here is an immense range of plants, many exceedingly rare and beautifully grown. Alpines are grown on raised beds and there are some excellent groups of particular plants – several varieties of witch-hazel, for example. Winding paths, decorative interludes and a yew arbour give the impression of space. The level of interest is unflagging – many far bigger gardens have much less to admire.

DOCWRA'S MANOR
Cambridgeshire

COLLECTIONS OF plants can be extremely boring to gardeners if they are not given a harmonious setting. Mrs Raven and her late husband took a particular interest in natural species, especially those from Mediterranean countries, and gave them a home

Shepreth,
nr Royston SG8 6PS
In Shepreth village, 8m S of
Cambridge off A10
Tel: 01763 261473/260235

Owner: Mrs John Raven

Open: All year, Wed and Fri
10–4.30; Apr to Oct, also
1st Sun in month 2–5.
2 1/2 acres

in this cold but very dry part of England. Many of them flourished and the Ravens designed a layout which would both provide a satisfactory habitat for the plants and make an attractive garden for non-botanists. In this they were triumphantly successful. There is just enough formality, such as a decorative tunnel of pears and clematis, to prevent a mere jungle but there is no artificial regimentation of plants. Old outhouses and courtyards give protection from the wind on this flat and well-drained site. Some interesting plants are propagated for sale.

DODDINGTON HALL

Lincolnshire

Doddington,
nr Lincoln LN6 4RU
5m W of Lincoln by B1190;
signposted off A46 Lincoln
bypass
Tel: 01522 694308
Fax: 01522 682584

Owner:
Mr and Mrs A.G. Jarvis

Open: Mar and Apr, Sun
2–6; May to Sept, Wed, Sun
and Bank Hol Mon 2–6.
12 acres. House open

ROBERT SMITHSON, the greatest Elizabethan architect, designed this lovely brick mansion which casts its spell over the gardens that surround it. Rare Elizabethan garden walls enclose the courts at back and front, making a wonderfully ornamental background to the varied planting that they enclose. The courtyard of the entrance front has a simple pattern of lawns edged with box, mounds of clipped yew, and borders flanking the porch. In the walled garden on the west side, ebullient box parterres make a brilliant display, in which crown imperials and many irises are followed by roses, and where deep herbaceous borders line the walls. A wild garden has ancient sweet chestnuts and many decorative incidents – a turf maze, an elegant Temple of the Winds, and a water garden.

EUSTON HALL

Suffolk

Euston, Thetford IP24 2QP
3m S of Thetford by A1088
Tel: 01842 766366

Owner: The Duke and
Duchess of Grafton

Open: 4 Jun to 24 Sept,
Thur (also Sun 28 Jun and
Sun 6 Sept) 2.30–5.
70 acres. House open

EUSTON HALL was built by the Earl of Arlington in
the 1670s, and in the early 18th century a pioneer
landscape garden was laid out by William Kent; later
in the century 'Capability' Brown was consulted by the
3rd Duke of Grafton. South of the house, a formal
terraced garden is ornamented with summer planting
in urns, and a balustrade. To one side, the King
Charles Gate, a survival from the 17th century, leads
out into the park, and in the far distance Kent's lovely
domed temple rises on an eminence. From the formal
garden a beautiful wrought-iron gate leads through a
high wall with a very successful mixed border. Beyond,
to the west, the remains of a great lime avenue
stretches out towards Kent's arched lodge. The present
Duke has added new borders to the east of the house
and contrived a charming setting for a wooden William
Kent summerhouse.

THE FAIRHAVEN GARDEN TRUST

Norfolk

WITH AN exceptional setting on the broads, this
unique woodland garden was started in 1947 by
Lord Fairhaven, of the same family that made the
garden at Anglesey Abbey. In marvellous old
woodland of beech and oak, some of great age and
beauty, exotic plantings are unostentatiously slipped

South Walsham,
Norwich NR13 6EA
E of South Walsham
village, 9m NE of Norwich
by B1140
Tel and Fax: 01603 270449

Owner:
The Fairhaven Garden Trust

Open: Easter to Sept, Tue
to Sun and Bank Hol Mon
11–5.30 (Sat 2–5.30).
170 acres

into the scenery – azaleas, cherries, dogwoods,
enkianthus and mahonias. In the spring immense
spreads of bluebells are followed by candelabra
primulas glittering along shady walks. Occasional
glades and clearings give calm views of South
Walsham Inner Broad. This is not a place for great
rarities or fortissimo displays of flower power. But
there is no other garden quite like it – where a lovely
piece of natural landscape has been gently shaped by
the restrained hand of the gardener.

FELBRIGG HALL

Norfolk

Roughton,
Norwich NR11 8PR
2m SW of Cromer by A148
and B1436
Tel: 01263 837444

Owner: The National Trust

Open: 28 Mar to 1 Nov,
daily except Thur and Fri
11–5.30. Parkland open
daily dawn–dusk.
6 1/2 acres. House open

A WINDY PLAIN surrounds the mansion at Felbrigg,
with its curious contrasting Jacobean and mid-
Georgian facades. Handsome parkland – dating from
the 17th century and with some survivals from that
time – is planted with beech, oak and sweet chestnut.
In the magnificent old walled kitchen garden at a
distance from the house gravel paths and low box
hedges divide the area in which productive plants –
vines, figs, pears and plums – are trained against the
walls. Borders line the walls – peonies and lilies under
shrub roses. An orchard is underplanted with spring
bulbs and a collection of thorns is planted in formal
rows. An octagonal dovecote with white doves stands in
the centre of the north wall, forming an eyecatcher at
the head of the central path. Of particular interest is
the collection of colchicums, of which Felbrigg has the
National Collection.

FISKS CLEMATIS NURSERY
Suffolk

Westleton,
Saxmundham IP17 3AJ
5m NE of Saxmundham by
A12 and minor roads
Tel: 0172 648263

Open: Mon to Fri 9–5; also
Sat and Sun, summer only
10–1, 2–5

IT IS hard to imagine any garden without at least one or two clematises. Here at Jim Fisk's admirable nursery, which has its own display garden, the visitor can see an immense range of varieties. The large-flowered hybrids as well as the species and other small-flowered sorts are stocked in variety, and many of them are rare – such as 'Louise Rowe' with frilly double and single mauve flowers. There is always something of interest flowering from spring to late autumn. A model catalogue (three 1st-class stamps) gives much valuable information on cultivation. Fisks supplies by mail, with meticulous planting instructions sent out with each order.

GANNOCK GROWERS
Hertfordshire

Illustration:
Lathyrus latifolius

Gannock Green, Sandon,
Buntingford SG9 0RH
1/2m NW of Sandon
church, 2 1/3m from A505;
SE off A505 towards
Sandon midway between
Baldock and Royston.
Tel: 01763 287386

Open: Apr to Sept, Thur to
Sat and Bank Hol Mon
10–4; also by appointment

GANNOCK GROWERS specialises in unusual hardy herbaceous plants. The range is wide, with many plants suitable for the border and some smaller items verging on alpines. Penny Pyle has several aquilegias, good campanulas, an unusual range of centaureas, eryngiums, one of the very best ranges of geraniums, lychnis, several species penstemons and some decorative sedges and grasses. There are countless individual plants, rarely seen in nurseries, that will seduce any gardener. Attractive display beds have recently been added. Most plants are priced by pot size and prices are modest. A list is published (three 1st-class stamps) and plants are sold by mail order.

THE GARDENS OF THE ROSE
Hertfordshire

Chiswell Green,
St Albans AL2 3NR
2m SW of St Albans by
B4630
Tel: 01727 850461

Owner: Royal National
Rose Society

Open: Mid Jun to mid Oct,
Mon to Sat 9–5, Sun and
Bank Hol Mon 10–6.
25 acres

THOUSANDS OF roses, including well over 1,700 varieties, are displayed here, and although there is a strong emphasis on modern varieties there are also interesting reference collections of the main historic groups. The site is flat and windswept and some vertical emphasis is given by Irish yews and pergolas on which the climbing roses are trained. Modern roses are generally arranged in large beds, often with a single block of one variety making a vast splash of colour. The Royal National Rose Society, one of the leading specialist plant societies, publishes a journal and provides expert advice to members.

GLEN CHANTRY
Essex

Ishams Chase,
Wickham Bishop CM8 3LG
1m W of Wickham Bishop,
8m NE of Chelmsford by
A12
Tel: 01621 891342

Owners:
Wol and Sue Staines

Open: 3 Apr to 16 Oct, Fri
and Sat 10–4. 3 1/2 acres

GLEN CHANTRY is both a garden and a nursery, of equal interest in both departments. It started as a hobby but over the years assumed a dominating role in the owners' lives. It is superlatively gardened and all visitors will relish the sight of exceptionally good and varied plants bursting with vigour. It was not a particularly propitious place for a garden – a wind-blasted hill with relentlessly stony soil in a famously dry corner of England. A certain amount of wind protection has been planted and the Staineses have greatly enriched their soil. Apart from a pretty, formal white garden east of the house the layout is informal with sinuous beds sweeping across close-mown turf. An immense range of plants is grown, with an especially good rock garden to the west of the house. The nursery specialises in herbaceous perennials and alpine or rock garden plants. A catalogue is produced (four 1st-class stamps) but there is no mail order. But the whole point of Glen Chantry is to see the garden and to buy plants, so a visit is essential.

GUNBY HALL

Lincolnshire

nr Spilsby PE23 5SS
7m W of Skegness by A158
Tel: 01909 486411

Owner: The National Trust

Open: Apr to Sept, Wed and Thur 2–6.
7 acres. House open

GUNBY PRESENTS an elegant pastoral scene – the Georgian brick mansion looking out over serene parkland. In the old walled kitchen garden there is more excitement, with a rumpus of roses, burgeoning herbaceous borders, apples trained over arches and underplanted with irises, and a dinky domed gazebo painted a celestial blue. A second walled garden has beds of fruit and vegetables, and old pear trees growing out of herbaceous borders. There is a rose walk, a bed of hydrangeas and, hidden behind a yew hedge, a stately walk of Irish junipers along a canal. On the far side of the house lawns are ornamented with specimen trees and there is a wild flower walk.

HATFIELD HOUSE

Hertfordshire

Hatfield AL9 5NQ
In the centre of Hatfield, 20m N of London; Jnct 3 of A1(M)
Tel: 01707 262823
Fax: 01707 275719

Owner: The Marquess of Salisbury

Open: 25 Mar to 14 Oct, daily 11–6 (closed Good Fri); East Garden open only Mon 2–5 (closed Bank Hol Mon). 30 acres. House open

HATFIELD HOUSE, a Jacobean extravaganza of pink brick, was started in 1607 by Robert Cecil and the family has owned it ever since. There has always been a notable garden here, but over the last twenty years the present Marchioness of Salisbury has brought dazzling new life to it. Near the house there are formal gardens, most of which have ancient origins. By the Old Palace Lady Salisbury has made a new knot garden with old varieties of plants, including many of those introduced by John Tradescant the Elder who worked for the Cecils when the garden was started. The Privy Garden and the Scented Garden to the west of the house have been replanted, and in summer are very beautiful. The East Garden is decorated with formal rows of clipped holm oaks

Illustration opposite:
The Privy Garden at
Hatfield House

(*Quercus ilex*) and brimming beds of shrubs, especially roses, underplanted with herbaceous plants. Beyond are avenues of apple trees, a Victorian yew maze (alas, not open) and the New Pond which is full of atmosphere. There are few great historic gardens that demonstrate so visibly the excitement of gardening. A shop, near the entrance, sells a few good plants.

HAUGHLEY PARK
Suffolk

nr Stowmarket IP14 3JY
4m NW of Stowmarket off
A14
Tel: 01359 240205

Owner: R.J. Williams

Open: May to Sept, Tue
and 1st two Suns in May for
bluebells 2–5.30. 8 acres
plus 260 acres woodland
and parkland

THE GABLED house was built in 1620, with a pretty Georgian wing added in 1820 and the whole restored by A.J. Williams after a fire in 1961. Handsome old woodland, with some exceptional individual specimens, makes a fine setting for the gardens which are almost entirely of the 20th century. North of the house a broad apron of grass opens out, edged with mixed borders; to one side is an immense hollow oak, hundreds of years old. The vista is continued by an old lime avenue stretching across parkland into the distance. A dell has shady walks fringed with hostas, and the woodland garden, ablaze with bluebells in spring, has many azaleas and rhododendrons planted among majestic beeches and Scots pines.

HELMINGHAM HALL
Suffolk

nr Stowmarket IP14 6EF
9m N of Ipswich by B1077
Tel: 01473 890363
Fax: 01473 890776

Owner: Lord Tollemache

Open: 26 Apr to 6 Sept, Sun
2–6; groups of over 30 by
appointment. 10 acres

AT HELMINGHAM, house, parkland and garden together create an exceptional work of art. The brick house, with its romantic moat and drawbridge, is of several periods, starting in 1500, and has always been owned by the Tollemaches. It overlooks a deer park with a double avenue of oaks. To one side, also moated, a walled kitchen garden has been turned to ornamental purposes. At the entrance a box-edged parterre with santolina is surrounded on three sides by borders of Hybrid Musk roses and hedges of lavender. Winged horses cap the piers of the gates into the walled garden, which is divided into eight parts by two superb double herbaceous borders running down and across. Leading off them are paths through tunnels of

sweet peas, runner beans or gourds, and behind the
ornamental borders fruit and vegetables grow in
impeccable beds. On the banks of the moat a grassy
walk with narrow borders encircles the walls. On the
far, eastern, side of the house a herb and knot garden
made since 1982 is hedged in yew. Within are low
hedges of clipped box or lavender, and a pattern of
beds of old roses which are underplanted with bulbs
and herbaceous perennials. Few great historic houses
have gardens so attractive as those at Helmingham.

HOECROFT PLANTS

Norfolk

THIS ADMIRABLE nursery specialises in an
increasingly popular type of ornamental plant:
Margaret Lister sells wonderfully attractive grasses
and plants with especially distinguished foliage – both
herbaceous and woody. It is the grasses, though, that
are the special excitement of her list. These are really
valuable border plants, mixing easily with any other

Severals Grange, Holt
Road, Wood Norton,
Dereham NR20 5BL
6m E of Fakenham by
A1067 and B1110
Tel: 01362 844206

Open: May to Sept, Fri and
Sat 10–4

plantings. Hoecroft carries a very wide range of the
best, some of which you will scarcely find in any other
nursery in the country. New kinds are constantly being
added and now over 220 varieties are stocked,
including reeds, sedges and bamboos. The catalogue
(£1.00) is outstanding, with much valuable information
on the garden use of the plants.

HOPLEYS PLANTS

Hertfordshire

Illustration:
Paeonia mlokosewitschii

High Street,
Much Hadham SG10 6BU
5m SW of Bishop's
Stortford by B1004
Tel: 01279 842509
Fax: 01279 843784

Open: Mar to 25 Dec, Mon
to Sat (closed Tue) 9–5, Sun
2–5

YOU WOULD have to be a gardener of steely resolve
to avoid buying something at Hopleys. Their list
ranges widely and every year new and exciting plants –
hardy and non-hardy – are offered. Some groups are
especially well represented (for example, salvias); the
striking quality of Hopleys is the very careful choice of
particular cultivars of a single species (e.g. 16 different
varieties of *Diascia*). The beautifully kept 4-acre
garden, alongside the nursery, is open to visitors.
There is an impeccable catalogue (£1.20) and a mail
order service is provided in the autumn only.

HYDE HALL

Essex

WHEN THE Robinsons came here to farm in 1955
there was no garden, merely a handful of trees
on top of a famously windswept hill in one of the
driest parts of the country. The garden they made is
now enormous, full of wonderful plants in diverse
habitats – a brilliant tribute to their gardening skill.

Rettendon,
nr Chelmsford CM3 8ET
7m SE of Chelmsford by
A130
Tel: 01245 400256
Fax: 01245 401363

Owner: The Royal
Horticultural Society

Open: 26 Mar to 26 Oct,
daily except Mon and Tue
(open Bank Hol Mon) 11–6.
24 acres

An immensely wide range of plants is grown –
daylilies, irises, peonies, roses, snowdrops and
countless ornamental trees and shrubs. Hyde Hall has
two National Collections: of crab apples (*Malus*) and
of viburnums. This is not merely a plant collection, for
many parts of the garden have carefully worked out
colour harmonies – a gold garden, for example, and a
series of herbaceous borders with hot or cool schemes.
No gardener could come here without being informed
and delighted. A nursery sells excellent plants but there
is no mail order. Hyde Hall is now owned by the RHS
and it is hoped that the charm of the Robinsons'
garden will survive intact.

ICKWORTH

Suffolk

Horringer, Bury St
Edmunds IP29 5QE
3m SW of Bury St Edmunds
by A143
Tel: 01284 735270

Owner: The National Trust

Open: 21 Mar to 1 Nov,
daily 10–5; 2 Nov to Mar
1999, Mon to Fri 10–4. Park
open all year 7–7. 33 acres
(garden), 1,800 acres
(estate). House open

THERE IS no other house like Ickworth – a dumpy,
domed cylinder with curving wings, designed in
the late 18th century by Francis Sandys with help from
his patron, the Earl of Bristol, Bishop of Derry. The
garden is influenced by the shape of the house. At the
front a sweeping herbaceous border, echoing the
wings, is well planted in blues and purples – acanthus,
campanulas, geraniums and sage – with clumps of
purple-leafed cotinus. Behind the house there is a more
formal arrangement, again related to the shape of the
house, with a curved terrace and box-hedged alleys. A
marvellous walk about the estate of Ickworth – there
are 1,800 acres of it in all – affords splendid views
back to the house and to the Earl's obelisk in the
distance. The park proper is a wonderful combination
of ancient woodland and the tactful hand of
'Capability' Brown.

KNEBWORTH

Hertfordshire

Knebworth SG3 6PY
28m N of London; Jnct 7
of AI(M)
Tel: 01438 812661
Fax: 01438 811908

Owner: Lord Cobbold

Open: 4 to 20 Apr, daily
11–5.30; 26 Apr to 17 May,
Sat, Sun and Bank Hol
Mon 11–5.30; 23 May to 7
Sept, daily 11–5.30; 12 to 27
Sept, Sat and Sun 12–5.30.
25 acres. House open

THE LYTTONS have lived here since the late middle ages and the house, a wild and woolly gothic fantasy, was partly designed by Bulwer Lytton, the best-selling Victorian novelist. Edwin Lutyens married a Lytton daughter and between 1907 and 1911 he simplified the immensely complicated Victorian garden. From the facade of the house a pair of cool pleached lime walks leads towards a formal rose garden flanked by herbaceous borders. Beyond a screen of clipped yew, with statues half-embedded in niches, a circular pool has gold borders on either side and a path leads to a formal garden of old roses underplanted with artemisias, catmint and lamb's ears. To one side of the house an attractive little herb garden has been recreated from a Gertrude Jekyll design of interlocking circles.

MANNINGTON HALL

Norfolk

MANNINGTON HALL, with its moat, towers and crenellations, has a wildly romantic air. It dates from the late 15th century but was much changed in the 19th century. The moat is splashed with water-lilies and walled with yew on the inner bank. Behind the hedges are beds of modern roses and stone busts on plinths surveying the scene. Lawns and specimen trees – some fine cedars of Lebanon – lie on the far

nr Saxthorpe NR11 7BB
18m NW of Norwich by
B1149 and minor roads
Tel: 01263 874175
Fax: 01263 761214

Owner:
Lord and Lady Walpole

Open: May to Sept, Sun
12–5; Jun to Aug, also Wed
to Fri 11–5. 20 acres

side of the moat, and a classical pavilion with a statue of Diana gives architectural contrast to beds of shrub roses. In a large walled garden a little distance from the house, the Heritage Rose Garden displays a very large collection of roses of all the representative types, trained on pergolas or walls, and in beds. Part of the garden is laid out to show the use of roses in different period styles. A visit at rose time is a heady experience but the beauty of house and setting is worth seeing at any time. A nursery sells a good selection of roses.

MELFORD HALL

Suffolk

Long Melford,
Sudbury CO10 9AH
In Long Melford village,
4m N of Sudbury by A131
Tel: 01787 880286

Owner: The National Trust

Open: Apr, Sat, Sun and
Bank Hol Mon 2–5.30; May
to Sept, daily except Mon
and Tue (open Bank Hol
Mon) 2–5.30; Oct, Sat and
Sun 2–5.30. 9 acres. House
open

IF IT were not for the gazebo at Melford Hall the garden would only just be worth visiting – but what a gazebo! It is octagonal, built of brick, and it bristles with pediments and finials. Gertrude Jekyll visited it and, recognizing its architectural distinction, criticised it for being smothered in ivy. Today it is revealed in its full eccentric glory. Steep steps lead up to it, and from tall sash windows there are views on one side over the dry moat and on the other of the garden with its curving herbaceous borders, old weeping ash and mulberry, and a pretty little herb parterre planted with low hedges of yew and patches of purple sage, germander, lavender and rue.

MONKSILVER NURSERY

Cambridgeshire

Oakington Road,
Cottenham CB4 4TW
In Cottenham village,
4 1/2m N of Cambridge by
B1049
Tel: 01954 251555

Open: Mar to Jun, Fri and
Sat 10–4

HERE IS one of the most fascinating collections of herbaceous plants that you will find anywhere. The Monksilver list (six 1st-class stamps) is the sort you take to bed on a winter's evening for a long, happy and richly inspiring browse. There are rare plants here, some exceedingly rare, but there are also countless more common (or garden) things that should not be overlooked. The catalogue describes the plants well, and in terms of naming and botanical precision has the highest standards. National Collections of deadnettles (the closely related genera *Galeobdolon* and *Lamium* – 23 species and 60 cultivars) and periwinkle (*Vinca* – 5 species and 45 cultivars) are held at the nursery. Chiefly a mail order business, the

Illustration opposite:
The gazebo at Melford Hall

Illustration: Centaurea macrocephala

nursery has fairly restricted opening times. Prices are very fair, although in a few cases, for extreme rarities, they do not quote a price but invite bids (of money or of *even rarer plants*). Do not miss the chance of a visit to this unique place.

NORFOLK LAVENDER

Norfolk

Caley Mill,
Heacham PE31 7JE
13 1/2m N of King's Lynn
on A149
Tel: 01485 570384
Fax: 01485 571176

Open: Daily 10–5 (closed
23 Dec to 14 Jan)

NORFOLK LAVENDER is the largest lavender farm in England and is a delightful place to visit. It holds a National Collection of lavender (55 different species and varieties); display beds show vividly the variations in foliage and flower, and in late summer fill the air with their scent. A new fragrant plant meadow also perfumes the air. Many lavenders and a few other plants are sold in a small nursery and a mail order service is provided.

THE OLD VICARAGE GARDEN

Norfolk

THIS IS one of the most remarkable and enjoyable gardens made in recent years. Created by Alan Gray and Graham Robeson, scarcely ten years old and expanding at a rate of knots, it is a feast of formal design, decorative exuberance and brilliant planting. It is quite close to the sea and well protected from the full blast of the wind by dense windbreaks, making it possible to grow remarkably tender things – *Pittosporum tobira*, *Buddleja crispa*, *Chamaerops humilis*, *Eucomis comosa* and countless others.

East Ruston,
Norwich NR12 9HN
Near East Ruston Church,
off A149 signposted Bacton,
Happisburgh; left at T
junction and ignore three
signs to East Ruston
Tel: 01603 632350
Fax: 01692 650233

Owner: Alan Gray and
Graham Robeson

Open: 12 Apr to 25 Oct,
Wed, Sun and Bank Hol
Mon 2–5. 12 acres

Clustering about the Arts and Crafts vicarage, walled and hedged compartments vary strongly in mood – from cool formality to explosions of colour and form. Much of this is inward-looking but occasional exhilarating vistas borrow distant church towers as eyecatchers. Sculptures, lavishly planted pots and finely detailed walls and gates also play their decorative part. Above all, the place is finely gardened and plants appear to be bursting with rude health. If you feel stuck in a horticultural groove and that nothing new is possible in gardening, a visit to the Old Vicarage will be an intoxicating pick-me-up.

OXBURGH HALL

Norfolk

R ISING FROM its moat, the 15th-century manor house is wonderfully romantic. It was built by the Bedingfields whose descendants gave it to the National Trust in 1952. To the east of the hall a splendid Frenchified parterre was made in the 19th century after the Bedingfields saw a similar one on a visit to France in 1845. Against a background of gravel, swirling beds hedged in box are filled with a permanent planting of rue and santolina, which is enlivened by summer

Oxborough,
nr King's Lynn PE33 9PS
In Oxborough 9m E of
Downham Market by
A1122 and A134
Tel: 01366 328258

Owner: The National Trust

Open: 7 to 22 Mar, Sat and
Sun 11–4; 28 Mar to 1 Nov,
daily except Thur and Fri
11–5.30. 18 acres. House
open

bedding of ageratums, marigolds and pelargoniums. Parterres of this sort were intended to be viewed from above, as this one can be from the windows of the hall or from the terrace to one side. A yew hedge separates a very handsome long mixed border from the parterre. A 19th-century brick-walled kitchen garden has been planted with a formal orchard of medlars, mulberries and different varieties of plum, with clematis and roses trained on the walls.

PADLOCK CROFT

Cambridgeshire

19 Padlock Road,
West Wratting,
Cambridge CB1 5LS
14m SE of Cambridge by
A1307 and minor roads
Tel and Fax: 01223 290383

Open: Apr to mid Oct,
visitors welcome at most
times except Sun but please
phone first. 1 acre

S USAN AND Peter Lewis are famous for campanulas, of which their garden houses the National Collection; their splendid list (four 2nd-class stamps) leads with no less than fifteen pages of them, and nearly 300 different species and cultivars may be seen growing in the garden. In addition they hold National Collections of the related genera of adenophora (10 species), platycodon (16 species and cultivars) and symphyandra (9 species); other genera of the Campanulaceae family are also stocked. Some of these are of chiefly botanical interest but many are marvellous garden plants. Garden and nursery blend indistinguishably at Padlock Croft, forming a maze of alpine troughs, glasshouses and packed beds. Alpines and smaller border plants are the speciality of the nursery, and there are very good collections. In every part of the list there are desirable things, but a visit is especially rewarding to see the many unlisted plants growing in the garden.

PARADISE CENTRE
Suffolk

Illustration:
Anemone nemorosa

Twinstead Road,
Lamarsh, Bures CO8 5EX
In Lamarsh village, 4m S of
Sudbury by minor roads
Tel and Fax: 01787 269449

Open: Easter to 1 Nov, Sat,
Sun and Bank Hol Mon
10–5; also by appointment

T HE HEART of this unusual nursery garden is its
collection of bulbs and herbaceous perennials.
Among the bulbs are exceptionally long lists of
alliums, crocuses, erythroniums, many fritillaries, and
species narcissi and tulips. Among the herbaceous
plants are excellent groups of epimediums, hardy
geraniums, hostas, a wonderful list of primulas and
several saxifrages. All the plants are well chosen and
are available by post from an attractively produced and
very informative catalogue (four 1st-class stamps). As
with many small and interesting nurseries of this kind,
there are always excellent plants available at the
nursery which have not been listed. The nursery is, in
effect, the owners' own garden – made by them from
virtually nothing – and it is delightful.

PARK GREEN NURSERIES
Suffolk

Wetheringsett,
Stowmarket IP14 5QH
6m NE of Stowmarket, E of
A140
Tel: 01728 860139
Fax: 01728 861277

Open: Mar to Sept, daily
10–5

R ICHARD AND Mary Ford grow over 300 different
species and varieties of hosta, and there are few
gardens for which an appropriate and beautiful
specimen cannot be found. Hostas are invaluable
plants for moist shady places – but some also flourish
in a sunny position. Many of the plants are hard to
come by, and some are available only here. As well as
their chief speciality, the Fords also have choice
collections of astilbes, of which they have many named
varieties, and of ornamental grasses. Hostas only are
sold by mail order and are despatched from November

to March when dormant. A good catalogue (four 1st-class stamps or £1) is produced, with excellent descriptions of plants. Seeds are also sold and, as hostas cross-pollinate with abandon, you may well germinate something new and interesting yourself.

PECKOVER HOUSE

Cambridgeshire

North Brink,
Wisbech PE13 1JR
In the centre of Wisbech
Tel: 01945 583463

Owner: The National Trust

Open: 28 Mar to 1 Nov,
daily except Thur and Fri
12.30–5.30; groups at other
times by arrangement with
tenant. 2 acres. House open

WHEN YOU have got over the surprise of finding a garden as big as this behind an elegant town house in the middle of Wisbech, you can get down to admiring its distinctive charms. Lawns slope away from the back of the house with many substantial specimen trees of a Victorian character, and a rustic summerhouse adds to the period flavour. To one side of the main lawn, hidden behind brick walls, a pair of mixed borders leads up to a pool and an elegant little gazebo. The borders are ornamented with slender metal pillars for roses and clematis, and a pair of topiary yew peacocks. In a separate part of the garden a conservatory houses oranges (reputedly over 300 years old – and still productive), daturas and other tender plants, and there is an unusual 19th-century glasshouse for tender ferns.

POTTERTON & MARTIN
Lincolnshire

Moortown Road, Nettleton,
Caistor LN7 6HX
18m NE of Lincoln by A46
Tel and Fax: 01472 851792

Open: Daily 9–5

POTTERTON & MARTIN call themselves 'The Cottage Nursery', which is misleading. In fact they sell a wide range of alpine plants, dwarf bulbs, ferns and orchids, with interesting excursions into such oddities as carnivorous plants, some of which are hardy and make good plants for the edges of ponds. There is generally a strong emphasis on species and forms, with an exceptionally good list of anemones; dozens of crocuses; virtually every species of cyclamen that is hardy out-of-doors (and several that are not), including some of the forms with especially pretty foliage; a good collection of the smaller irises; an excellent range of primulas; a long and interesting selection of saxifrages; and all sorts of other tempting things of the smaller kind. Catalogues are issued (50p stamp) and a mail order service is provided.

READS NURSERY
Norfolk

Hales Hall,
near Loddon NR14 6QW
10m SE of Norwich by
A146
Tel: 01508 548395
Fax: 01508 548040

Open: Tue to Sat 10–5 or
dusk if earlier; May to Oct,
also Sun and Bank Hol
Mon 2–5

THIS OLD-ESTABLISHED (1890) nursery specialises in fruit, especially citrus fruits, of which Reads has the largest selection commercially available in Britain – not just oranges and lemons but all sorts of exotics like mandarins and kumquats. It also sell desert and wine grapes, several different varieties of peaches, apricots and nectarines, mulberries and tender climbing plants. Among the last is a large reference collection of bougainvilleas, including many far better colours than the rather bilious purple kind. A connoisseur's collection of conservatory plants includes 20 cultivars of oleanders. The nursery also holds one of the National Collections of cultivars of the fig (*Ficus carica*), with no less than 39 varieties. Reads occupies a particularly attractive group of old brick buildings – the potting shed is housed in the largest medieval brick barn in England – and possesses a most attractive atmosphere. A very informative catalogue (four 1st-class stamps) is produced and plants are supplied by post.

THE ROMANTIC GARDEN NURSERY

Norfolk

The Street, Swannington,
Norwich NR9 5NW
In Swannington village,
9m NW of Norwich by
A1067 and minor roads
Tel: 01603 261488

Open: Wed, Fri and Sat
10–5

THE ROMANTIC Garden Nursery swarms with ready-made topiary – a menagerie of animals clipped from box. More unusual are the many standard-trained and mop-headed plants – *Arbutus unedo*, bay, holly, privet and others. Plants for the conservatory, including oleanders with three-part trunks prettily plaited together, and a range of hand-thrown frost-proof Italian terracotta pots, are also sold. A list is produced (four 1st-class stamps) and there is a mail order service.

SALING HALL

Essex

Great Saling,
nr Braintree CM7 5DT
6m NW of Braintree by
A120
Tel: 01371 850141
Fax: 01371 850274

Owner:
Mr and Mrs Hugh Johnson

Open: May to Jul, Wed 2–5.
12 acres

Illustration opposite:
Spring at Saling Hall

SOME GOOD gardens fall too easily into genteel ossification but at Saling Hall there is a constant buzz of horticultural activity. The present owners came in 1971 and found an old garden already full of interest surrounding the long, curvaceously gabled brick house of the early 17th century. They redefined the best parts (including a very pretty walled garden south of the house and a water garden with tall swamp cypresses) and expanded boldly into the woodland with new ventures. Here is an excellent collection of trees, many rare, skilfully deployed with vistas and ornaments (including a Temple of Pisces as an

eyecatcher), and a deft sketch of a Japanese garden with a cascade, billowing mounds of clipped box and a snow-lantern. If you don't like what you see here you have probably lost interest in gardening.

SANDRINGHAM HOUSE
Norfolk

Sandringham,
King's Lynn PE35 6EN
9m NE of King's Lynn by
B1440
Tel: 01553 772675
Fax: 01485 541571

Owner: H.M. The Queen

Open: Easter to late Jul,
early Aug to Oct, daily
10.30–5. House open

THERE ARE not many gardens belonging to the royal family that are regularly open to the public; this is one of the few places where its taste in gardening may be seen. First, it is on a huge scale and the chief impression is one of immense and impeccable lawns punctuated with specimen trees, many of which are 19th-century plantings of conifers. On this sandy, acid soil rhododendrons do well and they flourish in the protection of the trees. Nearer the house there is an attractive formality with lime walks, hedges of yew and a series of herbaceous beds enclosed in tall box hedges. On the far side of the house a stream feeds two lakes whose fringes are rich with conifers, maples and other ornamental trees and shrubs.

SHERINGHAM PARK
Norfolk

Upper Sheringham,
Sheringham NR26 8TB
2m SW of Sheringham by
A148
Tel: 01263 823778

Owner: The National Trust

Open: Daily dawn–dusk.
90 acres

HUMPHRY REPTON was the genius behind this place of woods and rambling walks around a shallow combe by the sea. It was commissioned by Abbot Upcher's family, for whom Repton also built a new house between 1812 and 1819 in a more picturesque position embowered by trees – many of them marvellous 18th-century oaks – on one side of the valley. In the woods across fields to the south of the house is a collection of rare rhododendrons started by Abbot Upcher's son Henry who helped finance plant-hunting expeditions to the Himalayas. Many of these rhododendrons have grown to great size in the sheltered combe. In 1975 Thomas Upcher built an arcaded temple, to Repton's design, on an eminence with marvellous views back towards the house and the sea beyond.

SHRUBLAND GARDENS

Suffolk

Coddenham,
Ipswich IP6 9QQ
7m NW of Ipswich by A14
and minor roads; follow
signs to Barham from
Beacon Hill roundabout
Tel: 01473 830221
Fax: 01473 832202

Owner: Lord de Saumarez

Open: Apr to beginning
Sept, Sun and Bank Hol
Mon 2–5. 40 acres

THE HOUSE at Shrubland, rising on an eminence over the Gipping valley, was built by James Paine in the 1770s and radically rebuilt by Sir Charles Barry in palatial Italianate style in the 1840s. He also laid out the splendid formal garden which lies below the western facade of the house. From a broad terrace a spectacular staircase – the Grand Descent – plummets down the slopes, ending in a formal garden with circular pool and waterjet, parterres with Prince of Wales feathers of clipped santolina, and an elegant arcaded loggia. Beyond lies the wild garden, about which William Robinson advised in the 1880s. To the south the Hot Wall, a long curving wall decorated with stone fretwork and urns, has elaborate arches at each end filled with vases of flowers. At the higher

Illustration opposite:
The grotto/fernery at the
Swiss Garden

level, north of the house, the Brownslow Terrace is a fine walk along a row of superlative ancient sweet chestnuts, culminating in a balustraded semicircle and a stucco figure of Diana the huntress turning her back on the enticing old parkland beyond.

SOMERLEYTON HALL
Suffolk

nr Lowestoft NR32 5QQ
5m NW of Lowestoft by
B1074
Tel: 01502 730224/732950
Fax: 01502 732143

Owner:
Lord and Lady Somerleyton

Open: Easter Sun to Sept,
Thur, Sun and Bank Hol
Mon 12.30-5.30; Jul to
Aug, also Tue and Wed
12.30–5.30. 12 acres.
House open

S OMERLEYTON HAS a big, bold Victorian house and a garden to suit. The garden entrance leads through the former kitchen garden which now has a spanking pair of herbaceous borders marching down the middle. The well-maintained glasshouses were designed by Joseph Paxton, and on the outside south walls of the kitchen garden there are rare peach cases. Wellingtonias and monkey puzzles on the lawn beyond the kitchen garden were part of the 19th-century layout, but among them are much older trees, including some superb sweet chestnuts. From the Victorian parterres by the house, planted with roses and columns of clipped yew, there are views of the remains of an ancient avenue of limes disappearing towards the horizon. There is also a hedge maze of yew built in 1846, and a magnificent winter garden of the same date in which the tea-room is now housed. Few places give such a vivid idea of the entire world of gardening at the height of the Victorian period.

THE SWISS GARDEN
Bedfordshire

Old Warden, nr
Biggleswade
2 1/2m W of Biggleswade
by minor roads; signposted
from A1 and A600
Tel: 01767 627666
Fax: 01234 228921

Owner: Managed by
Bedfordshire County
Council

Open: Mar to Sept, daily
except Tue 1.30–6; Jan, Feb
and Oct, Sun 11–3 (also
open 1 Jan). 9 acres

I N THE early 19th century there was a fashion for everything Swiss, and here at Old Warden the Lord Ongley made an enchanting 'Swiss' garden full of rustic thatched houses, precipitous rocky descents and picturesque views. The site, well wooded and gently undulating, has interconnected ponds with ornamental islands, and paths wind about, revealing views of garden houses, delicate iron-work arched bridges, a kiosk with stained glass, statues and urns, and a magnificent glass-domed grotto *cum* fernery. This last, now beautifully restored, is entered through stained-glass doors which open into a passage dripping with tufa stalactites, which, in turn, leads into the airy

fernery. The wonderfully elegant fernery dome was made between 1830 and 1833 and is one of the earliest known glass structures with a cast-iron frame. All around the garden are excellent trees and it makes an enchanting place in which to walk. It has, over the years, been beautifully restored by the county council. There is, surely, nothing like this in Switzerland but it is fine entertainment.

WIMPOLE HALL

Hertfordshire

Arrington,
Royston SG8 0BW
8m SW of Cambridge by
A603
Tel: 01223 207257

Owner: The National Trust

Open: 14 Mar to 1 Nov,
daily except Mon and Fri
1–5 (open Bank Hol Mon
and Good Fri); Aug, also
open Mon and Fri 1–5. Park
open daily 8–10. 20 acres.
House open

ON THIS windy, open site on the borders of Hertfordshire and Cambridgeshire the 18th-century house rises on a slight eminence, commanding wide and distant views. In the very early 18th century there had been a great formal garden here, and an immense avenue of elms, planted by Charles Bridgeman in the 1720s, survived until it was killed by the elm disease; it has now been replanted in limes. In the 1750s the formal garden began to be dismantled by 'Capability' Brown. North of the house he naturalised the landscape, creating a lake with, on a slight eminence in the distance, a towered folly. A little later Repton made a formal flower garden below the north facade, enclosed in railings and with fine views over fields and Brown's parkland. In recent years the National Trust has restored some of the formality (including brightly coloured parterres on the north side) but have respected the different layers of garden style that give Wimpole its interest.

WOLTERTON PARK

Norfolk

nr Erpingham NR11 7LY
2m N of Aylsham by A140
Tel: 01263 874175
Fax: 01263 761214

Owner:
Lord and Lady Walpole

Open: 9–5 or dusk if earlier.
100 acres

WOLTERON PARK is a handsome house of orange brick and stone, built in the 1730s for Horatio Walpole. It has remained in the family but was abandoned in the 19th century, lived in once again in the 20th century, and badly damaged by fire in 1952. Now the present Lord Walpole has taken it in hand and a programme of restoration is under way. The visitor starts with a wonderful rural amble, skirting fields and woods, passing a romantically ruined church tower and eventually emerging in a vast open space dotted with exceptional oaks. The south front of the house is then revealed, embowered in trees, overlooking in the far distance a great lake. Hedges and trees are being replanted in the park. The hall and the formal gardens south of the house, glimpsed from the park, are occasionally open (see local press).

WOOTTEN'S PLANTS

Suffolk

Blackheath, Wenhaston,
Halesworth IP19 9HD
3m SE of Halesworth by
A144 and minor roads
Tel and Fax: 01502 478258

Open: Nursery: daily 9.30–5
(closed 25 Dec–2 Jan);
Garden: open May to Sept,
Wed 9.30–3

MICHAEL LOFTUS started his nursery in 1991 and by now it has a distinctive, and distinguished, character. He sells chiefly herbaceous plants, not all hardy, and what makes the nursery different is the meticulous choice of plants and the care with which they are grown; plants are regularly potted on and all visitors will be struck by their size and vigour. Here are many campanulas, diascias, euphorbias, geraniums, lychnis, penstemons, salvias and countless other things such as large daturas in pots, and the very finest pelargoniums. An excellent catalogue (£2.00) is produced. Virtually everything in it is desirable but you will have to go to the nursery, for there is no mail order. Michael Loftus's own very attractive garden alongside is occasionally open.

WREST PARK
Bedfordshire

Silsoe MK45 4HS
3/4m E of Silsoe by A6
Tel: 01525 860152

Owner: English Heritage

Open: 22 Mar to Oct, Sat and Sun 10–6. 80 acres

THE GARDEN at Wrest Park has only fragments left – but they are wonderfully attractive. The de Grey family had lived at Wrest since the 13th century but the present palatial house was built in the 1830s in the French style. A Frenchified parterre south of the house dates from the same time and has bedding schemes and fine classical statues. Nearby, designed by Earl de Grey himself in 1836, is an ebullient conservatory, pale apricot with arched windows, caryatids flanking the entrance and rows of urns on the parapet. All that remains of the elaborate formal garden of the early 18th century is a slender canal and a swagger domed classical pavilion designed by Thomas Archer in 1710 with, between the two, a jaunty lead figure of William III. A garden of woodland vistas and a serpentined pool has a pretty Chinese gazebo and traces of 'Capability' Brown who worked here from 1758 to 1760. One of the charms of the place is the mixture of his informal landscaping overlaid on the fine survivals of the earlier formal garden.

THE
NORTH
OF
ENGLAND

County Durham
Cumbria
Humberside
Lancashire
Northumberland
Tyne and Wear
Yorkshire

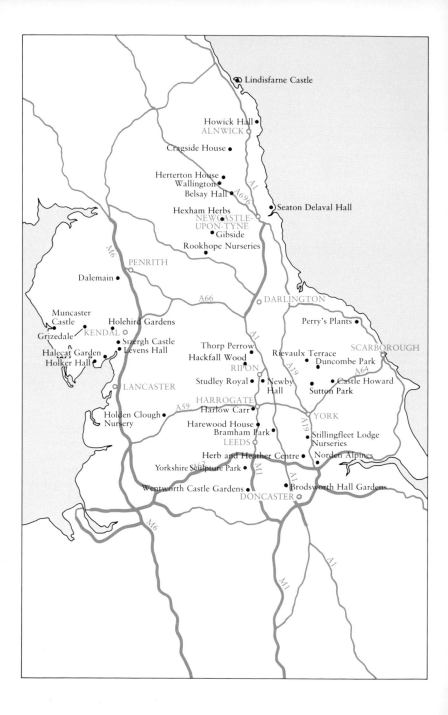

Lindisfarne Castle

Howick Hall •
ALNWICK ◦

Cragside House •

Herterton House •
Wallington •
Belsay Hall •

Hexham Herbs •
NEWCASTLE-
UPON-TYNE
• Gibside

Rookhope Nurseries •

Seaton Delaval Hall •

A1
A696

Dalemain •

PENRITH ◦

M6

A66

DARLINGTON ◦

Muncaster
Castle •

Grizedale •

Holehird Gardens •
KENDAL ◦

Sizergh Castle •
Levens Hall •

Perry's Plants •

Halecat Garden •
Holker Hall •

Thorp Perrow •
Hackfall Wood •

Rievaulx Terrace •
Duncombe Park •

SCARBOROUGH

Studley Royal •

RIPON ◦

• Newby
Hall

Castle Howard •
Sutton Park •

A1
A19
A64

LANCASTER ◦

HARROGATE ◦

Holden Clough
Nursery •

A59

Harlow Carr •

Harewood House •
Bramham Park •

YORK ◦

M6

LEEDS ◦

Herb and Heather Centre •

Yorkshire Sculpture Park •

Wentworth Castle Gardens •

Stillingfleet Lodge
Nurseries •

Norden Alpines •

Brodsworth Hall Gardens •

DONCASTER ◦

M62

M1

A1

M6

M1

A1

BELSAY HALL

Northumberland

Belsay, nr Newcastle-upon-
Tyne NE20 0DX
14n NW of Newcastle by
A696
Tel: 01661 881636
Fax: 01661 881043

Owner: The Belsay Trust. In
guardianship of English
Heritage

Open: Apr to Oct, daily
10–6 or dusk if earlier; Nov
to Mar, daily 10–4 (closed
25–27 Dec). 50 acres. House
open

THE NEO-CLASSICAL brown stone mansion at Belsay was built to the design of its owner, Sir Charles Monck, in the early 19th century. The stone was quarried on the site and the resulting rocky hollows and ravines were made by Sir Charles into an unforgettable wild and romantic garden. The planting is boldly appropriate to the setting, with the striking foliage of Chusan palms, the larger-leafed rhododendrons, *Gunnera manicata* and the handsome angelica tree (*Aralia elata*) looking wonderful against the cliffs and outcrops. A path winds gently upwards between the walls of stone fringed with ferns, and emerges in meadows above the quarry. Here is a surprise – the substantial remains of 14th-century Belsay Castle rising up in the long grass. Near the house formal terraced gardens overlook woodland of conifers with a large collection of rhododendrons, and an unusual 'winter garden' is planted with different kinds of heather for winter colour.

BRAMHAM PARK

West Yorkshire

Wetherby LS23 6ND
5m S of Wetherby by A1
Tel: 01937 844265
Fax: 01937 845923

Owner: Mr and Mrs
George Lane Fox

Open: Easter weekend,
spring Bank Hol weekend,
1.15–5.30; 21 Jun to 6 Sept,
Sun, Tue, Wed and Thur
and Bank Hol Mon
1.15–5.30. 100 acres.
House open

A GARDEN LIKE Bramham is an exciting place, giving unique and special pleasure. There are borders and rose beds but the really wonderful thing here is the great formal garden of immense alleys of clipped beech, distant views of lonely statues, exquisite garden buildings commanding wide views, and refreshing vistas out into the surrounding countryside. It was designed in the very early 18th century for Robert Benson, the 1st Lord Bingley, who probably masterminded the building of the beautiful house as well as the making of the garden. On the Grand Tour he had seen the latest French gardens and wanted to make something of the sort for himself. The garden he made has a definite French accent – but with an attractively playful English irregularity. It is certainly grand, but never entirely solemn. Still owned by descendants of its maker, Bramham is maintained to wonderfully high standards; of its kind, there is nothing in England to touch it.

Brodsworth,
nr Doncaster DN5 7XJ
In Brodsworth village,
5 1/2m NW of Doncaster;
Jnct 37 of A1(M)
Tel: 01302 722598
Fax: 01302 337165

Owner: English Heritage

Open: Apr to Oct, daily
12–6. 15 acres. House open

THE HALL is a swagger Italianate mansion built in the 1860s, with splendid views to the south over rural landscape. The garden is a romantic Victorian affair with great character. The flower gardens west of the croquet lawn are a knickerbocker glory of bedding schemes, ivy ribbons, marble vases, soaring monkey puzzles and a gushing fountain. In the woods beyond, the quarry garden is a rocky ravine with a long archery lawn; at one end is a classically ruinous eyecatcher and at the other the delicious Palladian gothic Swiss cottage style Archery House. Beyond it an immense iron rose pergola curves round flower beds edged in box. English Heritage have breathed new life into this rare place and continue to do so.

CASTLE HOWARD

North Yorkshire

BIG IS the word for Castle Howard but the garden gives pleasures that are both grand and intimate. Vanbrugh's gigantic early 18th-century palace is set in dramatic country that is matched for drama by the

nr York YO6 7DA
14m NE of York by A64
Tel: 01653 648444
Fax: 01653 648462

Owner:
The Hon. Simon Howard

Open: Late Mar to late Oct,
daily 10–5. 50 acres. Castle
open. Much of the grounds
also open in winter; check
by phone

house. To the south a vast formal arrangement of clipped yew hedges surrounds a fountain with a figure of Atlas supported by Tritons, designed by W.A. Nesfield in 1850. To one side, in a secluded walled garden, yew hedges and screens of hornbeam divide rose beds edged in dwarf box, lavender and purple berberis. The very large collection of roses – old and new – is beautifully arranged, underplanted with grey and silver artemisias, phlomis, pinks and santolina. On the slopes far beyond the house a completely different atmosphere reigns. Ray Wood is an immense woodland garden with winding walks and a marvellous collection of trees and shrubs.

CRAGSIDE HOUSE
Northumberland

Rothbury,
Morpeth NE65 7PX
13m SW of Alnwick by
B6341
Tel: 01669 20333/20266

Owner: The National Trust

Open: Apr to 1 Nov, daily
except Mon (open Bank
Hol Mon) 10.30–6.30; Nov
to Dec, Sat, Sun and certain
weekdays 10.30–4.
1,000 acres. House open

CRAGSIDE WAS designed by Norman Shaw for the industrialist Lord Armstrong, and built in 1870. The very name makes one think of a Grimm fairy tale, and the appearance of the house rising high above a rocky bluff overlooking the Debdon Valley has more than a touch of Wagner. This is no place for genteel borders, and below the house a precipitous rockery cascades down the slopes. Giant steps lead down to a sombre and beautiful pinetum spreading along the banks of the river below, which is spanned by an elegant steel bridge. On the way down there are views of marvellous trees, the fern-fringed stream below and the wild house rearing on the cliff above. Recently the National Trust has acquired additional parts of the garden, including glasshouses with hydraulically driven turntables to allow tender fruit to ripen evenly. These have been beautifully restored, as well as one of the grandest bedding schemes in the north of England.

DALEMAIN
Cumbria

ON ONE side of the handsome 18th-century house at Dalemain a broad gravelled terrace, fringed with tumbling shrub roses, looks out over fields. Behind the house a knot of box-edged compartments is filled with artemisias, astilbes, campanulas,

nr Penrith CA11 0HB
3m SW of Penrith by A66
and A592
Tel: 01768 486450

Owner: R. Hasell McCosh

Open: Sun before Easter to
first Sun in Oct, daily
except Fri and Sat 11.15–5.
3 acres. House open

penstemons and violas, and in summer, pots of lilies
are arranged about a pool. A gravel walk with a border
of shrub roses leads under old fruit trees to a door.
Beyond this is Lobb's Wood where a wild woodland
walk follows the banks of the Dacre beck. On the
other side of the beck the wild garden is occasionally
revealed, with azaleas, rhododendrons and ornamental
trees. This is the kind of garden, unpretentious and
filled with good plants, that many think of as
quintessentially English.

DUNCOMBE PARK

North Yorkshire

Helmsley YO6 5EB
On the W edge of
Helmsley, 12m E of Thirsk
by A170
Tel: 01439 770213
Fax: 01439 771114

Owner: Lord Feversham

Open: Apr and Oct, daily
except Fri and Sat 11–6;
May to Sept, daily except
Fri 11–6. 485 acres

THE STORY of Duncombe Park is a splendid
reversal of fortune. The great early 18th-century
house had been leased for over 60 years to a girls'
school when Lord Feversham took it back as a private
residence. He has also restored the garden with its
exquisite views. In the 18th century Thomas
Duncombe, capitalising on its unique setting, created a
great boomerang-shaped terrace, giving views over the
ancient castle and rooftops of Helmsley and of the
sparkling waters of the curving river Rye below. The
terrace is ornamented by two fine temples – at one end
a rotunda almost certainly designed by Sir John
Vanbrugh, at the other a domed Doric temple by an
unknown architect. A long, slow walk to absorb the
Arcadian scenery is one of the greatest treats that any
garden can offer. It was Thomas Duncombe who was
also responsible for the similarly beautiful terrace at
Rievaulx nearby (see page 269).

GIBSIDE

Tyne and Wear

nr Rowlands Gill,
Burnopfield, Newcastle-
upon-Tyne NE16 6BG
On B6314 between
Burnopfield and Rowlands
Gill, 6m SW of Gateshead
Tel: 01207 542255

Owner: The National Trust

Open: Apr to 1 Nov, daily
except Mon (open Bank
Hol Mon) 11–5. 350 acres

HERE ARE the seductive fragmentary remains of a splendid landscape park – spacious, calm and dramatic. Gibside was the home of the Bowes family which, in the 18th century, embarked on ambitious landscape schemes along the Derwent Valley – 'one of the grandest idylls of the 18th century' as Christopher Hussey called it. The house is now a shell but the essence of the place survives with James Paine's beautiful Palladian chapel at one end of a vast avenue of oaks leading towards an immense Column of Liberty. To one side winding paths lead through the woods towards the lovely gothic Banqueting House which commands wide views. This is in the separate ownership of The Landmark Trust and it may be rented for holidays (01628 825925).

GRIZEDALE

Cumbria

Grizedale, nr Hawkshead,
Ambleside LA22 0QJ
3m S of Hawkshead by
B5285
Tel: 01229 860373

Owner: Forestry
Commission

Open: Daily dawn–dusk.
9,000 acres

GRIZEDALE FOREST lies between Coniston and Windermere, at the heart of some of the most beautiful scenery in the Lake District. It is an ancient place – the name is Norse for 'valley of the pigs' – and rich in trees. The Forestry Commission has opened it up for walking or biking, with over twenty miles of pathways. The Grizedale Society had the bright idea of enriching the forest with splendid sculptures made of

fallen timber, brushwood, slabs of stone and roughly hewn wood. Many of these are made by distinguished artists such as Sue Berger, Andy Frost, Andy Goldsworthy and others. These are, for the most part, designed to be ephemeral – and new ones are added from time to time. To the gardener they are of intense interest for they show vividly the magical power of such things powerfully to animate the scene.

HACKFALL WOOD

North Yorkshire

Grewelthorpe, nr Ripon
1/2m NW of Grewelthorpe village, 6 1/2m NW of Ripon

Owner: Woodland Trust

Open: Daily dawn–dusk. 112 acres

THIS WONDERFUL wild landscape garden was conjured out of a piece of dramatic country by William, son of John Aislabie of Studley Royal (see page 273), between 1730 and 1750. A natural wooded gorge, 100 metres deep, overlooks a lovely loop of the river Ure. Aislabie added buildings, paths, waterfalls and rills to animate the woods of beech and oak. Today you may wander at will, pushing through thickets of bracken, and marvel at the romantic prospects within the woods or high above them from the crest of the gorge. A famous beauty spot until the 1930s, it fell into decay; rediscovered by local enthusiasts, it is now cared for by the Woodland Trust

and accessible to all. It has a secret atmosphere and its present state of controlled dishevelment seems perfectly in tune with its exceptional character. It encourages a feeling of intrepid exploration. Its charms yield themselves only gradually and are the more memorable for it. It is certainly not a place for a hurried visit – a protracted leisurely amble is needed, perhaps with a picnic at the banqueting house.

HALECAT GARDEN NURSERIES

Cumbria

Witherslack, Grange-over-Sands LA11 6RU
5m NE of Grange-over-Sands by B5277 and A590
Tel: 01539 552229

Open: Mon to Fri 9–4.30, Sun 2–4

HALECAT HOUSE is an early 19th-century mansion looking south over terraced gardens and fields to exquisite, far-reaching views of Arnside Knott. The private garden is open to visitors, which gives an additional reason for coming to the very good nursery. Stone-paved terraces run along the south side of the house and a path skirts an unadorned lawn edged on two sides with generously planted mixed borders. A handsome gothic gazebo designed by Francis F. Johnson clings to the slope and provides an eyecatcher for a pair of borders with many shrub roses and a background of dark purple cotinus. In the nursery, on the far side of the house from the garden, an especially choice collection of over 60 cultivars of hydrangea (mostly *H. macrophylla*) is the star of the list, but there are many good things, herbaceous and woody, in other departments. A well-produced catalogue is issued but there is no mail order.

HAREWOOD HOUSE

West Yorkshire

Harewood, Leeds LS17 9LQ
7m N of Leeds and 7m S of
Harrogate by A61
Tel: 0113 2886331
Fax: 0113 2886467

Owner: The Earl and
Countess of Harewood

Open: Mar to Oct, daily
10–6. 36 acres. House open

HAREWOOD HOUSE is a palatial mansion designed by John Carr of York and Robert Adam, and built in the 1760s. In the 19th century Sir Charles Barry made many changes, laying out the Italianate south terrace which survives today and has been meticulously replanted according to his original designs. A parterre with arabesques filled with seasonal carpet bedding changed twice a year, stone urns and cones of clipped yew, is embellished with a fine statue by Astrid Zydower – a nobly proportioned bronze figure of Orpheus with a leopard draped over his shoulders, standing on a black marble plinth veiled with falling water. But the view from the terrace over 'Capability' Brown's landscape park is the most beautiful thing at Harewood. A lake is masked by trees and the land rises and falls with belts and clumps of trees alternating with meadows in which cattle graze. No building or ornament is visible and the simplicity of it is a splendid foil to the imposing house. Barry's lavish terrace is a cheerful period piece and not without charm – but it is a coarse piece of work in comparison with Brown's sublime Arcadian scene.

HARLOW CARR BOTANICAL GARDENS

North Yorkshire

Crag Lane,
Harrogate HG3 1QB
1 1/2m W of Harrogate by
B6162
Tel: 01423 565418
Fax: 01423 530663

Owner: The Northern
Horticultural Society

Open: Daily 9.30–6 or dusk
if earlier. 68 acres

THIS IS the northern equivalent of Wisley Gardens and is crammed with the same sort of garden attractions. The site is a very handsome one: a shallow valley with a stream and well wooded on its south-western slopes. There are sections devoted to particular groups of plants, such as a bulb garden and an arboretum. Display areas have three different kinds of rockeries – peat, limestone and sandstone – and a winter garden. Much space is devoted to vegetables and a fruit cage. Something different is arranged for each season in the trial gardens, with displays of new cultivars. A seasonal leaflet is produced, giving background information about what is going on in the season in question, and about the plants displayed. It is a lively place in which to learn about gardening.

HERB AND HEATHER CENTRE
North Yorkshire

West Haddlesey,
nr Selby YO8 8QA
4m SW of Selby by A19
Tel: 01757 228279

Open: Daily except
Christmas week 9.30–5.30
or dusk in winter

Herb gardens spring up all the time and vary considerably in their interest. Carole Atkinson's is a particularly good one, and apart from herbs she sells a wide range of heathers (over 200 varieties) and a good collection of conifers. All her plants are raised organically, and most may be seen in the adjacent display gardens which contain over 500 varieties of herbs and a National Collection of cotton lavender (*Santolina*). A list (£1.50) is issued and orders are supplied by mail order.

HERTERTON HOUSE GARDENS AND NURSERY
Northumberland

Hartington,
nr Cambo NE61 6BN
2m N of Cambo by B6342
Tel: 01670 774278

Owner:
Frank and Marjorie Lawley

Open: Apr to Sept, daily
except Tue and Thur
1.30–5.30. 1 acre

Few gardens so small give so much pleasure and interest as Herterton. Stone outhouses and beautifully made walls frame a series of enclosed gardens, each with distinctive character. A flower garden has hedges of box and yew, and beds edged in stone. Filled with unstaked herbaceous plants, these give generous informality to the ordered design of the layout. A physic garden, overlooked by an arcaded loggia, has a great clipped drum of silver pear at the centre, surrounded by beds edged in London pride or thrift. On the road side of the house the formal garden has topiary of yew and of box, and square box-edged beds brim with different varieties of dicentra. The important thing throughout the garden is the strength and simplicity of the design. The nursery sells only herbaceous perennials and although the stock is not large the choice is fastidious.

HEXHAM HERBS
Northumberland

In lovely country hard by Hadrian's Wall, Hexham Herbs has found a happy home in a 2-acre walled former kitchen garden. Here are gravel paths, ebullient box-edged borders and, beautifully displayed on a sloping gravel bed, the National Collection of thymes

Chollerford,
nr Hexham NE46 4BQ
On the W edge of
Chollerford, 4m NW of
Hexham by A6079
Tel: 01434 681483

Open: Easter to Oct, daily
10–5; phone for winter
opening hours

– over 120 species and cultivars. A formal pool has
recently been added, and a knot garden, laid out from
a design in William Lawson's *The Country Housewife's
Garden* (1617) – the first gardening book written for
women. Indeed the garden is now so attractive that it
is best to think of it as both a nursery *and* a garden.
The nursery sells herbs, herbaceous plants and native
species of wildflowers. There is no mail order but a
catalogue is available (£1.50).

HOLDEN CLOUGH NURSERY

Lancashire

Holden,
Bolton-by-Bowland,
Clitheroe BB7 4PF
7m NE of Clitheroe by
A671, A59 and minor roads
(turn off at Sawley)
Tel: 01200 447615

Open: Mar to Sept, Mon to
Thur 1–5, Sat 9–5 (Apr to
May, also Sun 2–5); Oct to
Feb, daily 9–5. Weather or
shows can interfere; best to
phone first

THIS IS an outstandingly good nursery, specialising
in alpines above all, but with many other
worthwhile hardy perennials. The alpine department
will excite even veteran fans with its splendid
collections of, for example, gentians (over 20 species
and cultivars), very many saxifrages, dozens of sedums
and so on. New plants are constantly being added.
Apart from these there are some excellent ornamental
grasses and a connoisseur's selection of ferns, heaths,
herbaceous perennials, shrubs and climbers. The 176-
page catalogue (£1.20) is exceptional – a chunky little
bible of its subject, packed with valuable information.
A mail order service is provided.

HOLEHIRD GARDENS

Cumbria

Patterdale Road,
Windermere LA23 3JA
1m N of Windermere by
A592
Tel: 01539 446238

Owner: The Lakeland
Horticultural Society

Open: Daily dawn–dusk.
3 1/2 acres

IN A well-wooded position on slopes above the eastern shore of Lake Windermere, Holehird has a marvellous site. The garden owes much of its present interest to William Groves who, in the early years of the 20th century, sponsored the plant-hunting expeditions of Reginald Farrer and William Purdom to north-west China. The Lakeland Horticultural Society took over in 1969 and is responsible for the impeccable upkeep and high level of plant interest that visitors can enjoy today. The soil is acid and rainfall is famously high, giving excellent conditions for azaleas, ferns, heathers, Himalayan poppies, maples and rhododendrons. These are decoratively disposed on slopes intricately laced with winding walks. A fine walled garden, recently restored, gives protection to many surprisingly tender plants – callistemon, carpenteria, diascia and *Eucryphia glutinosa*. Holehird has National Collections of astilbes – probably the largest in the world – hydrangeas and polystichum ferns. The plants are handsomely displayed in well-planned borders.

HOLKER HALL

Cumbria

Cark-in-Cartmel,
nr Grange-over-Sands
LA11 7PL
4m W of Grange-over-
Sands
Tel: 01539 558328
Fax: 01539 558776

Owner: The Lord
Cavendish of Furness and
Lady Cavendish

Open: Apr to Oct, daily
except Sat 10–6. 25 acres.
House open

SOME OF the most worthwhile gardens manage to juggle very different ingredients with complete success, and Holker Hall is a prime example. The late 16th-century house has a splendid neo-Elizabethan wing built in 1871 after a disastrous fire. Inventive formal gardens near the house provide secluded sitting places and much to admire: an alley of glistening Portugal laurels, herbaceous borders with well-judged colour harmonies, stately gravel walks, yew hedges and elegant thorns (*Crataegus orientalis*) set in squares of box hedging. A gate pierces the wall and leads to a meadow garden, a brilliant contrast to the formal enclosures by the house. To one side gardens of a woodland character spread out; eucryphias, hoherias, magnolias, rhododendrons and stewartias ornament a background of venerable beeches and oaks. Among the trees an ornamental staircase, with cascades of water

on either side, leads to a 17th-century Italian figure of Neptune. Everywhere there are distinguished plants and the garden will give immense pleasure in any season, not least for the inspiringly high standard of its upkeep. The garden holds the National Collection of Styracaceae – a genus of plants that sounds vaguely forbidding but which includes such exceptional trees as *Styrax japonica*, possibly the loveliest of all smallish trees for the garden. Holker Hall is an admirable source of inspiration and knowledge.

HOWICK HALL

Northumberland

Alnwick NE66 3LB
6m NE of Alnwick by
B1340 and minor roads
Tel and Fax: 01665 577285

Owner:
Howick Trustees Ltd

Open: Apr to Oct, daily
1–6. 14 acres

HOWICK, VERY near the wild Northumberland coast, has a secluded and romantic air. The grand late 18th-century house overlooks a series of balustraded terraces linked with steps. Thickets of *Choisya ternata* and *Carpenteria californica* flank the steps leading down from the uppermost terrace to a pool and to mixed borders rich with roses and lavender with, in late summer, great waves of blue agapanthus. Beyond the last terrace a meadow, brilliant in spring with narcissi and tulips, is planted with maples, birches and shrub roses. Although this is limestone country, part of the garden at Howick has acid soil and here, between the wars, an excellent woodland garden was made, with azaleas, camellias, outstanding magnolias and rhododendrons under a canopy of old oaks, beeches and sweet chestnuts. Later in the season eucryphias, hydrangeas and viburnums continue interest, and in the autumn there is brilliant colour from cercidiphyllums and maples.

LEVENS HALL
Cumbria

Kendal LA8 0PD
5m S of Kendal by A591
and A6
Tel: 01539 560321
Fax: 01539 560669

Owner: C.H. Bagot

Open: Apr to 15 Oct, daily
except Fri and Sat 11–5.
3 acres. House open

A MYSTERIOUS FRENCHMAN, Guillaume Beaumont, came to Levens Hall in 1690 and by 1694 had laid out an exotic formal garden – a forest of topiary and cool beech alleys – which still survives in splendid old age. Fanciful shapes of yew, both golden and common, and of box, many billowing and misshapen with age, are scattered about. Among them, bedding plants making blocks of colour, their brilliance contrasting well with the monumental topiary. Rising above all this is the grey stone house with its great square pele tower. On one side, behind castellated yew hedges, are excellent new borders, a herb garden and an ornamental *potager*. Beaumont's extraordinary beech alley opens out into a giant circle and a path leads to a field with a ha-ha – the first in England – and an avenue of sycamore.

LINDISFARNE CASTLE
Northumberland

Holy Island, Berwick-upon-
Tweed TD15 2SH
11 1/2m SE of Berwick-
upon-Tweed by A1 and
causeway at low tide; check
tide times, which are also
posted at each end of the
causeway
Tel: 01289 89244

Owner: The National Trust

Open: Apr to 29 Oct, daily
except Fri (open Good Fri)
1–5.30 (Jul to Aug 11–5.30,
tide and staff permitting)

E DWIN LUTYENS restored the castle as a holiday home for Edward Hudson, the famous editor of *Country Life*. Lytton Strachey thought it 'very dark, and nowhere to sit'. A garden by Gertrude Jekyll was an essential accompaniment, and she laid out a little walled enclosure at some distance from the castle across sheep pastures. It survives today; aquilegias, irises, Jacob's ladder, lady's mantle and lamb's ears spread among stone flags, and roses are trained on walls and wooden frames. It is so surprising, and such an appropriately simple layout, that any gardener will enjoy seeing it in this remote and wonderfully beautiful setting.

MUNCASTER CASTLE
Cumbria

M UNCASTER IS a wonderfully romantic place. Rising over ravines near the wild Cumbrian coast is a granite medieval castle, rebuilt by Anthony Salvin in 1862. From the entrance lodge the drive

Ravenglass CA18 1RQ
1m SE of Ravenglass by
A595
Tel: 01229 717614
Fax: 01229 717010

Owner: Mrs P. Gordon-
Duff-Pennington

Open. Daily 11–5. 77 acres.
House open

plunges down towards the castle, and marvellous old rhododendrons line the way. Many of these were planted by Sir John Ramsden, who financed some of Frank Kingdon-Ward's plant-hunting expeditions in the 1920s. Near the castle a grassy terrace walk snakes along the valley, giving unforgettable views of the Esk and the mountains beyond. The slopes above the terrace are richly planted with cherries, magnolias, maples, rhododendrons and other ornamental trees and shrubs. Along the other side of the walk a box hedge has regularly spaced topiary piers of golden and common yew; on the precipitous slopes below, marvellous trees include probably the biggest sweet chestnut you will ever look down on. The walk culminates in a thatched rustic summerhouse.

NEWBY HALL GARDENS

North Yorkshire

NEWBY HALL has one of the best private gardens in England, with outstanding collections of plants beautifully arranged and cared for. The gardens lie to the south of the house on a magnificent site that slopes gently down to the river Ure. Giant double herbaceous

Ripon HG4 5AE
4m SE of Ripon by B6265
Tel: 01423 322583
Fax: 01423 324452

Owner: R.J.E. Compton

Open: Easter to Sept, daily
except Mon (open Bank
Hol Mon) 11–5.30.
25 acres. House open

borders, hedged on either side in yew, sweep down to
the river edge, and paths lead off enticingly to other
formal enclosures or into the surrounding woodland.
Among the formal parts are a dramatic 19th-century
statue walk; striking seasonal gardens designed
specifically for spring and autumn; an excellent garden
of old roses; and Sylvia's Garden in which herbs and
grey-leafed plants flourish round paved paths. In the
woodland are many excellent trees, especially maples,
birch and dogwoods (a National Collection). Although
full of rarities, this is a garden that can be relished
even by those who cannot tell a dandelion from a
daffodil. Intensely visited in the summer months, it is
big enough to absorb the numbers and provide all
kinds of intimate corners where the visitor may be
virtually alone.

NORDEN ALPINES
Humberside

Hirst Road, Carlton,
nr Goole DN14 9PX
8m W of Goole by A614
and A1041
Tel: 01405 861348

Open: Mar to Sept, Sat, Sun
and Bank Hol Mon 10–5;
also by appointment

THIS NURSERY is, in the words of its owners, the
result of a hobby that got out of hand. It sells only
alpines, of which it has a dazzling selection: over 2,500
varieties, with marvellous groups of campanulas,
gentians, irises, primulas (including many auriculas),
saxifrages (well over 70 varieties) and sedums, all
propagated on the premises, often in quite small
quantities. There is a catalogue (four 2nd-class stamps)
and a mail order service.

PERRY'S PLANTS
North Yorkshire

River Gardens, Sleights,
Whitby YO21 1RR
2 1/2m SW of Whitby on
B1410
Tel: 01947 810329

Open: Easter to Oct, daily
10–5

PATRICIA PERRY specialises in herbaceous perennials
with a few woody plants, and has charming
gardens on the river Esk – Victorian tea-gardens with
all sorts of amusements of the period: croquet, putting
and, of course, tea. The nursery has a fine selection of
anthemis, good hebes, excellent lavateras and other
mallows, and a choice range of perennial wallflowers
(erysimums). An intriguing group of euphorbias
includes the splendidly named *E. characias* 'Winter
Blusher', which sounds like an essential plant. A list is
issued (large s.a.e.) but there is no mail order.

RIEVAULX TERRACE

North Yorkshire

Rievaulx,
Helmsley YO6 5LJ
2 1/2m NW of Helmsley by
B1257
Tel: 01439 798340

Owner: The National Trust

Open: Apr and Oct, daily
10.30–5; May to Sept, daily
10.30–6. 15 acres

IT WAS one of the new ideas of 18th-century landscape gardening to make a terrace from which to admire fine views of the countryside and other beauties. At Rievaulx, high above the astonishing remains of the 12th-century abbey, a grassy terrace curves through woodland, giving wonderful views of the abbey, the valley and distant countryside. At each end of the terrace a little temple provides a punctuation mark; the plain round Tuscan temple has a simple interior but the Ionic temple is sumptuously furnished, with a table laid for a feast, and decorated with a noble painted ceiling. All this was made in the late 1750s by Thomas Duncombe (see page 256), an early exercise in picturesque landscape design that still has the power to enchant. Modest in scale, it is the perfect place to grasp the genius of the 18th-century landscape revolution.

ROOKHOPE NURSERIES

County Durham

Rookhope,
Upper Weardale DL13 2DD
22 1/2m NW of Bishop
Auckland by A68 and A689
Tel: 01388 517272

Open: Mid Mar to mid
Oct, daily 9–4

KAREN AND Alan Blackburn's nursery on the Upper Pennine moors is over 1,000 feet up and, among other things, provides a tough hardiness test-ground for garden plants. The most extensive part of the list is a representative collection of alpines, with many good campanulas, erodiums, gentians, the smaller geraniums, helianthemums, saxifrages, thymes and violas. In addition, there are dwarf conifers and heathers, and a good range of herbaceous perennials

Illustration:
Eryngium alpinum

and of shrubs. The adjacent garden shows what may be done in this cold, windy place which has regular heavy snowfalls. If you garden in similarly extreme conditions a visit is especially instructive. A catalogue (three 1st-class stamps) is issued and there is a limited mail order service.

SEATON DELAVAL HALL

Northumberland

Seaton Delaval,
Whitley Bay NE26 4QR
9m NE of Newcastle-upon-
Tyne on the A190
Tel: 0191 2373040/237 1493

Owner: Lord Hastings

Open: May, Bank Hol Sun
and Mon 2–6; June, Wed
and Sun 2–6; Jul to Aug,
Wed, Thur, Sun and Bank
Hol Mon 2–6. 3 acres

T HE HOUSE at Seaton Delaval, completed in 1726, is one of Sir John Vanbrugh's ripest confections, with a memorably dramatic position on the Northumberland coast, frequently veiled in sea mist. A few traces survive of the original garden (including bastions of a Vanbrughesque kind) but the existing scheme has been almost entirely made by the present Lord Hastings who, in 1947, commissioned from James Russell a new formal garden to the west of the house. He laid out a splendidly theatrical arrangement of yew hedges and topiary, with lively patterns of box hedges, to which fine urns and a fountain were later added. On one side of the house a box parterre is planted with roses, making a lovely patchwork in late June. Nearby, a pair of mixed borders sweeps round a wonderful old weeping ash. Behind yew hedges Lady Hastings has added a lily pond and a laburnum tunnel leading towards the Norman church. Everywhere, the eye is caught by Vanbrugh's beautiful swaggering house, a dramatic contrast to the light-hearted decorativeness of the garden.

Illustration opposite:
Seaton Delaval Hall

SIZERGH CASTLE

Cumbria

nr Kendal LA8 8AE
3 1/2m S of Kendal by A591
Tel: 01539 560070

Owner: The National Trust

Open: Apr to 29 Oct, Sun
to Thur 12.30–5.30. 14
acres. House open

THE GREAT thing at Sizergh, lying in the shadow of the late medieval stone castle, is one of the best rock gardens in England. It was laid out in 1926 by a local firm, T.R. Hayes & Son of Ambleside, and is now a densely planted jungle of conifers and Japanese maples, laced with winding walks and a splashing stream, and underplanted with a marvellous collection of hardy ferns – over 100 species and varieties. South of the castle steps lead down to an ornamental lake, and to the west an avenue of rowans leads through a Rose Garden with species and shrub roses.

STILLINGFLEET LODGE NURSERIES

Yorkshire

Illustration: Iris douglasiana

Stillingfleet,
York YO4 6HW
In Stillingfleet village (turn
opposite the church), 7m S
of York by A19 and B1222
Tel and Fax: 01904 728506

Open: Apr to mid Oct,
daily except Mon, Thur and
Sun 10–4; garden also open
May to Jun, Wed 1–4

VANESSA COOK specialises in herbaceous perennials, although she also sells some of the more versatile woody plants such as artemisias, cistus, daphnes, hebes and lavenders. Her careful selection of herbaceous plants is particularly attractive, with good euphorbias, a long list of hardy geraniums, penstemons, primulas, pulmonarias (of which she holds a National Collection of 11 species and over 90 cultivars) and veronicas. There are also several interesting grasses, or grass-like plants. The nursery is specially rich in those smaller ornamental items which find a decorative home in odd corners of the garden and immensely add to its character. A catalogue is issued (five 1st-class stamps), from which plants may be supplied by post.

STUDLEY ROYAL

North Yorkshire

Fountains, Ripon HG4 3DZ
4m W of Ripon by B6265
Tel: 01765 608888/601005

Owner: The National Trust

Open: Nov to Jan, daily
except Fri (closed 24–25
Dec) 10–5; Mar, daily 10–5;
Apr to Sept, daily 10–7
(closes early 10 and 11 Jul
and 1 Aug); Oct to Mar
1999, daily 10–5 or dusk if
earlier. 900 acres

JOHN AISLABIE was Chancellor of the Exchequer in 1720 when the South Sea Bubble collapsed, and he subsequently retired to his Yorkshire estate to lick his wounds and make a garden. In the wooded valley of the river Skell he laid out a great water garden ornamented with statues of lead and stone, and in the woods above built a banqueting house, an octagonal tower, a Temple of Piety and a Temple of Fame. John Aislabie's son William later acquired the ruins of the nearby Cistercian Fountains Abbey, and these were incorporated into the landscape scheme – suddenly revealed round a curve of the river, like a gigantic and celestial garden ornament.

SUTTON PARK

North Yorkshire

Sutton-on-the-Forest,
York YO6 1DP
8m N of York by B1363
Tel: 01347 810249
Fax: 01347 811251

Owner: Sir Reginald and
Lady Sheffield

Open: Easter to Sept, daily
11–5.30. 8 acres

THE APPROACH to the garden at Sutton Park is oblique, through groves of ornamental trees, with the pretty garden facade of the 18th-century house gradually revealed. A series of terraces, filled with decorative planting, leads down from the house. The second terrace has a geometric pattern of beds, with standard roses underplanted with *Alchemilla mollis*, artemisia, catmint and rue, and a weeping silver pear at each corner. Vertical emphasis is given by a series of soaring cypresses and the last terrace has a long, calm lily pond. Across a lawn a beech hedge dips down in the middle to reveal the peaceful countryside beyond.

THORP PERROW ARBORETUM
North Yorkshire

Bedale DL8 2PR
2m S of Bedale off B6268
Tel: 01677 425323

Owner: Sir John Ropner Bt

Open: Daily dawn–dusk.
85 acres

THIS WAS started by Colonel Sir Leonard Ropner in 1931 as a private plant collection. Old trees, especially conifers planted in the 1840s, provided both protection and a fine sombre background to the more colourful ornamental trees. Only a complete list would give a full idea of the range and depth of the woody plants represented here; it is a vast collection, with great rarities and excellent specimens of individual trees. For the gardener there are admirable collections of flowering shrubs and of the smaller ornamental trees such as cherries and crab apples.

WALLINGTON
Northumberland

Cambo,
Morpeth NE61 4AR
12m W of Morpeth
Tel: 01670 774283

Owner: The National Trust

Open: Gardens: Apr to
Sept, daily 10–7; Oct, daily
10–6; Nov to Mar 1999,
daily 10–4 or dusk if earlier;
Grounds: daily all year
during daylight hours. 100
acres. House open

THE HOUSE at Wallington looks out over a ha-ha and parkland. The pleasure garden lies at some distance from the house, hidden in woodland across the road. Overlooking a pond there remains from the 18th century the handsome Portico House, a classical gardener's cottage. In the heart of the woods an immense walled garden bursts into view – long and narrow, irregularly shaped and built on a slope. A high terrace is planted with a long white and silver border, and its retaining wall is crested with lead statues. From the gravelled terrace walk there are views over grassy paths sweeping between mixed borders in the lavishly planted gardens spread out decoratively like an intricate patchwork below.

WENTWORTH CASTLE GARDENS
South Yorkshire

Illustration opposite: The
Portico House at Wallington

SANDWICHED BETWEEN the ghastly M1 to the east and surprisingly unspoilt rural scenes to the west, Wentworth Castle is caught between present and past. The Wentworth family built the great house in the early 18th century and laid out an elaborate garden, at first following the formal style of the day but, later in the century, becoming increasingly informal. The early

Stainborough,
Barnsley S75 3ET
4m SW of Barnsley, W of
M1 between Jncts 36 and 37
Tel: 01226 285426
Fax: 01226 284308

Owner: Barnsley
Metropolitan District
Council

Open: Spring Bank Hol Sun
and Mon 10–4.30; May and
Jun, guided tours every Tue
(10 am) and Thur (2 pm)
50 acres

18th-century parterres are now a car park but behind the house, where the land sweeps uphill, are fine surviving features. A memorial obelisk to Lady Mary Wortley Montagu (who introduced innoculation against small-pox in 1720) stands out on the skyline, and to one side is the splendid gothic folly of Stainborough castle – dating from the late 1720s and one of the earliest gothic garden buildings in the country. In the surrounding woodland there are fine trees and shrubs – the garden holds National Collections of species rhododendrons and of magnolias. Restoration progresses in this lovely landscape and visitors will follow it with interest.

YORKSHIRE SCULPTURE PARK
West Yorkshire

Bretton Hall, West Bretton,
Wakefield WF4 4LG
1m NW of Jnct 38 of the
M1
Tel: 01924 830302
Fax: 01924 830044

Open: Daily 10–6 (in winter
10–5). 200 acres

SCULPTURES OF all kinds are often seen at their best in handsome landscape rather than in the cooped-up confines and hushed atmosphere of the museum. The sculpture park is a 20th-century idea as a public amenity and this one, in the grounds of University College Bretton Hall, is very successful. The landscape benefits from the points of emphasis given by the works of art, and the undulating lie of the land and the fine trees provide a good background to exhibits which range widely from French neo-classicism to outrageous modernism. The Park has its own substantial loan collection, from Barbara Hepworth to Grenville Davey, and changing selections from it are displayed throughout the year. In addition to the permanent collection there are temporary exhibitions, sculpture courses, crafts workshops and other events.

SCOTLAND

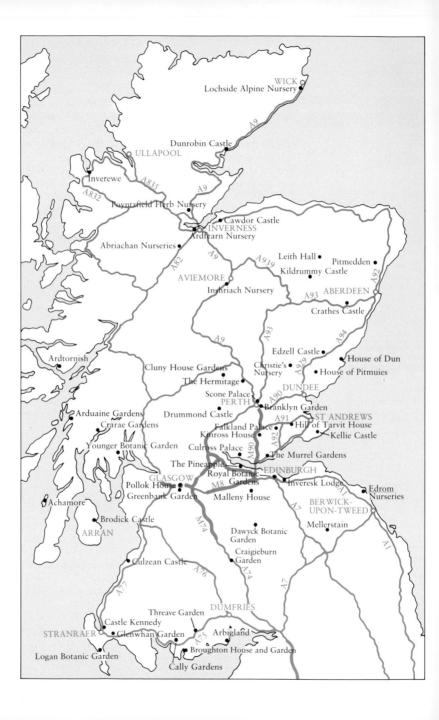

WICK

Lochside Alpine Nursery

A9

Dunrobin Castle

ULLAPOOL

Inverewe

A835

A832

A9

Poyntzfield Herb Nursery

Cawdor Castle

INVERNESS

Ardfearn Nursery

Abriachan Nurseries

A82

A9

Leith Hall

Pitmedden

Kildrummy Castle

A92

AVIEMORE

A939

Inshriach Nursery

A93

ABERDEEN

Crathes Castle

A93

A94

Ardtornish

Edzell Castle

House of Dun

Cluny House Gardens

Christie's
Nursery

A929

House of Pitmuies

The Hermitage

DUNDEE

Scone Palace

PERTH

Branklyn Garden

Arduaine Gardens

Drummond Castle

A91

ST ANDREWS

Crarae Gardens

Falkland Palace

Hill of Tarvit House

Younger Botanic Garden

Kinross House

A92

Kellie Castle

Culross Palace

M90

The Murrel Gardens

The Pineapple

Royal Botanic

EDINBURGH

GLASGOW

Gardens

Pollok House

M8

Inveresk Lodge

Edrom

Greenbank Garden

Malleny House

Nurseries

Achamore

BERWICK-
UPON-TWEED

A7

A1

Brodick Castle

Mellerstain

ARRAN

Dawyck Botanic
Garden

M74

Culzean Castle

Craigieburn
Garden

A74

A7

A76

A7

DUMFRIES

Threave Garden

Castle Kennedy

STRANRAER

Glenwhan Garden

Arbigland

A75

Logan Botanic Garden

Broughton House and Garden

Cally Gardens

ABRIACHAN GARDEN AND NURSERY

Highland

Loch Ness Side,
Inverness IV3 6LA
9m SW of Inverness on A82
Tel: 01463 861232

Open: Feb to Nov, daily 9–7
or dusk if earlier

O N THE banks of Loch Ness, Abriachan has an enviable south-facing site. Here are excellent dianthus, foxgloves, a good range of hardy geraniums, several meconopsis, an immense collection of primulas and many thymes. In the alpine department are gentians, a vast range of helianthemums, lewisias, the smaller phlox and a large number of saxifrages. Well-planted beds surround the nursery, and paths entice the visitor uphill to an attractive further garden area – which keeps expanding and now extends to an area of three acres, making an attraction in its own right. An excellent catalogue is produced (three 1st-class stamps) and plants are supplied by mail order.

ACHAMORE

Strathclyde

Isle of Gigha PA41 7AD
Off W coast of Kintyre;
ferry from Tayinloan
Tel: 01583 505267/505254
Fax: 01583 505244

Owner: Derek Holt

Open: Daily dawn–dusk.
50 acres

G IGHA IS a small island in the Inner Hebrides. Here Sir James Horlick came in 1944 and started to make a woodland garden, his new plantings protected by evergreens and old broad-leafed trees. Rhododendrons now reign supreme, constituting one of the best collections in Scotland, with the aristocratic, large-leafed species such as *R. falconeri* and *R. macabeanum* growing to exceptional size and beauty in this mild climate of high rainfall. Apart from the rhododendrons there is much else to admire, not least the rich underplanting of herbaceous and bulbous plants and the very wide range of ornamental trees and shrubs with excellent camellias, magnolias, mahonias, many shrub roses, viburnums and tender trees such as the New Zealand Christmas tree, *Metrosideros umbellata,* and other very unusual things from the southern hemisphere. The wide range of plants growing in such a mild climate means that something interesting is happening in the garden on any day of the year.

ARBIGLAND

Dumfries and Galloway

Kirkbean,
Dumfries DG2 8BQ
14m SW of Dumfries by
A710
Tel: 01387 880283

Owner: Captain and Mrs
J.B. Blackett

Open: May to Sept, daily
except Mon (open Bank
Hol Mon) 2–6. 20 acres

SOME GARDENS provide the thrill of exploration and discovery, gradually unlocking their charms to the visitor. Arbigland, with its elegant mid-Georgian house handsomely framed in fine trees, does not at first reveal signs of any particular garden interest. But behind the house the Broad Walk plunges down through woodland towards the hidden sea. From this central axis enticing paths lead to Japan – a bosky water garden; to a hidden rose garden built on the site of old Arbigland Hall; and to glades planted with ornamental trees and shrubs that flourish in this climate of high rainfall and mild winters. There are wonderful rhododendrons such as the tender giant *R. sinogrande*; beautiful old maples; eucryphias grown to great size; and very fine conifers giving shelter from the coastal winds. The cry of seagulls and the sound of unseen waves provides a curious further dimension to the pleasures of this rare garden.

ARDFEARN NURSERY

Highland

Bunchrew,
Inverness IV3 6RH
4m W of Inverness by A862
Tel: 01463 223607
Fax: 01463711713

Open: Daily 9–5

JAMES SUTHERLAND and his son Alasdair have established this relatively new nursery as an excellent source of alpine plants. A courtyard of old cow byres makes an attractive setting for the plants, many of which are displayed in beautifully planted raised beds and troughs. Over 1,000 species and varieties are available, and there is a constant stream of new introductions – some from the wild by plant-hunting expeditions to which the nursery subscribes – and even expert alpinists will find unfamiliar things.

For the non-alpinist there is a good range of herbaceous perennials and shrubs. An alpine catalogue is produced (four 2nd-class stamps) in September, and orders are fulfilled by post between October and March. There remain plenty of good plants for visitors to the nursery – but rarities are snapped up quickly.

ARDTORNISH

Highland

Morvern,
by Oban PA34 5XA
30m SW of the Corran
ferry (and A828 from
Oban) by A861 and A884
Tel: 01967 421288
Fax: 01967 421211

Owner: Mrs John Raven

Open: Apr to Oct, daily
10–5

THE ARDTORNISH estate lies in one of the most beautiful parts of Scotland, in the south-western part of the Morvern peninsula. The house and garden command splendid views from the head of Loch Aline, looking south-west across to the Sound of Mull. The garden was largely the creation of the present owner, her late husband, John Raven, and her parents. Its character is informal and its great strength is the admirable collection of acid-loving trees and shrubs – cercidiphyllums, enkianthus, eucryphias, hoherias, maples, rhododendrons and many others. There are also many herbaceous perennials and underplantings of bluebells, colchicums, daffodils and snowdrops. The keen gardener will rent one of the flats or cottages on the estate, all of which give free access to the gardens. John Raven's excellent book, *A Botanist's Garden*, now back in print, vividly describes the planting here and at the Ravens' other garden, Docwra's Manor near Cambridge (see page 221). The two gardens, each with its own character, could scarcely be more different.

ARDUAINE GARDENS

Strathclyde

Kilmelford PA34 4XG
20m S of Oban by A816
Tel and Fax: 01852 200366

Owner: The National Trust
for Scotland

Open: Daily 9.30–sunset.
18 acres

THE GARDEN at Arduaine was started in 1897 by James Arthur Campbell, a tea planter and friend of Osgood Mackenzie the maker of Inverewe. It is on a splendid site which slopes gently down towards the shores of Loch Melfort. The first part of the garden is fairly open, with many smaller azaleas and rhododendrons planted in island beds, and enlivened by a stream and pools. There is rich underplanting of superb Himalayan poppies, groves of gunnera, hostas and trilliums. Paths lead up the hill and the visitor soon experiences the full Himalayan effect. Immense rhododendrons are at their most impressive against a backdrop of coniferous planting. It is essential to keep going to the top of the hill where a viewpoint gives an wonderful panorama of the calm waters of Loch Melfort below.

BRANKLYN GARDEN

Tayside

Dundee Road,
Perth PH2 7BB
On the E edge of Perth by
A85
Tel: 01738 625535

Owner: The National Trust
for Scotland

Open: Mar to Oct, daily
9.30–sunset. 1 3/4 acres

JOHN AND Dorothy Renton started to make this garden in 1922. On a south-facing slope with acid soil they built up a wonderful collection of appropriate plants – smaller rhododendrons, maples, daphnes, magnolias and many woodland plants such as erythroniums, fritillaries, meconopsis and trilliums. Narrow paths of turf wind along the contours of the land, bringing the visitor nose-to-nose with all kinds of distinguished plants beautifully grown. The combination of woody plants underplanted with spring bulbs and later with herbaceous plants is executed with brilliant aplomb.

BRODICK CASTLE

Strathclyde

BRODICK CASTLE occupies a splendid position, well protected from westerly winds and looking east across the Firth of Clyde. The castle with its castellated towers is partly medieval but was rebuilt in the early 17th century and in 1844. The present garden

Isle of Arran KA27 8HY
2m from Brodick Ferry
Tel: 01770 302202
Fax: 01770 302312

Owner: The National Trust
for Scotland

Open: Daily 9.30–sunset.
80 acres. Castle open

dates from 1923 when the Duchess of Montrose
started an ambitious woodland garden with a
collection of rhododendrons, many of them recent
introductions from the great plant hunters, in
particular George Forrest; among them the huge-leafed
R. macabeanum and *R. sinogrande*. From the castle
paths wind downhill towards the seashore, and in a
shady place there is a fernery and a delightful Bavarian
summerhouse embellished with rustic work and lovely
inlaid panels of pine-cones. In spring the woodland,
with meconopsis and primulas flourishing about the
ornamental shrubs, is a brilliant sight. A walled
garden, dated 1710, has been restored with Victorian-
style carpet bedding, and mixed borders which prolong
the flowering interest to the very end of the summer.

BROUGHTON HOUSE AND GARDEN

Dumfries and Galloway

12 High Street,
Kircudbright DG6 4JX
In the centre of
Kircudbright
Tel: 01557 330437

Owner: The National Trust
for Scotland

Open: Apr to Oct, daily
1–5.30. 1 acre. House open

KIRCUDBRIGHT IS an enchanting town which from
the 1880s attracted a fascinating community of
artists. One of the most successful, one of the
'Glasgow Boys', was E.A. Hornel, the original owner
of this beautiful 18th-century house. Between 1901 and
1933 he embellished the house and created a delightful
garden which lies behind it, with views over the river
Dee at its foot. Here is a lively sketch of a Japanese
garden, with a hint of a scarlet bridge over a pool
traversed by stepping stones and fringed with Japanese

maples, junipers clipped into cones and stone troughs. Two parallel box-edged paths lead straight down the garden, linking many enclosures which are full of good plants and peaceful sitting places. Untouched by horticultural trendiness the garden is full of aristocratic plants – *Aralia elata*, *Acer griseum* and *Cornus controversa* 'Variegata'. It is the sort of immediately attractive place which makes visitors exclaim, 'Oh, I would love to live here!'

CALLY GARDENS

Dumfries and Galloway

Gatehouse-of-Fleet,
Castle Douglas DG7 2DJ
E of Gatehouse on B727
Dumfries road
Tel: 01557 815029

Open: Easter weekend to
first weekend of Oct, Sat
and Sun 10–5.30

A 3-ACRE WALLED garden is the setting for this treasure trove of plants. Michael Wickenden has around 3,000 different species and varieties, of which about 500 are in stock at any one time. His sources are exchanges from other collectors, seeds from botanic gardens, and his own finds on plant-collecting trips. The catalogue (three 1st-class stamps) is therefore a moveable feast, but a feast nonetheless, and you may always find something unfamiliar and extremely desirable (like several species of the tender South African *Watsonia* in the current list). A mail order service is provided but a visit is essential to inspect the stock, much of which is handsomely displayed in deep borders against the walls.

CASTLE KENNEDY

Dumfries and Galloway

Rephad,
Stranraer DG9 8BX
5m E of Stranraer by A75
Tel: 01776 702024
Fax: 01776 706248

Owner: The Earl and
Countess of Stair

Open: Easter to Sept, daily
10–5. 75 acres

M ANY GARDENS seem interesting enough at the time but later fade in the memory to a blur of borders. Castle Kennedy is a vast place, a piece of heroic landscaping with intimate moments, that would be hard to forget. The garden lies between two castles – the ruins of the 15th-century Castle Kennedy and the 19th-century Lochinch Castle – which make splendid eyecatchers to vistas through woods and up hills. North of the old castle are the rare remains of the early 18th-century formal gardens – extraordinary terraces and turf mounds sculpted in the ground. Woodland is embellished with an immense collection of distinguished trees and shrubs: many very large conifers, exceptional rhododendrons and eucryphias which grow to immense size. By the old castle a walled garden has fine borders, and an avenue of eucryphias and embothriums plummets down to the loch.

CAWDOR CASTLE

Highland

Cawdor IV12 5RD
11m N of Inverness by A96 and B9090
Tel: 01667 404615
Fax: 01667 404674

Owner: The Dowager Countess Cawdor

Open: May to 11 Oct, daily 10–5.30. 20 acres. Castle open

CAWDOR IS exactly what a Highland castle should be. To one side of it, ancient stone walls enclose a flower garden where a broad grass path runs between a pair of herbaceous borders with old apple trees rising behind. A rose garden, its oval beds edged in lavender, is given height by soaring columns of common and golden yew. Here, too, are a rose tunnel, a peony walk and a virtuoso pair of beds brimming with *Galtonia candicans* and pale orange lilies. On the far side of the castle a new 'paradise garden' has a beautiful and mysterious fountain, a prickly thistle garden and a knot garden with box-edged beds. A maze of holly is enclosed on three sides by a laburnum cloister.

CHRISTIE'S NURSERY

Angus

HIGH UP on the north side of the Sidlaw hills, Christie's sells a marvellous range of acid-loving plants with an emphasis on alpines. Some of these need cosseting in an alpine house but many others have proved their out-of-doors toughness at the nursery.

Downfield, Main Road,
Westmuir DD8 5LP
1m W of Kirriemuir by
A926
Tel and Fax: 01575 572977

Open: Mar to Oct, daily
except Tue 10–5 (Sun 1–5)

The stock ranges widely with, among much else, a dazzling range of cassiopes, corydalis, lovely fritillaries, many gentians (species and cultivars), lewisias, a very long list of primulas, saxifrages and trilliums. They also have a particularly interesting range of hardy and cool house orchids. A catalogue is produced (two 1st-class stamps) and a mail order service is available.

CLUNY HOUSE GARDENS
Tayside

by Aberfeldy PH15 2JT
3 1/2m NE of Aberfeldy.
W from Aberfeldy to bridge
over Tay and turn right at
Weem–Strathtay road
Tel: 01887 820795

Owner: Mr J. and Mrs W.
Mattingley

Open: Mar to Oct, daily
10–6

THIS PART of Perthshire, 600ft above the river Tay, has an alpine character, and the name Cluny means in Gaelic 'meadow place'. The house is a pretty, early 19th-century mansion with gothic touches, and the garden is disposed on the slopes below it. Here are many shrubs and trees relishing the acid soil and high rainfall, but its greatest glory is the range of herbaceous plants. The National Collection of Asiatic primulas, well over 100 species, is kept here, and many of these exquisitely delicate plants line the paths which thread their way through the woods. Apart from these there are lovely crocuses, fritillaries, gentians, spectacular examples of the giant lily *Cardiocrinum giganteum*, narcissi and trilliums. This is very much a garden to walk in and to explore, and gradually, as you get your eye in, you will discover more and more – many of the best things are tucked away in odd corners. A small nursery has some admirable, and often rare, plants for sale.

CRAIGIEBURN GARDEN
Dumfries and Galloway

Craigieburn House, by
Moffat DG10 9LF
2m E of Moffat by A708
Tel: 01683 221250

Open: Mid Apr to Oct,
daily except Mon 12.30–6.
7 1/2 acres

FEW THINGS are more exciting to gardeners than new nurseries and new gardens. Craigieburn started in 1991 and Bill Chudziak and Janet Wheatcroft have built up an excellent collection of plants and made a solid start on restoring the woodland garden. Behind the house the Craigie burn plummets down a spectacular ravine with wooded slopes crowding in all about. In front of the house an ambitious formal garden, already containing some lively ornamental planting, is evolving. The true spirit of the place lies in the beautiful natural lie of the land. Bill is a former computer programmer who saw the light and has made himself an expert on Himalayan poppies; the nursery sells the finest range of *Meconopsis* commercially available. The emphasis is on herbaceous perennials, particularly species and forms, with lovely aquilegias, digitalis, primulas and violas. An excellent catalogue (four 1st-class stamps) is produced but there is no mail order service.

CRARAE GARDENS

Strathclyde

Crarae,
by Inveraray PA32 8YA
10m S of Inveraray by A83
Tel: 01546 886614

Owner: The Crarae Garden Charitable Trust

Open: Summer, daily 9–6; winter, daily dawn–dusk.
50 acres

CRARAE GARDENS have a marvellous site in a precipitous glen on the north-west bank of Loch Fyne. At its centre is a romantic wooded ravine stuffed like a good plum pudding with plenty of rich delights. The great Asiatic flowering shrubs – azaleas, camellias, magnolias and rhododendrons – are well represented, together with choice collections of many other groups: several species of the southern beech *Nothofagus*, excellent rowans, lovely examples of styrax and much else. Paths girdle the glen which is occasionally traversed by wooden bridges, giving exceptional views of the magnificent plants and rushing waters of the rocky burn below. With its mild climate Crarae is worth visiting in any season, and there is always the piquant contrast of exotic introductions in a natural Scottish setting of special beauty.

CRATHES CASTLE

Grampian

nr Banchory AB31 3QJ
3m E of Banchory and 15m
SW of Aberdeen by the A93
Tel: 01330 844525
Fax: 01330 844797

Owner: The National Trust
for Scotland

Open: Daily 9–sunset.
92 acres. Castle open

ALTHOUGH THE bones of this garden are old – the superb yew hedges were planted in about 1700 and the romantic tower house dates from the 16th century – the garden is almost entirely of the 20th century. Sir James Burnett of Leys inherited the estate in 1926, and he and his wife started a new garden, much influenced by the Hidcote tradition of lavish plantings of often unusual plants within a firmly disciplined plan of enclosed areas. The Burnetts made a series of magnificent borders, some with single colour schemes – among the finest herbaceous borders in Britain. Gardeners from further south will note that herbaceous plants, because of the much longer daylight hours at this northern latitude, grow exceptionally well. All this is maintained impeccably, and visitors will learn much about practical gardening as well as enjoying an exceptionally beautiful place. In its day the garden at Crathes was a pioneer; today, it preserves its freshness and its power to inspire.

CULROSS PALACE

Fife

Culross KY12 8JH
In the centre of Culross,
14m SE of Stirling by A907
and B9037
Tel: 01383 880359

Owner: The National Trust
for Scotland

Open: Good Fri to Sept,
daily 11–5. 1/4 acre

THE LITTLE town of Culross is one of the most enchanting survivals in Scotland – a cluster of wonderfully preserved 17th- and 18th-century houses in a surprisingly isolated position hard by the banks of the Firth of Forth. The Palace has no royal associations; it was a grand merchant's house of the 17th century. The National Trust for Scotland recently completely restored it and had the excellent idea of recreating a period garden on the terraced slopes behind. The early 18th century was an important moment in Scottish garden history, when gardens were becoming increasingly cultivated for ornamental purposes. Period plants, culinary and ornamental, are arranged in a pattern of raised beds, and an arbour is covered with pleached mulberry and vines. The 'herbers', rough lawns, are cut with a hook to give the true shaggy texture of their time. It is a great success. The most memorable views of the garden are from the old leaded windows on the north side of the house.

CULZEAN CASTLE

Strathclyde

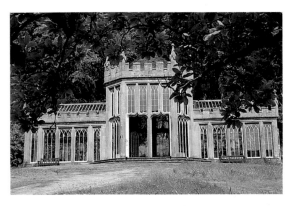

Maybole KA19 8LE
4m SW of Maybole and
12m S of Ayr by A719
Tel: 01655 760274
Fax: 01655 760615

Owner: The National Trust
for Scotland

Open: Daily 9.30–sunset.
120 acres. Castle open

Robert Adam's gothic castle – towered, turreted and irresistible – occupies a suitably dramatic site on the very brink of cliffs, looking north-west across the sea to the Isle of Arran. To the south of the castle, terraces with fine borders overlook a pool and fountain. Myrtles, cabbage palms, olearias and pittosporums flourish against the walls. In the walled former kitchen garden with its old glasshouses, fruit is still grown and there are rose and herbaceous borders. On the way, do not fail to visit the beautifully restored gothic camellia house (1818) – one of the prettiest garden buildings imaginable. The fine old woodland of the estate provides marvellous walks among magnificent 19th-century conifers, with huge numbers of bluebells, narcissi and snowdrops in spring.

DAWYCK BOTANIC GARDEN

Borders

Stobo EH45 9JU
8m SW of Peebles by A72
and B712
Tel: 01721 760254
Fax: 01721 760214

Owner: Royal Botanic
Garden Edinburgh

Open: Mar to Oct, daily
9.30–6. 60 acres

Dawyck is an enthralling place – a marvellous collection of plants set in beautiful country with a fascinating history. In the late 18th century Sir James Naesmyth came here and started planting up the garden. He subscribed to David Douglas's pioneer plant-hunting expedition to the Pacific north-west in the 1820s. Subsequent owners, in particular the Balfours, added to the collection which, in 1978, became part of the Royal Botanic Garden in

Edinburgh. The garden has a wonderful hilly site, with the sparkling Scrape burn rushing down a ravine under high-arched bridges. Ancient conifers – some of them the largest known specimens – dominate the scene but there are also many fine ornamental broad-leafed trees and shrubs, especially maples, berberis, cotoneaster and rhododendrons. A particularly interesting collection of Scottish native plants, some unique to Scotland, includes rowans and birches. There is much to see in any season and the lie of the land is so attractive that it makes a marvellous place for a long, varied and informative walk.

DRUMMOND CASTLE GARDENS

Tayside

Muthill, nr Crieff PH7 4HZ
2m S of Crieff by A822
Tel: 01764 681257
Fax: 01764 681550

Owner: Grimsthorpe and
Drummond Castle Trust

Open: Easter weekend 2–6;
May to Oct, daily 2–6.
15 acres

THE CASTLE is composed of buildings of different periods – chiefly a late medieval keep and a fine 17th-century house. Backed by old woodland, it sits at the top of a slope below which spreads one of the most extraordinary formal gardens in Britain. Inspired by 17th-century garden taste, it was laid out in the 1830s when garden makers looked to the past for inspiration. A huge rectangle is divided by paths forming a St Andrew's cross, with a magnificent multi-facetted sundial at the centre, and within the areas formed by this division an intricate symmetrical pattern of ornament and planting is laid out. Box-edged parterres are filled with roses, bedding schemes or gravel, and height is given by a profusion of stone urns, clipped cones of yew, Portugal laurels and purple Japanese maples. These varied ingredients are given order by the firm underlying pattern of the design, and the place has an exuberant and festive air.

DUNROBIN CASTLE GARDENS
Highland

Golspie KW10 6RR
1m N of Golspie by A9
Tel: 01408 633177
Fax: 01408 634081

Owner:
The Sutherland Trust

Open: Daily 10.30–5.30.
5 acres. Castle open

Dunrobin is the ancient estate of the earls and dukes of Sutherland, and at its centre is a wonderful 19th-century fantasy castle, with a touch of the Loire and a dash of Bavaria, rising cheerfully on the slopes above the Dornoch Firth. Sir Charles Barry rebuilt the house in its present form, and almost certainly laid out the formal gardens on terraces that descend to the sea. The first terrace wall gives shelter to a long border with bold mixed plantings. Below this, a circular parterre in Barry's full-blown formal style has box-edged compartments planted with roses, geraniums and potentillas, with clipped domes of yew rising above them.

EDROM NURSERIES
Borders

Illustration:
Roscoea cautleyoides

Coldingham,
Eyemouth TD14 5TZ
12m NW of Berwick-upon-Tweed by A1 and A1107
Tel: 01890 771386

Open: Mar to Sept, Mon to Fri 10–4.30, Sat and Sun 2–5

This is not a large nursery but it has a very carefully chosen list of excellent plants, some of which are rarely found for sale. The great speciality is alpines, but there are a few rhododendrons and various oddities that have caught the nursery's fancy (like *Zaluzianskya ovata* from Lesotho). In the alpine department there are androsaces, marvellous gentians,

lewisias, several meconopsis and one of the most
fastidiously selected collections of primulas you will
find anywhere. There is an excellent catalogue (s.a.e.
9 × 5in) from which mail orders are fulfilled.

EDZELL CASTLE

Tayside

Edzell, nr Brechin DD9 7UE
7m N of Brechin by A90
and B966
Tel: 01356 648631

Owner: Historic Scotland

Open: Apr to Sept, daily
9.30–6.30 (Sun 12–6.30);
Oct to Mar, daily except Fri
9.30–4.30 (Thur 9.30–2 and
Sun 2–4.30). 1 acre

IN THE early 17th century the now ruined castle of
the Lindsays had a fine ornamental garden, or
'pleasaunce', enclosed in walls carved with the Lindsay
arms and all kinds of symbolic motifs representing
virtues, the arts and planetary deities. To this rare and
beautiful survival was added in the 1930s a box-edged
parterre of vaguely 17th-century character – a pretty
sight viewed from the upper rooms of the castle and
towers of the garden walls.

FALKLAND PALACE

Fife

Falkland KY7 7BU
11m N of Kircaldy by A912
Tel: 01337 857397

Owner: The National Trust
for Scotland

Open: Good Fri to Oct,
Mon to Sat 11–5.30, Sun
1.30–5.30. 7 acres. Palace
open

HIDDEN BEHIND stone walls in the centre of
Falkland, the gardens still have the feeling of a
royal 'privy' garden. The 16th-century palace of the
Kings of Scotland, formerly a Stewart hunting lodge,
gives immense character to what is an almost entirely
20th-century garden. Large areas of lawn are broken
by island beds lavishly planted with shrubs and
ornamental trees – a scheme designed by Percy Cane in

the 1950s. These beds are straight where they run parallel to the perimeter walls but curved where they face each other across the lawn, forming a lively sinuous walk between them. A giant mixed border almost 500ft long faces west across the lawn to a blue and white herbaceous border and a dazzling border of delphiniums. At the southern extremity of the lawn, monumental yew hedges shelter a lily pond, and at an upper level there is a formal arrangement of yellow ('Allgold') and scarlet ('Frensham') roses – the heraldic colours of the Stewarts – underplanted with lavender and silver *Brachyglottis greyi* and given emphasis with pyramids of golden yew. This, although wholly modern, evokes the spirit of renaissance symbolism.

GLENWHAN GARDEN

Dumfries and Galloway

HIGH ABOVE the main road to Stranraer, Glenwhan Garden spreads out over a windy hilltop with marvellous views of Luce bay and the Mull of Galloway. Since 1979 the Knotts have made a very large, interesting and individual garden which is filled

Dunragit,
by Stranraer DG9 8PH
7m E of Stranraer by A75
Tel and Fax: 01581 400222

Owner:
Tessa and William Knott

Open: Mar to Oct, daily
10–5. 12 acres

with good plants. At its heart is an extensive pool divided by a grassy causeway and fed by a tumbling stream. The slopes above are lavishly planted with trees and shrubs. Several different habitats are provided by the lie of the land, and the wet, mild climate promotes luxuriant growth. There is no point in beginning to list plants – almost any gardener will find something unfamiliar here. But this is not just a plant collection for there are all sorts of well-planned ornamental schemes and wonderful views over water and hills. A nursery attached to the garden sells a wide range of herbaceous and woody plants of the kind seen growing in the garden.

GREENBANK GARDEN

Strathclyde

Flenders Road, Clarkston,
Glasgow G76 8RB
6m S of city centre
Tel: 0141 639 3281

Owner: The National Trust
for Scotland

Open: Daily 9.30–sunset
(closed 25–26 Dec and
1–2 Jan). 16 acres

Illustration opposite: The
cascade at the Hermitage

GREENBANK IS a very decorative 18th-century house of stucco and stone with a pediment capped with urns. South of the house an old walled kitchen garden, of the same date as the house, is divided into several enclosures with, at its heart, a rondel of clipped yew hedges and a sundial. In other enclosed areas there is that beguiling mixture, so often found in Scottish gardens, of ornamental planting and fruit and vegetables. Old espaliered apple trees rise out of mixed borders which are particularly rich in shrub roses, and orderly vegetable beds spread beneath the walls. A woodland garden threaded with walks provides further seclusion. The Glasgow suburbs press all around, but Greenbank preserves a delicious rural character.

THE HERMITAGE

Tayside

1m W of Dunkeld, 16m N
of Perth, signposted off the
A9
Tel: 01796 473233

Owner: The National Trust
for Scotland

Open: Daily dawn–dusk.
37 acres

THERE IS not much here for lovers of flower power, but for connoisseurs of dramatic atmosphere few places can beat it. A path winds along the banks of the fast-flowing river Braan through cool coniferous woods; all about are Douglas firs (*Pseudotsuga menziesii*), some of immense size. Soon a vast placid pool is seen, with a mossy stone bridge arching over a narrow ravine, and, on one side, the Hermitage itself. A tremendous roar increases as the visitor enters the

building. An open platform reveals the source of the noise – a spectacular broad waterfall, below the Hermitage on its far side, whose waters lunge between great boulders. The Hermitage was built in 1758 by the heir to the 2nd Duke of Atholl, who named it Ossian's Hall; deeper in the woods lies a rustic grotto, Ossian's Cave. William Wordsworth's sister, Dorothy, visited it in its heyday in 1805 and vividly described the Hermitage, much admiring 'the beauties of the place . . . dizzy and alive with waterfalls.'

HILL OF TARVIT HOUSE

Fife

nr Cupar KY15 5PD
2 1/2m S of Cupar by A916
Tel: 01334 653127

Owner: The National Trust for Scotland

Open: Apr to Oct, daily 9.30–9.30; Nov to Mar, daily 9.30–4.30. 10 acres. House open

ROBERT LORIMER rebuilt the 17th-century mansion at Hill of Tarvit in 1906, and gave it a new formal garden on the slopes below. Here an avenue of sentinel yews, blown sideways by the wind, links yew-hedged terraces which descend to the pastures below. A long border under the first terrace is planted with perennials and annuals and, specially planned for the blind and those with poor sight, a section of aromatic plants with labels in braille. On one side a lead satyr pipes at the centre of a formal rose garden, and by the house a well-head is decorated with a beautiful wrought-iron overthrow designed by Lorimer. Above the house, sweeping along a high wall interrupted by a grand iron gate, a deep border has repeated plantings of kolkwitzia, purple cotinus, philadelphus and *Rosa moyesii* underplanted with anemones, campanulas, geraniums and potentillas. The wonderfully atmospheric Edwardian potting shed, heady with compost, is also on view.

HOUSE OF DUN

Tayside

Angus DD10 9LQ
4m NW of Montrose by A935
Tel: 01674 810264
Fax: 01674 810722

Owner: The National Trust for Scotland

Open: Daily, 9.30–sunset. 45 acres. House open

THE HOUSE of Dun, a very pretty villa by William Adam, started in 1730, has an enviable position embowered in woodland on gently sloping land with views of Montrose Basin. To one side of the house Lady Augusta's Walk follows a tumbling burn through woodland, and has an air of agreeable melancholy. In front of the house a long gravel walk, hedged in yew on one side, runs along a wall on which are trained many old varieties of apple and pear, some of which are old Scottish cultivars for which these parts were particularly noted. At the end of the walk a restored formal rose garden is sheltered by old stone walls.

HOUSE OF PITMUIES

Tayside

Guthrie,
by Forfar DD8 2SN
8m E of Forfar by A932
Tel: 01241 828245

Owner:
Mrs Farquhar Ogilvie

Open: Apr to Oct, daily
10–5. 25 acres

TO THE front of the early Georgian house a gentlemanly atmosphere prevails – fine parkland beyond a ha-ha is framed by old trees, including an exceptional sweet chestnut. The flower garden lies behind the house where, in an old walled garden, lavishly planted borders are planned to maintain their flowering interest over a very long season. Colour schemes are fastidiously chosen; a double border, for example, seen from the drawing-room window, has a scheme of blue, cream, white and yellow to go with the colours of the room. Throughout this part of the garden use is made of shrub roses but abundant other planting, woody and herbaceous, extends the flowering period. The busy-ness of borders is alleviated by occasional simpler schemes – a collection of old delphinium cultivars; a stately walk of *Prunus serrula*

with its glistening, peeling bark; hedges of coppiced
Prunus pissardii; and an airy arch of clipped silver
pear. The kitchen garden has a very pretty formal
potager. Beyond the garden walls a riverside walk leads
past a castellated dovecote through old woodland.

INSHRIACH NURSERY
Highland

Aviemore PH22 1QS
2m SW of Aviemore by
B970
Tel: 01540 651287
Fax: 01540 651656

Open: Daily 9–5 (Sat 9–4,
Bank Hol Sun 1–5)

A MONG ALPINE plant enthusiasts this is one of the
best known nurseries in Britain. It was founded
before World War II by Jack Drake, a former colleague
of Will Ingwersen's. A very wide range is carried, and
rarities pop up all the time. The exceptionally
informative main list (£1.00) also includes plants
suitable for wild and bog gardens – supplementary
lists describe rare plants and alpine seeds. A mail order
service is provided. The nursery lies in fine birch and
juniper woodland and parts of it have been attractively
arranged to show the plants in action.

INVERESK LODGE GARDEN
Lothian

nr Musselburgh
EH21 6BQ
6m E of Edinburgh by
minor roads
Tel: 01721 722502

Owner: The National
Trust for Scotland

Open: All year, Mon to Fri
10–4.30, Sat and Sun 2–5.
13 acres

I NVERESK IS a charming village rich in distinguished
houses of the 17th and 18th centuries. Inveresk
Lodge belongs to the earlier period, and the
unpretentious walled garden with its decorative central
sundial complements it well. An excellent rose border

was designed by Graham Stuart Thomas; a raised alpine bed is filled with ericaceous plants; good use is made of smaller flowering trees like cherries; and the garden is a model of appropriate and floriferous planting in a modest space.

INVEREWE

Highland

Poolewe IV22 2LQ
6m NE of Gairloch by A832
Tel: 01445 781200
Fax: 01445 781497

Owner: The National Trust for Scotland

Open: 15 Mar to Oct, daily 9.30–9; Nov to 14 Mar 1999, daily 9.30–5. 62 acres

FAMOUS GARDENS do not always live up to their reputations but it would be hard to imagine any gardener failing to be excited by Inverewe. In 1862 Osgood Mackenzie came to this very remote corner of the western Highlands – a windswept, bare rocky site at the very edge of a sea loch. It was fifteen years before he got much to grow, but once windbreaks began to be established, the high rainfall and balmy Gulf Stream Drift climate promoted luxuriant growth. Today it is a jungle of mature exotic trees and shrubs, laced with winding walks, rising and falling, which give sudden glimpses of shimmering water through foliage. Spring is obviously the showiest season but flowering interest continues throughout the year; in any case, there is immense pleasure to be had at any time in admiring the exotic bark of giant eucalyptus, myrtles and rhododendrons and much strange and beautiful foliage.

KELLIE CASTLE

Fife

nr Pittenweem KY10 2RF
3m NW of Pittenweem by B9171
Tel: 01333 720271

Owner: The National Trust for Scotland

Open: Daily 9.30–sunset. 1 1/3 acre. Castle open

ON SOUTH-FACING slopes to the sea, Kellie Castle, with its crow-steps and turrets, is the perfect Scottish castle. It dates from the 16th to the 17th century but the little walled garden nestling against the castle walls was laid out in 1880 by Robert Lorimer when still a schoolboy. Here at Kellie, his family home, he made a romantic garden of gravel paths, box-edged beds and rose arbours – inspired by 17th-century Scottish gardens. His, too, is the gardener's house in the north-west corner with a jaunty carved stone bird on the ridge. Much replanting has recently been done, and organic methods used throughout the garden keep it in the pink of good health.

KILDRUMMY CASTLE GARDENS

Grampian

nr Alford AB33 8RA
10m from Alford by A944
Tel: 01975 571277/571203

Owner: Kildrummy Castle
Garden Trust

Open: Apr to Oct, daily
10–5. 15 acres

KILDRUMMY IS in the tradition of romantic Victorian gardens where the most important ingredient is the response to the site. Here, in a glen through which flows the burn of Backden, sandstone was quarried in the late Middle Ages to make Kildrummy Castle whose ruins rise above the old silver firs and beeches that clothe the glen. The estate was bought in 1898 by Colonel James Ogston, a soap tycoon, who developed the garden, using the old quarry, the linked pools of the burn, and its wooded banks. He commissioned a rock garden from the famous firm of Backhouse, and this today has a good collection of alpine plants. A high arched stone bridge spans the burn, and paths on its banks give views of rhododendrons and other flowering shrubs.

KINROSS HOUSE

Tayside

Kinross KY13 7ET
In the centre of Kinross

Owner:
Mr James Montgomery

Open: May to Sept, daily
10–7. 4 acres

DECORATIVE GATE-PIERS mark the entrance to Kinross House, and an avenue of limes leads straight as an arrow to the house itself – long, low and with a distinct whiff of something French. It was designed in the 1680s by Sir William Bruce for his own use, and he also designed the garden that goes with it. The entrance avenue forms a central axis which continues on the far side of the house to a gate with a beautifully carved stone surround, through which are glimpsed the ruins of Loch Leven castle. Romantically sited on an island, this is where Mary Queen of Scots was imprisoned in 1567. The garden between the house and the loch descends in gentle terraces with grassy walks and herbaceous borders. A deep border runs along the far wall, which is handsomely decorated with piers and heraldic animals. There is nothing like Kinross; it has unique character.

LEITH HALL

Grampian

Kennethmont,
by Huntly AB54 4QQ
1m N of Kennethmont, 6m
S of Huntly by B9002
Tel: 01464 831216

Owner: The National Trust
for Scotland

Open: Daily 9.30–sunset.
25 acres

THE HALL is a handsome mid 17th-century mansion, the ancestral home of the Leith and Leith-Hay family. Although there are traces of an early 18th-century layout, the present garden is an almost entirely 20th-century creation, chiefly by Charles and Henrietta Leith-Hay before World War I. Here are ebullient borders flourishing as they flourish nowhere better than in Scotland. A 1920s rock garden has been replanted by the Scottish Rock Garden Club and everywhere there are excellent plants to admire – in particular a splendid collection of primulas. The fine beech woods are full of wood anemones, and views of the Coreen Hills and the surrounding rural landscape make a beautiful backdrop.

LOCHSIDE ALPINE NURSERY

Highland

Ulbster KW2 6AA
7m S of Wick by A9
Tel: 01955 651320

Open: Mar to Oct, daily
10–6; also by appointment

TERRY AND Jane Clarke's nursery is almost certainly the northernmost supplier of good plants in Britain – and possibly in Europe; it is about the same latitude as Stockholm. It is so remote that it offers its visitors bed and breakfast hospitality, which is an arrangement that makes even more sense now that they no longer provide a mail order service. Their stock is chiefly herbaceous and full of good things at exceptionally reasonable prices: campanulas in variety, cyclamen, outstanding gentians, many phlox, a long list of primulas and wonderful saxifrages. It is never possible for them to list everything that is for sale at the nursery so a visit is to be recommended.

LOGAN BOTANIC GARDEN

Dumfries and Galloway

Port Logan,
Stranraer DG9 9ND
12m S of Stranraer by A716
Tel: 01776 860231
Fax: 01776 860333

Owner: Trustees of the
Royal Botanic Garden
Edinburgh

Open: Mar to Oct, daily
10–6.30. 30 acres

PORT LOGAN lies in the middle of a narrow spit of land, the Mull of Galloway, which juts out into the sea in the extreme south-west of Scotland. A grove of Chusan palms immediately announces the character of this place – sub-tropical plants flourish here and provide some rare and beautiful sights. The garden was started by the McDouall family who lived here for 800 years, and since 1969 it has been in the care of the Royal Botanic Garden at Edinburgh. But this is not just a botanic garden, for it is beautifully laid out, particularly in the walled garden which has fine terraces and well planned borders under an avenue of cabbage palms (*Cordyline australis*). The climate is exceptionally mild and different habitats provide conditions for a huge range of tender plants. A small selection of plants is offered for sale.

MALLENY HOUSE GARDEN

Lothian

Balerno EH14 7AF
In Balerno, 7m SW of
Edinburgh by A70
Tel: 0131 449 2283

Owner: The National Trust
for Scotland

Open: Apr to Oct, daily
9.30–7; Nov to Mar, daily
9.30–4. 2 acres

THE HOUSE at Malleny is an ornamental riddle, with features of the 17th and 18th centuries and hints of something much older. Its tower and conical roof on the garden side contribute much to the atmosphere of the place. A walled enclosure divided by a yew hedge lies at the heart of the garden, with a splendid quartet of ancient yew trees clipped into the shape of pointed mushrooms. Roses are everywhere, and Malleny has a National Collection of 19th-century shrub roses which are mingled with other plants in handsome mixed borders on two sides of the walled garden. There is, in addition, a separate collection of modern roses. Displayed in a corner of the garden behind the greenhouse is a collection of bonsai arranged by the Scottish Bonsai Society. Despite being in the suburbs of Edinburgh, Malleny has a rare quality – the remote and soothing atmosphere of an old-fashioned garden in the depths of the country.

MELLERSTAIN

Borders

nr Gordon TD3 6LG
9m NW of Kelso by A6089
Tel: 01573 410225
Fax: 01573 410636

Owner: The Earl of Haddington

Open: Easter weekend 12.30–5; May to Sept, daily except Sat 12.30–5. House open

THE GREAT early 18th-century house at Mellerstain, designed by William Adam and later added to by his son Robert, originally had a formal garden that was removed in the 18th-century landscape gardening craze. In the early 20th century, however, a version of it was reinstated by the architect Sir Reginald Blomfield. A row of clipped cones of yew runs across the back of the house, and balustraded terraces descend in stately progression – starting with a splendid double staircase – ornamented with parterres of modern roses, lavender, clipped shapes of box and generous lawns. All this provides a contrastingly formal but decorative foreground for the curvaceous lake set in woodland below – with idyllic views of the Cheviot Hills in the distance.

THE MURREL GARDENS

Fife

Aberdour KY3 0RN
1m N of Aberdour on B157
Fax: 01383 860157

Owner: Mrs J. Milne

Open: Apr to Oct, daily except Sat and Sun 10–5 (weekends by appointment). 7 1/2 acres

HIDDEN IN a fold of land facing south towards the Firth of Forth, The Murrel has a rare site. Designed in 1908 by Frank Deas in the Arts and Crafts style, the house and garden have been excellently restored since 1984 by a new owner. To one side of the house, on south-facing slopes, a walled garden gives protection to many tender plants such as *Buddleja crispa* and *Pittosporum tobira*, rarely seen out-of-doors in these parts. Below the walled garden a formal sunken garden with rose beds leads to a water garden overhung with old rhododendrons and ornamental trees. A ravine-like wild garden, still being replanted but already memorably beautiful, leads back up the hill where, to the west of the house, a large rock garden is laid out with scree beds. An excellent range of plants, some unusual and propagated in the garden, is for sale.

THE PINEAPPLE

Central

Dunmore, nr Stirling
On the Dunmore Estate
(enter by East Lodge) 6m
SE of Stirling by A905
Tel: 01628 825925

Owner: The National Trust
for Scotland

Open: Daily 10–sunset

THE PINEAPPLE is a wonderful survival, a banqueting house of lovely eccentricity. Built in 1761 in the great kitchen garden of Dunmore Castle, it was given to The National Trust for Scotland which leased it to The Landmark Trust which has beautifully restored it. No architect is known but the craftsmanship is superb – the pineapple leaves are exquisitely carved in stone, and curvaceous gothic windows ornament the second floor. The former kitchen garden has been replanted as a formal orchard with rows of fruit trees planted in turf. The interior of The Pineapple is private; it may, however, be rented as a holiday house from The Landmark Trust (Shottesbrooke, Maidenhead, Berkshire SL6 3SW. Tel: 01628 825925).

PITMEDDEN

Grampian

IN THIS remote corner of Aberdeenshire is one of the most beguiling gardens you could hope to see. There was a garden here in the 17th century but in 1818 the house was burnt down, the estate changed hands and the original garden disappeared. However, the garden

nr Pitmedden,
Ellon AB4 0PD
14m N of Aberdeen by
A920 and B999
Tel: 01651 842352

Owner: The National Trust
for Scotland

Open: May to Sept, daily
10–5.30. 4 3/4 acres

walls, elegant pavilions, garden steps and gate-piers all survived, and in 1954 The National Trust for Scotland planted immense formal parterres with a central avenue of clipped yew pyramids and a fountain. The parterres are edged in intricately shaped box hedges with compartments filled with coloured chippings and arrangements of annuals, blocks of a single colour, changing every year. Looking down from the surrounding terraces with their beautiful gazebos, the effect is marvellous. Running along the south- and east-facing walls are a pair of good borders, and above the walled garden a tunnel of old varieties of apples leads to a formal herb garden. Pitmedden has an enchanting atmosphere, unlike any other garden.

POLLOK HOUSE

Glasgow

2060 Pollokshaws Road,
Glasgow G43 1AT
3m SW of the city centre by
A77 and B762
Tel: 0141 632 0274

Owner: City of Glasgow
District Council

Open: Daily except 25 Dec
and 1 Jan, Mon to Sat 10–5,
Sun 11–5. 361 acres

ALTHOUGH NOW engulfed by urban sprawl, the Pollok House estate, for 800 years the property of the Maxwell family, preserves the beautiful character of old parkland. The dashing grey stone house was built in the mid 18th century and has pretty formal gardens spreading out below the house. From box-edged parterres and a gravel walk a double staircase leads to a lower terrace with lovely views of the parkland on the far side of the river. Elegant ogee-roofed pavilions overlook the terrace, and to one side a path leads up to a grassy walk between beds planted with Himalayan birches underplanted with hostas and backed by rhododendrons. Nearby, through the woods, is the famous Burrell Collection.

POYNTZFIELD HERB NURSERY

Highland

Poyntzfield, Black Isle,
by Dingwall IV7 8LX
5m W of Cromarty on
B9163
Tel and Fax: 01381 610352

Open: Mar to Sept, Mon to
Sat 1–5 (Jun to Aug, also
Sun 1–5)

THIS IS one of the northernmost nurseries in Britain, which gives it a special interest. It specialises in herbs and, over the years, a collection of varieties has been built up that are hardy in this climate. Thus, anyone buying plants here may be confident that they are acquiring pretty tough customers. Over 300 varieties are stocked, all organically grown, and there is a particularly attractive collection of culinary and medicinal plants native to

Scotland. An excellent catalogue (three 1st-class stamps and s.a.e.) is produced, the only one I know of that gives common names in Gaelic, where they exist. A mail order service is provided.

ROYAL BOTANIC GARDEN

Edinburgh

Inverleith Row,
Edinburgh EH3 5LR
1m N of the city centre
Tel: 0131 552 7171
Fax: 0131 552 0382

Owner: Trustees of the
Royal Botanic Garden
Edinburgh

Open: Nov to Jan, daily
9.30–4 (closed 25 Dec and 1
Jan); Feb, daily 9.30–5;
Mar, daily 9.30–6; Apr to
Jun, daily 9.30–7; Jul to
Aug, daily 9.30–8; Sept,
daily 9.30–6; Oct, daily
9.30–5. 67 acres

THE ROYAL Botanic Garden was founded in 1670 and moved to its present site in 1820. The beauty of the setting – high, undulating land with sweeping views of the city to the south and the hills beyond the Firth of Forth to the north – the exemplary standards of upkeep, and the liveliness of it all make it exceptional. Unlike other botanic gardens, Edinburgh seems to have the interests of the ordinary gardener close to heart. There are areas of specific habitats – an unforgettable rock garden, a woodland garden and a peat garden; collections of rhododendrons, heaths and alpines; several glasshouses; marvellous trees everywhere; and excellent demonstration gardens. Newly opened in 1997 is an admirable garden of Chinese plants – an old interest of the garden's – with a cascade, pool and elegant pavilion.

SCONE PALACE

Tayside

Illustration: The bark of
Chamaecyparis lawsoniana

THE BROWN stone palace, 16th-century but richly gothicised in the early 19th century, lies in beautiful parkland. The ornamental gardens by the palace are fairly perfunctory and the chief garden pleasure at Scone is a splendid and atmospheric

Scone, Perth PH2 6BD
2m NE of Perth on A93
Tel: 01738 552300
Fax: 01738 552588

Owner: Trust for Viscount
Stormont

Open: Good Fri to 12 Oct,
daily 9.30–5.15. 100 acres

pinetum. Started in 1848 by the 4th Earl of Mansfield, it contains many mature specimens, some of which date back to the original plantings. Several of these are trees of tremendous character – a Chinese fir (*Cunninghamia lanceolata*) with glowing cinnamon bark and gleaming fronds of foliage like demented bottle-brushes; a lovely old western hemlock (*Tsuga heterophylla*) with gnarled trunk and wide spreading branches. All these, disposed in attractive glades, are impeccably labelled. To one side – an encouraging sight – is a newly planted pinetum. Also at Scone is a Douglas fir (*Pseudotsuga menziesii*), the first planted in Britain and raised from seed sent by David Douglas in 1826. Douglas was a local man, from Dunkeld, and this historic tree is a memorable sight.

THREAVE GARDEN

Dumfries and Galloway

Stewartry,
Castle Douglas DG7 1RX
1m W of Castle Douglas by
A75
Tel: 01556 502575
Fax: 01556 502683

Owner: The National Trust
for Scotland

Open: Daily 9.30–sunset.
65 acres

THE NATIONAL Trust for Scotland has its own school of horticulture here, and the gardens, largely created by the students since the school started in 1960, are of great interest. Mature woodland of beech, conifers and oak forms the background to a large collection of shrub roses, sweeping mixed borders, many dwarf heathers and conifers, peat and rock gardens, a collection of over 200 narcissi and a youthful arboretum that is already showing its paces. A walled kitchen garden has splendidly blowsy borders and superbly maintained glasshouses. Threave holds a National Collection of penstemons.

YOUNGER BOTANIC GARDEN BENMORE

Argyll

Illustration:
Rhododendron morii

Benmore,
Dunoon PA23 8QU
7m N of Dunoon by A815
Tel: 01369 706261
Fax: 01369 706369

Owner: Trustees of The
Royal Botanic Garden
Edinburgh

Open: Mar to Oct, daily
9.30–6. 120 acres

THE YOUNGER Botanic Garden Benmore is a country annexe of the Royal Botanic Garden in Edinburgh. Its history starts in the 1820s with the first plantings of conifers, and today superb old specimens of Douglas firs, larches, Scots pines and a splendid avenue of Wellingtonias (*Sequiaodendron giganteum*) make a wonderful background to later collections of ornamental shrubs and trees. The mild climate and very high rainfall promotes spectacular growth in conifers, and some of the spcimens here are among the largest in the British Isles. The climate also makes this an ideal place for rhododendrons, and today there are about 250 different species, 100 subspecies and forms, and a further 300 hybrids and cultivars. There are excellent specimens, too, of deciduous trees such as southern beeches (*Nothofagus* species) and *Davidia involucrata*, and autumn is brilliant with the foliage of azaleas, cercidiphyllums, enkianthus and maples.

IRELAND

ALTAMONT GARDENS

County Carlow

Tullow
Between Tullow and
Bunclody, signposted off
N80 and N81
Tel: 0503 59302
Fax: 0503 59128

Owner: Mrs North

Open: Apr to Oct, Sun and
Bank Hol Mon 2–6; also by
appointment. 40 acres

ALTAMONT HAS a secret air and one of the charms of the place is that visitors may feel that they are making a private visit. The gardens lie behind a pretty 18th-century house, with a bold axial path leading gently downwards towards a lake. The path is overarched from time to time by venerable Irish yews trained to meet in the middle, and lined with borders, becoming narrower as they descend, in which shrub roses are the chief feature. On either side lawns – dotted with the occasional clucking domestic fowl – are backed by substantial groves of shrubs and trees, and half way down the drooping form of a fine deodar (*Cedrus deodarus*) makes a bold ornament. All this has a charmingly sleepy air but it is with the lake that Altamont becomes truly memorable. This is girdled with walks from which lovely views, especially those back towards the house, are revealed. A path plunges away from the water down the Ice Age Glen in which the occasional aristocratic rhododendron reminds you that this is not untouched primeval woodland.

ANNES GROVE

County Cork

THERE ARE two gardens at Annes Grove, each different and both memorably attractive. Just north of the handsome 18th-century house is a large walled garden with burgeoning herbaceous borders, beds of patterned box hedging, a mount with a rustic

Castletownroche
Signposted from the centre
of Castletownroche
Tel and Fax: 022 26145

Owner: Patrick Annesley

Open: mid Mar to Sept,
daily 10–5 (Sun 1–6).
40 acres

summerhouse and, all about the substantial walls, fine shrubs – hoherias, olearias, magnificent embothriums and much else. Annes Grove, however, is most famous for its Robinsonian woodland garden, laid out on a beautiful site above and along the looping river Awbeg. Dating from the early years of the 20th century, and drawing on newly introduced plants from the expeditions of Frank Kingdon-Ward and George Forrest, it has a lovely naturalistic character. In spring, magnolias and brilliant rhododendrons provide eye-stopping interludes among the trees, while fine groups of plants in a more restrained key adorn the banks of the river – waves of *Primula florindae*, the giant foliage of *Gunnera manicata* and *Lysichiton americanum*, all flourishing below the graceful spreading branches of *Cercidiphyllum japonicum*. For long walks in marvellous scenery animated by distinguished plants there are few places to beat Annes Grove, in Ireland or anywhere else.

ARDNAMONA

County Donegal

ARDNAMONA HAS a marvellous position hard by the banks of Lough Eske. The garden is an old one, going back to the 1830s when the Wray family started planting trees. Several beautiful specimens survive from these early plantings, among them monkey puzzles, *Sequoiadendron giganteum* and *Picea orientalis*. A second wave of planting took place towards the end of the 19th century when Sir Arthur

Lough Eske
On the W shore of Lough
Eske
Tel: 073 22650
Fax: 073 22819

Owner:
Amabel and Kieran Clarke

Open: Jan to May, daily
10–8; remainder of year by
appointment. 40 acres

and Lady Wallace, with connections at the National
Botanic Garden, introduced fine flowering shrubs. All
this was in a state of collapse when the Clarkes came
here in 1990. Embarking on an ambitious restoration,
they have already cleared the most important areas,
opening out fine vistas and revealing the beauty of
countless magnificent specimens. The tender large-
leafed species rhododendrons such as *R. sinogrande*
are particularly lovely and the whole place has
remarkable character. The Clarkes also receive guests
for B & B and for dinner.

BALLINLOUGH CASTLE

County Westmeath

Clonmellon
25km W of Navan by N51
and R154; or by Kells and
N52
Tel: 046 33135
Fax: 046 33331

Owner:
Sir John and Lady Nugent

Open: Apr to Sept, daily
except Fri 11–6 (Sun 2–6).
40 acres

A S SOON as you climb the winding drive (or avenue
as it is called in Ireland), with its beautiful
parkland trees all about, it is easy to succumb to the
romantic mood of Ballinlough. The towered and
battlemented castle is perched enticingly on a grassy
eminence above a lake. Views of it from the far side of
the lake are an essential part of a visit. To the north-
east of the castle is a pretty water garden with a rustic
summerhouse, and the banks of a stream attractively
planted with aconitums, dicentras, ferns, hellebores,
primulas, rodgersias and much else. The magnificent
old 3 1/2-acre walled kitchen gardens, at a little
distance from the castle, have been well restored,
giving a vivid impression of the great days of an Irish
estate. Here are newly planted beech hedges, attractive
herbaceous borders, a walled rose garden with a
gazebo, and a large formal orchard of apples,
damsons, medlars and mulberries.

BALLYMALOE COOKERY SCHOOL GARDENS

County Cork

Shanagarry, Midleton
30km E of Cork by N25
and R632
Tel: 021 646785
Fax: 021 646909

Owner:
Tim and Darina Allen

Open: Apr to Oct, daily
9–6. 10 acres

TIM ALLEN'S parents, Myrtle and Ivan, started the legendary Ballymaloe House Hotel. The cookery school, not far away at Shanagarry, is the particular province of Tim and his wife, Darina, who have also created a charming, rapidly expanding garden. Part of this is given over to formal gardens of fruit, vegetables and herbs but other parts are purely ornamental and have recently been extended on a grandiose scale. A magnificent pair of double herbaceous borders now leads out to an elegant little summerhouse. Nothing quite prepares you for the exquisite interior – it is encrusted in shells arranged in inventive abstract patterns – the work of Blot Kerr-Wilson. To one side is a vast newly planted hedge maze of yew – and more features are being planned for the garden.

BIRR CASTLE DEMESNE

County Offaly

Birr
On the edge of the town
Tel: 0509 20023/20056
Fax: 0509 21583/20425

Owner: The Earl of Rosse

Open: Daily 9–6 or dusk if
earlier. 120 acres.

THE BIRR Castle estate has been in the possession of the same family since the beginning of the 17th century. The demesne was finely landscaped in the 18th century and the last three generations of the family have been assiduous plant collectors and patrons of several of the great plant-hunting expeditions – of E.H. Wilson, George Forrest, Augustine Henry and others. The demesne today is not only magnificently endowed with fine plants in a beautiful landscape but also possesses, to one side of the castle, most attractive formal gardens, largely the creation of the parents of the present Earl. Two rivers meet at Birr, so the grounds are well watered and the river Camcor, rushing past quite close to the castle, has a particularly ornamental presence. It has a romantic cascade, is spanned by an elegant early iron suspension bridge, and has beautiful terrace walks and much distinguished planting along its banks. North-west of the castle is the 3rd Earl's giant telescope, mounted in a castellated building like some exotic medieval keep. With this telescope, in 1845, the 3rd Earl first observed and described the spiral shape of constellations. In 1995 his descendant celebrated the 150th anniversary of this discovery by planting a whirlpool pattern of *Tilia cordata* nearby. The formal gardens to the north of the castle have soothing cloisters of clipped hornbeam, a parterre-like arrangement of lilac in box-edged beds, beautiful 17th-century stone urns and a pair of white-painted wooden benches whose backs trace the initials of Anne and Michael Rosse.

BUTTERSTREAM GARDEN

County Meath

Kildalkey Road, Trim
On the edge of Trim village, 40km NW of Dublin by N3 and R154
Tel: 046 36017
Fax: 046 31702

Owner: Jim Reynolds

Open: Apr to Sept, daily 11–6. 8 acres

Butterstream is a key garden in modern Irish gardening. It shows a striking mixture of ingredients, woven together in distinctive harmony, and it is impossible to imagine any gardener failing to be delighted by it. There are traces of Robinsonian natural gardening – an unspoilt stream winds its way through the garden – contrasted with highly sophisticated passages of formal design and subtle juxtaposition of plants. The site is a flat one and the garden, divided into many compartments, is essentially inward-looking – although a new arrangement of canals under construction when I visited in 1997 directed the eye to the far horizon, with hints of Versailles-like ambitions. The owner and passionate gardener, Jim Reynolds, started the garden in the early 1970s, inspired by the 'irrational desire to possess a few roses'. A marvellous collection of roses, kept in check by trim box-edged enclosures, is one of the delights of the garden today. Wherever you look there is something to enchant and educate the eye, providing inspiration for owners of gardens of any size.

CASTLE WARD

County Down

Strangford,
Downpatrick BT30 7LS
7m NE of Downpatrick on
A25
Tel: 01396 881204
Fax: 01396 881729

Owner: The National Trust

Open: Daily dawn–dusk.
40 acres. Castle open

CASTLE WARD is a knockout 18th-century house, coolly classical on one side and vivaciously gothick on the other. With a beautiful position on the southern banks of Strangford Lough, its grounds make a wonderful place for a long walk punctuated by many stops to admire both the scenery and exceptional trees. The microclimate here is amazingly benign, wet and warm, promoting vigorous growth in trees. In the old woodland, chiefly of oak and beech, are exotics, particularly conifers, which have grown to giant size. Here are notable examples of *Sequoiadendron giganteum*, an extraordinary many-stemmed western cedar (*Thuja plicata*) and, a tender rarity, the Patagonian cypress, *Fitzroya cupressoides*. The fine remains of an 18th-century park include a lake overlooked by a pedimented Doric Temple and, at some distance from the house, Old Castle Ward is a fortified tower dating from the early 17th century.

CASTLEWELLAN NATIONAL ARBORETUM

County Down

THE ANNESLEY family started this great arboretum and plant collection in the 1870s. It benefits from a fine site in the foothills of the Mourne Mountains near the coast in southern County Down. On the wooded slopes east of the castle is the original 12-acre walled arboretum, now called the Annesley Garden,

Castlewellan BT31 9BU
30m S of Belfast by A24
and minor roads
Tel: 03967 78664
Fax: 013967 71762

Owner: Department of
Agriculture (Northern
Ireland)

Open: Daily 10–dusk.
108 acres

which has fine borders and exceptional flowering
shrubs and trees, many of them rare and tender species
from the southern hemisphere, such as the evergreen
Carpodetus serratus from New Zealand and
Librocedrus uvifera from the Andes. North of the
walled garden, azaleas, camellias and rhododendrons
thrive under the canopy of beech and oak. An area of
woodland by the curving lake is planted with
deciduous trees chosen for especially brilliant autumn
colouring. Throughout the arboretum there are
outstanding specimens, several of which date from the
original 19th-century plantings, giving great character
to the place.

CREAGH GARDENS
County Cork

Skibereen
6km SW of Skibereen by
R595
Tel and Fax: 028 22121

Owner: Gwendoline
Harold-Barry Trust

Open: Daily 10–6. 20 acres

THE HANDSOME bow-fronted late Georgian house,
swathed in rich reddy brown stucco, is repeatedly
glimpsed rising on its eminence among trees in the
gardens at Creagh. This woodland garden capitalises
on an exquisite setting by the calm waters of Baltimore
Bay. South-west of the house a little thatched
summerhouse is overshadowed by a strange and tender
shrub, the very rare Tasmanian waratah, *Telopea
mongaensis*, with startling scarlet flowers in May like
many-legged spiders wriggling upside down.
Ornamental flowering shrubs are all about, in jungly
profusion, and a meandering former millpond is edged
with *Gunnera manicata* and ferns. If you follow the
pond you will come to the ruins of the mill itself,
looking amazingly like some carefully placed
picturesque folly, and to the very waters of the bay
where a grassy quay, with benches, affords delicious

views over the water. South of all this the magnificent walled kitchen garden has been beautifully restored, with box-edged beds of orderly produce and a most luxurious poultry house with chickens, ducks and geese. Near the walled garden a sign reads 'Ladies & Gentlemen will not, & others must not, pick the flowers or shrubs. Thank you.' This is a gentlemanly place, beautifully restored by new owners, with a charming atmosphere of peaceful melancholy.

DERREEN
County Kerry

Lauragh
On the edge of Lauragh village, 20km SW of Kenmare by N71 and R571
Tel: 064 83103

Owner:
The Hon. David Bigham

Open: Apr to Sept, daily 10–6. 80 acres

THE SCENERY in this part of County Kerry is spectacularly beautiful and Derreen occupies a dramatically undulating site with views of the pointed silhouette of the mountain Knockatee. The estate was acquired in the 17th century by the Petty family, one of whose descendants, the 5th Marquess of Lansdowne, greatly enriched the planting of the garden from 1870 onwards. The climate is wet and mild, and the soil acid, providing ideal conditions for the wild woodland garden that may be seen today. Many plants survive from the 19th century, some grown to huge size, such as the recumbent *Cryptomeria elegans* under which visitors may walk. The rust-coloured trunks of old rhododendrons and the speckled bark of *Luma apiculata* are magnificent. In the King's Ooze there is a splendid grove of tree ferns looking quite at home and Derreen is rich in other tender rarities, such as the Australian blackwood, *Acacia melanoxylon*.

THE DILLON GARDEN
County Dublin

45 Sandford Road,
Ranelagh, Dublin 6
2km S of the city centre
Tel and Fax: 01 497 1308

Owner:
Val and Helen Dillon

Open: Mar, Jul, Aug, daily
2–6; Apr to Jun, and Sept,
Sun 2–6. 3/4 acre

HELEN DILLON has become a great force for good in Irish gardening, and her books, television appearances and spreading renown lure keen gardeners from far afield to see her remarkable Dublin garden. Three qualities make it exceptional – a most fastidious plantsmanship, a strong sense of design and the highest standards of practical horticulture. There is a newly laid out front garden but it is the space behind the fine Georgian house that contains the Dillon essence. Although it is divided into enclosures, each with its own intense atmosphere, there are no solid walls to impede the view; low box hedges, airy trellis work or an arbour of apples, roses and honeysuckle provide firm but not unyielding structure. There is a lightness about the planting, too, with clouds of the variegated foliage of the dogwoods *Cornus mas* 'Variegata' and *C. controversa* 'Variegata', giving substance without dominating oppressively. Helen Dillon has a taste for the rare and aristocratic, such as the beautiful *Paeonia tenuifolia* 'Flore Pleno', but she values equally the old Bramley apple tree which was in the garden when she came. The planting is dense but it is interspersed with the relieving space of beautifully kept lawns, purposeful paths and alluring eyecatchers. A strong colour sense excludes any sense of jumble – the sombre purple foliage of cimicifuga, berberis, *Euphorbia* 'Chameleon' and bronze-leafed Queen Anne's lace is spiked with deep magenta *Knautia macedonica* and rich red *Astrantia* 'Ruby Wedding'. Few gardens of this size provide such exhilaration; Helen Dillon's passion for gardening is infectious.

DOWNHILL CASTLE
County Londonderry

42 Mussenden Road,
Castlerock,
Coleraine BT51 4RP
5m NW of Coleraine on A2
Tel: 01265 848728

Owner: The National Trust

Open: Daily dawn–dusk.
147 acres

DOWNHILL WAS the creation of an extraordinary 18th-century figure, Frederick Augustus Hervey, 4th earl of Bristol and Bishop of Derry who, from 1772 onwards, animated this beautiful site with some remarkable buildings and monuments. The burnt-out house is a shell only, but a distinguished one, rising up behind its ha-ha among grazing sheep and cattle. The most beautiful and memorable building here is the Mussenden Temple – domed, girdled with columns, and teetering on the very brink of a 200ft cliff, below which Atlantic rollers crash on sandy strands. Views from it are breathtakingly lovely. The gardens of the Bishop's Gate entrance lodge were prettily refashioned by the late Miss Jan Eccles from 1962. She replanted a decorative bog garden and added distinguished trees to the walk which leads to the ruined house.

DUNLOE CASTLE GARDENS
County Kerry

Dunloe
8km NW of Killarney by
R582
Tel: 064 31900
Fax: 064 32118

Owner:
Hotel Dunloe Castle

Open: 24 Apr to 1 Oct,
daily dawn–dusk. 3 acres

THE REMAINS of Dunloe Castle, with its gothic windows, form a pretty eyecatcher in the grounds of a large modern hotel. Here is a fine collection of trees, for which Roy Lancaster has written an admirable guide (available from the hotel reception). The climate here is very mild and some of the trees, such as the beautiful *Cupressus torulosa* 'Cashmeriana' and the South American *Lomatia ferruginea*, will be quite unfamiliar to gardeners from harsher climates. Some are of special Irish interest, such as the lovely hornbeam *Carpinus henryana*, introduced by the great Irish plant hunter Augustine Henry. The gardens are finely kept and no visitor will fail to find beautiful, and often rare, plants to admire.

EMO COURT GARDEN
County Laois

Illustration opposite:
The Mussenden Temple at
Downhill Castle

THE SPLENDID neo-classical house, originally called Emo Park, was built in the 1790s to the designs of James Gandon for the first Earl of Portarlington. Leading from the entrance is a spectacular avenue of

Emo
10km SW of Monasterevan
by N7
Tel and Fax: 0502 26573

Owner: Department of Art,
Heritage, Gaeltacht and the
Islands

Open: Daily dawn–dusk.
Guided tours by
appointment. 80 acres

Wellingtonias (*Sequoiadendron giganteum*), dating
from the 1840s, when it provided the entrance drive
from the Dublin road. To the east and north of the
house a solemn walk of Irish yews is embellished with
urns and statues, and from here the ground descends, a
grassy sward with oaks, limes and beeches. Mad
Margaret's Walk winds downhill through the woods to
a lake, and there is good recent decorative planting
between the lake and the house, including a fine walk
lined with *Davidia involucrata*. The place has the
stately character of an 18th-century landscape park,
with the the beautiful ruin of a domed gazebo.

FAIRFIELD LODGE

County Dublin

Monkstown Avenue,
Monkstown
7km S of the centre of
Dublin off road to Dún
Laoghaire (car ferry)
Tel and Fax: 01 280 3912

Owner: John S. Bourke

Open: May to Sept, Sun,
Wed and Bank Hol Mon
2–6; groups any day by
appointment

THIS VERY pretty miniature late Georgian house in
the suburbs of Dublin has a delightful garden
which shows what a creative imagination can do with
very limited space. The formal front garden is planted
with white and silver plants, some familiar – such as
'Iceberg' roses – others much less so – such as the
beautiful silvery *Celmisia semicordata*. Passing by an
enclosure in which a baby Neptune rules the placid
waters of a pool and golden foliage illuminates the
shade, the visitor comes to a rectangular space on the
far side of the house. Here, a Buddha presides over the
large leaves of *Fatsia japonica* and clumps of bamboo,
giving an Oriental feel, and at the far end a grand Pope
(the poet not the Pontiff) urn emerges from a sea of
Melianthus major. Everywhere there is good planting
and an unfettered decorative liveliness from which all
gardeners could learn.

FERNHILL

County Dublin

Sandyford
11km S of Dublin by R117
Tel: 01 295 6000

Owner: Mrs Sally Walker

Open: Mar to Oct, Tue, Sat
and Bank Hol Mon 11–5;
Sun 2–6. 40 acres

FERNHILL, ONE of the most attractive gardens in Ireland, has a potent and beguiling atmosphere. South of the house a superlative old sweet chestnut marks the beginning of the Broad Walk, a stately gravel path laid out in about 1860 by Mr Justice Darley. It is shaded by giant old Wellingtonias (*Sequoiadendron giganteum*) against a background of oak and beech woodland. At its far end a curious 'laurel lawn', a vast expanse of low-growing laurel, forms a sheet of glistening green about the trunks of old beeches. Fine collections of ferns and flowering shrubs animate the woods. When you turn back after walking up the hill, marvellous views of Dublin Bay are revealed over trees to the east. On the far side of the house a rock garden and stream garden are richly planted. Beyond them is the original garden, going back at least 200 years, where fruit and vegetables intermingle with decorative plants. Among the many roses here one of the most memorable is an old HT introduced by Dicksons in 1905 – 'Irish Elegance', with graceful single flowers of red suffused with apricot. Any visitor will succumb to the atmosphere of Fernhill and even the most knowledgeable plant-lover will find something unfamiliar and lovely.

FOTA ARBORETUM

County Cork

Fota Estate, Carrigtwohill
14km E of Cork by N25 and
R624
Tel: 021 812728/088 279908
Fax: 021 270244

Owner:
The Office of Public Works

Open: Daily, 10–5.30 (Sun
11–5.30). 32 acres

THE FOTA estate is on an island (connected by road to the mainland) in the estuary which opens out into Cork Harbour. It is an exceptionally protected site, with rich soil in which woody plants flourish as they do in few parts of the British Isles. The collection was started early in the 19th century by James Hugh Smith-Barry and some of the most remarkable specimens date back to this time – such as a marvellously battered Monterey pine (*Pinus radiata*) planted in 1847. Newly introduced conifers such as these are among the stars of the collection but there are also beautiful deciduous trees (including a lovely fern-leafed beech, *Fagus sylvatica* 'Asplenifolia') and tender shrubs such a gigantic *Drimys winteri*. A placid lake is surrounded with some of the best trees.

GLENVEAGH CASTLE

County Donegal

Church Hill
In Glenveagh National
Park, 16km NW of
Letterkenny by R251
Tel: 074 37090/37262
Fax: 074 37072

Owner: National Parks and
Wildlife Service

Open: Easter to first Sun in
Nov, daily 10–6.30. 28 acres

GLENVEAGH HAS a setting of unbeatable splendour on the shores of Lough Beagh, with the spectacular Derryveagh Mountains rearing up on the far side. The castle – wild, woolly and romantic rather than beautiful – was built by John Adair in the 1870s. It was bought in 1937 and restored by Henry McIlhenny, a cultivated American whose ancestors came from Donegal. With advice from a fellow American, Lanning Roper, and from James Russell, he made a most attractive garden on the slopes above. Its centrepiece lies immediately behind the castle: a walled garden of the traditional Irish kind in which the kitchen garden is embellished with ornamentals. Running across the middle is a pair of pretty borders with repeat planting of *Geranium psilostemon*, *G.* 'Johnson's Blue', *G. endressii*, catmint, loosestrife and *Eryngium alpinum*. An elegant conservatory jollifies the stern castle walls and all about are decorative details – lead cherubs on spheres of stone, florid cast iron benches and fine lead urns. The wooded slopes round about are finely planted with distinguished trees and shrubs, and from a lofty viewpoint there are beautiful views of the grand surrounding scenery.

GLIN CASTLE

County Limerick

Glin
W of Glin village, 50km W
of Limerick by N69
Tel: 068 34173
Fax: 068 34364

Owner: The Knight of Glin
and Madam Fitz-Gerald

Open: May and Jun, daily
10–12, 2–4; at other times
by arrangement. Castle
open. 5 acres

ON STRICTLY horticultural grounds it would be hard to justify the inclusion of this marvellous place. However, taken all in all, it has as potent a character as any place I know. The dashingly romantic castle looks northwards over the broad waters of the Shannon estuary on one side and, on the other, into its own well-wooded demesne. Near the castle formality reigns, with an axial walk leading from two clipped bays by the castle, between crescents of yew hedging, to a billowing *Parrotia persica* at the centre of of a long wall with sweeping parapet. Above it an apron of grass sparkles with daffodils and bluebells in spring. To the west a great sloping walled kitchen garden, now fully functional, provides fruit and vegetables for the castle and its guests. The castle interior is exceptional – with marvellous furniture, pictures and china, and it is possible to stay here as a paying guest or, indeed, rent the whole caboodle fully equipped with staff, including a chef of brilliant skills.

GRAIGUECONNA

County Wicklow

THIS WAS the garden of a notable alpine gardener, L.B. Meredith, whose book, *Rock Gardens*, published in 1908, appeared at the height of the craze for such things. There are beautiful views of the Little Sugar Loaf Mountain, and enticing paths through

Old Connaught, Bray
18km SE of Dublin by N11
Tel: 01 282 2273

Owner:
Mr and Mrs John Brown

Open: May to Jul, by
appointment only, to
groups of not less than four.
2 1/2 acres

rocky passages lead the visitor into planting all about.
Here, the more you look the more you will certainly
see – from a giant 100-year-old *Eucalyptus globulus* or
a beautiful *Cornus capitata* to the exquisite tender
evergreen maidenhair fern (*Adiantum venustum*) or
choice forms of *Helleborus orientalis*. In the lower
part of the garden, the Paddock, there is a long border
with many shrub roses and much pretty, simple
planting – for example a white cherry underplanted
with white tulips, *Geranium macrorrhizum*, forget-me-
nots, white comfrey and silver dead-nettle.

HEYWOOD

County Laois

Ballinakill
On the edge of Ballinakill
village, 8km SE of
Abbeyleix
Tel: 0502 33563/056 21450

Owner: Department of
Arts, Heritage, Gaeltacht
and the Islands

Open: Daily dawn–dusk.
45 acres

T HE FORMAL garden at Heywood is one of the
most satisfying designs of Sir Edwin Lutyens. His
client was Lt.-Col. William Hutcheson-Poë who
commissioned a new garden between 1909 and 1912.
The house was 18th-century, rebuilt in the 19th
century, preserving fine 18th-century parkland to the
south. Below the house Lutyens made a vast lawn with
views over the park and, to the east, formal enclosures
culminating in one of his most dazzling ideas. Here a
steeply terraced oval garden with a pool at its centre is
overlooked by an elegant Italianate pavilion. The
surrounding walls on the park side are pierced by oval
windows which afford glimpses of the countryside.
Above the oval garden, connected by a beautifully
fashioned curving staircase, a series of yew-hedged
gardens is undergoing restoration. The architecture of
the garden is in fine condition but the planting, some
of which was originally designed by Gertrude Jekyll, is
not yet worthy of its beautiful surroundings.

ILNACULLIN (Garinish Island)

County Cork

S OME GARDENS become so well known that their
reputation quickly outstrips the actuality. Ilnacullin
is, if anything, even more beautiful than one expects it
to be. The passage across to the island is enchanting,
with marvellous scenery and seals frolicking on some
of the smaller islands. The garden, commissioned from
Harold Peto, was made for Annan Bryce in 1910. Peto's

Illustration opposite:
Ilnacullin

Garinish Island, Glengarriff
On an island in Bantry Bay;
boats from Glengarrif
Tel: 027 63040
Fax: 027 63149

Owner: The Department pf
Arts, Heritage, Gaeltacht
and the Islands

Open: Mar and Oct, daily
10–4.30 (Sun 1–5); Apr to
May, Sept, daily 10–6.30
(Sun 1–7); Jul to Aug, daily
9.30–6.30 (Sun 11–7). 30
acres

elegant Italianate *casita* overlooking a sunken garden is familiar from countless photographs, but at the end of the rectangular pool a smaller pavilion has a viewing platform on its far side, with commanding views of the Caha Mountains. The Jungle at the island's centre presents a bewildering array of ornamental trees and shrubs, including many that are tender (like the large-leafed rhododendrons) and several conifers such as *Cupressus torulosa* 'Cashmeriana' with its cascades of fine leaves. South of the Jungle a long vista links a Martello Tower to a temple on an elevation, with beautiful views of the estuary and distant mountains. The beauty of Ilnacullin comes from this deft intermingling of the formal and the wild.

JOHNSTOWN CASTLE GARDENS

County Wexford

Murrintown
5km S of Wexford by N25
Tel: 053 42888
Fax: 053 42004

Owner: TEAGASC – The
Food and Agriculture
Authority

Open: Daily 9–5 (closed 25
Dec). Castle open. 50 acres

THE CASTLE at Johnstown is medieval but was gothicised in the 19th century. The ornamental grounds, rich in conifers, are a splendid survivor of that later period. South and east of the castle is a lake edged with bastion-like walls and with battlemented towers at vantage points. On the far side of the lake an Italianate walk with statues, designed by Daniel Robertson in the 1840s, has a stream and formal cascade. Deep in the surrounding woods are the picturesque remains of the medieval Rathlannon Castle. A walled garden has glasshouses and borders, but the most memorable thing at Johnstown is the authentic Victorian atmosphere of conifers, lugubriously dark or biliously golden, reflected in inscrutable water overlooked by formidable machicolated towers.

THE JOHN F. KENNEDY ARBORETUM

County Wexford

THIS HUGE arboretum, on a fine site, was opened in 1968 and now constitutes one of the finest collections of trees and shrubs in Ireland. The layout is ingenious – about half is disposed in geographical

New Ross
12km S of New Ross by
R733
Tel: 051 388171
Fax: 051 388172

Owner: The Office of
Public Works

Open: Apr and Sept, daily
10–6.30; May to Aug, daily
10–8; Oct to Mar, daily
10–5. 623 acres

plots with plants from the same regions, and the other half is laid out according to botanical genus. In all there are well over 4,500 different kinds of trees and shrubs. They are disposed atractively – those grouped by genus are largely arranged along the banks of a stream and lake with exceptional collections of individual groups. For tree-lovers it is a marvellous treat – and gardeners will relish a long walk among beautiful plants. The arboretum is open throughout the year, with plenty to see and admire in every season.

KILFANE GLEN

County Kilkenny

Thomastown
3km N of Thomastown and
16km SE of Kilkenny by
R700
Tel: 056 24558
Fax: 056 27491

Owner:
Susan and Nicholas Mosse

Open: 15 May to 15 Sept,
daily except Mon 2–6.
10 acres

THE GLEN, with its plummeting waterfall and exquisite cottage *ornée* must be the prettiest 18th-century picturesque garden in Ireland. At a little distance from the house, the wooded glen has a tumbling stream and mossy rocks; from a loop in the stream the cottage looks across to the waterfall tumbling into its pool. The cottage has lattice windows, rustic railings and furniture, and is crowned with an enveloping eiderdown of thatch. Its delightful ground floor is used as a tea-room for visitors; upstairs, the lucky guest may lie in bed gazing up at a *trompe l'oeil* painting of the sky, fringed with garlands of foliage and flowers and rustic trimmings, and be lulled to sleep by the gentle sound of falling water. I know; I have slept there. There are fine walks in the glen, but do not neglect the attractive formal gardens which the Mosses have made about the house. Here, a rectangular pool is edged with blocks of stone, a pergola is draped with roses and clematis, and a white, silver and variegated garden is planted with artemisias, hostas, cranesbills, aquilegias, campanulas and roses. A path leads into woodland, with modern sculptures disposed among the trees. A splendid bronze by Bill Woodrow has a giant wheel whose rim is inscribed with the endlessly repeated words 'to make it work to make it just to make it work . . .'

KILLRUDDERY

County Wicklow

Bray
20km SE of Dublin by
N11/M11
Tel and Fax: 01 286 2777

Owner: The Earl and
Countess of Meath

Open: May to Jun, Sept,
daily 1–5; other dates and
times for groups by
appointment. 41 acres

KILLRUDDERY IS a delightful and rare survivor: a fully-fledged 17th-century formal garden of powerfully French character, in its essence unchanged by later fashions. The estate has belonged to the Brabazon family since the early 17th century and it was they, with the help of a Frenchman named Monsieur Bonet, who laid out the gardens in the 1680s. South of the house a pair of slender pools draws the eye to a long lime avenue which extends the vista far into the distance. On one side are the 'Angles' – a series of triangular areas enclosed in hedges of beech, hornbeam and lime, very similar to the *bosquets* seen in French gardens of this time – and at the southern extremity a round pond with a fountain and the remains of formal cascades. West of this, half-concealed in woodland, are traces of earlier formality – an iron statue of a stricken warrior engulfed in spring by wild garlic, a tall figure of Venus beckoning from the heights of a plinth, and the sketchy remains of vistas. Closer to the house a pretty *théâtre de verdure* is hedged in bay with turf seats, and a huge circle of beech hedges encloses a round pool. Immediately west of the house a Victorian parterre with a scalloped pool is surrounded by marvellously lumpy yew hedges. To one side an enchanting octagonal dairy is shrouded in trellis and clematis. It has a lovely interior – stained-glass windows, a finely carved marble sink, blue tiles and elegant shelving supported on carved brackets.

KNOCKREE GARDEN
County Dublin

Glenamuck Road, Carrickmines, Dublin 18
11km S of city centre, W of N11
Tel and Fax: 01 2955 884

Owner:
John and Shirley Beatty

Open: Apr to Jul, Sun 2–6; groups on any day by appointment. 2 acres

KNOCKREE IS one of those irresistible gardens which you may feel, if you had possesssed Shirley Beatty's lively skills, you might have made yourself. It lies on the slopes of the foothills of the Dublin Mountains, and behind the house, where the land rises sharply, a dramatic outcrop of granite breaks the surface, like the back of some friendly subterranean monster. This giant natural shape dominates the mood of the garden, which is naturalistic in style with paths following the lie of the land. Here are substantial shrubs and trees – a purple-leafed Japanese maple, a huge *Crinodendron hookerianum*, many rhododendrons and a beautiful *Drimys lanceolata*. A narrow gravel path winds up the hill to one side of the rock with a profusion of herbaceous perennials on either side – aquilegias, cranesbills, pansies, peonies, variegated comfrey, plum-red astrantia and scatterings of a pretty pink-flowered strawberry. As you near the top of the garden there is an orchard among the rocks and a kitchen garden. Beyond is a rocky heath with gorse, foxgloves, Scots pines and lofty views. You may now descend the hill by an alternative path through a shady grove of Scots pines with rhododendrons and hollies underplanted with cranesbills, dicentras, ferns, Solomon's seal and trilliums. The front garden is also rich in fine plants but it is the garden at the back, with its inventive use of the site, that sticks in the mind.

LAKEMOUNT

County Cork

Barnavara, Glanmire
W of Glanmire, 5km E of
Cork by N25
Tel: 021 821052

Owner: Brian Cross

Open: Apr to Sept, by appointment 2–5. 2 acres

THE IMMEDIATE impression at Lakemount is of the jewel-like perfection of the planting and the flawless standards of maintenance. Many visitors will return home realising that their standards are not, remotely, as high as Brian Cross's. A vast range of plants is grown, ordered and disposed with a refined sense of their decorative possibilities: *Cornus controversa* 'Variegata' is underplanted with a sea of white *Camassia leichtlinii*; the silver bark of a Himalayan birch rises from the plum-coloured hummock of a Japanese maple; an onion-shaped pot is placed alongside a sheaf of New Zealand flax overshadowed by a Chusan palm. The site is a gently sloping one, with flowing beds, sweeping areas of velvety lawn, and strong planting shapes – pointy conifers among mounded rhododendrons. There is a profusion of sitting places, and ornaments skilfully woven into the planting scheme. All this sophistication contrasts strikingly with the lofty site of the garden with its splendid views over countryside to the south-east and the estuary of the river Lee.

LARCHILL ARCADIAN GARDEN
County Kildare

Larchill, Kilcock
25km W of Dublin by N4
Tel and Fax: 01 628 4580

Owner:
Michael de Las Casas

Open: May to Sept, daily
12–6; also by appointment.
63 acres

T HIS IS an excellent example of a forgotten garden brought thrillingly back to life: an 18th-century intimate landscape garden of a particularly attractive type, the *ferme ornée*, a working farm ornamented with decorative buildings. Alongside the pretty 18th-century house the walled garden, which is being restored, has a round tower whose interior is enlivened with patterns of native Irish shells. South of the house, on the far side of a stream, rare breeds of sheep and cattle graze in pastureland that runs down to a lake studded with eccentric decorative constructions: a gothic boathouse, a fort in the shape of the Rock of Gibraltar, a statue of Bacchus and a curious pillared temple. All this is country vernacular rather than Grand Tour classical – but nonetheless delightful. On the western side of the lake and field is a long walk along an avenue of beech, ash and limes, from which there are views of the house and other ornamental buildings – the bizarre Fox's Earth with dumpy columns, the Eel House and other monuments of a rural kind. It all has a magical charm, epitomized by the farmyard with pigs in ornamental sties, and with geese, chickens, ducks, fluttering white fantail pigeons and rare goats lurking in the background.

LISMORE CASTLE

County Waterford

Lismore
In Lismoret own, 25km W
of Dungarvan by N72
Tel: 058 54424
Fax: 058 54896

Owner:
The Duke of Devonshire

Open: 25 April to 26 Sept,
daily 1.45–4.45. 7 acres

THE CASTLE, looking north over the river Blackwater, has a spectacularly romantic setting. Its origins go back to the 12th century but it owes its present appearance to the rebuilding which took place in the first half of the 19th century under the 6th Duke of Devonshire. The garden has no horticultural fireworks but it does have the irresistible charm of a historic site which, changing gently from time to time, has been finely gardened for centuries. The Lower Garden is a vast expanse of lawn with an atmospheric walk of gnarled yews at its southern end. Along the terrace wall are big specimens of *Luma apiculata* with trunks the colour of milky coffee, and a giant *Drimys winteri*. Immediately to the east of the castle two rows of eucryphias make an unusual avenue. The Upper Garden, dating from the 17th century, is said to be the oldest surviving walled garden in Ireland. It is on two levels, with hedges of beech, hornbeam and box, and herbaceous borders ornamenting a large kitchen garden. A grassy walk at the back of the upper level, embellished with buttresses and topiary, has such tender plants as olearias, *Melianthus major* and mimosas flourishing against the retaining wall.

MALAHIDE DEMESNE

County Dublin

THE TALBOTS are a very ancient family; they built the first castle at Malahide in the 12th century. The castle's present romantically gothic appearance dates from the mid 19th century and it makes a beautiful ornament at the heart of the splendidly wooded demesne. The garden proper consists of about 20 acres immediately around the castle, with the

Malahide
13km NE of Dublin by
R105 and R106
Tel: 01 872 7777
Fax: 01 872 7530

Owner:
Fingal County Council

Open: Grounds: daily
dawn–dusk; *Talbot Botanic
Garden:* May to Sept, daily
2–5 (guided tours Wed at
2). 20 acres. Castle open

walled Talbot Botanic Garden in the middle. The
Talbots had Tasmanian connections in the 18th
century and the plants of the southern hemisphere,
many of which flourish so well in the balmy
microclimate here, dominated their plant-collecting
activities. The walled garden is chiefly the creation of
Lord (Milo) Talbot de Malahide after World War II.
Australasian plants are deeply represented –
Athrotaxis, eucalyptus, hebes, olearias, pittosporums
and many others. Outside the walled gardens grassy
walks are edged with shrub borders. By the castle are
exceptional trees – a superb cedar of Lebanon and a
stupendous sessile oak (*Quercus petraea*).

71 MERRION SQUARE

County Dublin

Dublin 2
In the centre of Dublin
Tel: 01 676 7281

Owner: Sybil Connolly

Open: By appointment to
groups only

MERRION SQUARE is one of the finest of Dublin's
Georgian squares and No 71 is owned by Sybil
Connolly whose exquisite designs – among them
Tiffany porcelain – are treasured all over the world.
Her garden is as fastidious, and delightful, as you
might expect. From a paved terrace with a clipped cone
of bay, a basket-weave brick path snakes across
flawless turf. Substantial shrubs and ornamental trees
animate the scene – a beautiful *Viburnum plicatum*, a
weeping silver pear, a golden sycamore and a Japanese
maple with plum-coloured feathery foliage, tree
peonies and shrub roses. The walls on either side are
garlanded with ivy, jasmine, clematis and wisteria. At
the far end an enchanting little brick mews house, with

arched windows and doors and gothick tracery glazing bars, is used as accommodation for guests. In the context of the garden design it assumes the role of a delicious eyecatcher.

MOUNT CONGREVE

County Waterford

Kilmeaden
8km W of Waterford by N25
Tel: 051 384115
Fax: 051 384576

Owner: Ambrose Congreve

Open: By appointment only, Mon to Fri 9–5 (closed Bank Hols). 180 acres

MOUNT CONGREVE is a woodland garden on a heroic scale. Its vast collection of trees and shrubs has much skilful herbaceous underplanting but it is intensively cultivated in a way that is different from any other garden I know. Paths follow the contours of undulating land, with dense planting on either side. The paths are edged with huge quantities of a single plant – hummocks of Japanese maple, seas of white azaleas, hostas, libertias or astilbes. The trees themselves often have their lower branches removed and are beautifully cared for; even quite ordinary species, if they are fine specimens, are given full weight in the landscape: for example, a group of superlative beeches is scattered across a giant close-mown lawn fringed with maples and rhododendrons. Many of the trees have climbers – clematis, roses or *Vitis coignetiae* – beautifully trained high up their trunks. Although there are other pleasures at Mount Congreve, among them vast walled gardens, glasshouses and the occasional well-placed temple or curious Chinese house, it is the finely manicured woodland garden, with plants in such huge quantities looking so startlingly healthy, that sticks in the mind.

MOUNT STEWART

County Down

Newtownards BT22 2AD
15m E of Belfast by A20
Tel: 01224 88387/88487
Fax: 01224 88569

Owner: The National Trust

Open: Easter to Aug, daily
except Tue 12–6; Sept to
Oct, Sat and Sun 12–6.
78 acres. House open

GOOD GARDENS often bear the stamp of one exceptional creator, but few so firmly as Mount Stewart. Edith, Marchioness of Londonderry came to Mount Stewart as a young wife in 1921 and plunged into the making of the garden which, restored by the National Trust, is today very much as she made it. The climate at Mount Stewart is exceptionally mild, with high humidity from the sea. This allows a great range of tender plants: huge eucalyptus, an avenue of the New Zealand cabbage palm (*Cordyline australis*) and tender conifers such as *Cupressus torulosa* 'Cashmeriana'. To the west of the house a sunken garden is surrounded on three sides by a pergola with roses, vines and the rare *Billardiera longiflora* with brilliant blue berries in autumn. Beds in the centre are brilliant in spring with orange azaleas, and in summer with a rich mixture of herbaceous plants. Behind the house the Italian garden is a giant parterre in which the beds – edged with purple berberis or golden thuya, have skilful and ebullient colour schemes – grey, white and blue to the west and orange, yellow and scarlet to the east. Curious statues of monkeys and other animals decorate the enclosing walls, and a menagerie of creatures lurks in the undergrowth. On the far side of the house, woodland, with many rhododendrons and ornamental trees, presses in on a lake whose banks are planted with drifts of iris, crocosmia or kniphofia. Mount Stewart is nothing if not bold, but its strong sense of design holds it brilliantly together and makes it one of the finest and most enchantingly varied gardens in Britain.

MOUNT USHER GARDENS

County Wicklow

Ashford
In Ashford village,
50km S of Dublin by N11
Tel: 0404 40116/40205
Fax: 0404 40205

Owner: Madelaine Jay

Open: 13 Mar to 2 Nov,
daily except Sun 10.30–6.
20 acres

THE GARDEN at Mount Usher was started in the 1860s by Edward Walpole, and developed by his three sons. Edward Walpole had the advantage of advice from Sir Frederick Moore, the Director of the National Botanic Garden, the great plant hunter Augustine Henry and E.A. Bowles. The garden is dominated by the lovely river Vartry and one of the Walpole sons, Thomas, an engineer by profession, made the weirs that punctuate it. The pools above the weirs are a vital part of the garden's charm, for their mirror-like surfaces reflect the lovely plantings which clothe the banks. There are at least 3,000 species here, with major collections of acers, eucalyptus, eucryphia and *Nothofagus*. Mount Usher exudes peace and everywhere there is something to admire – brilliant colours and bold shapes reflected in the river, waves of martagon lilies in the woods, an eyestopping azalea glade stretching between trees and, in the Island Garden, a delightful stream on whose banks are Asiatic primulas, dactylorhizas and the sweetly scented giant lily, *Cardiocrinum giganteum*.

MUCKROSS GARDENS AND ARBORETUM

County Kerry

THIS BEAUTIFUL place is part of the Killarney National Park, over 25,000 acres of magnificent protected countryside. The demesne is magnificently endowed with fine trees, some of which date back to the mid 19th century. A long terrace runs along the west side of the house with, to one side, a superlative

Killarney
4km S of Killarney by N71
Tel: 064 31440
Fax: 064 33926

Owner: The Office of
Public Works

Open: Daily 9–5.30.
50 acres. House open

Monterey pine (*Pinus radiata*). Beyond it the Lawns
spread out, a huge expanse of greensward dotted with
great trees (notice the immense Caucasian fir, *Abies
nordmanniana*, by the stream), and clumps of tree
rhododendrons. The arboretum beyond the stream has
beautiful old woodland, rich in such native trees as the
sessile oak (*Quercus petraea*) and the Scots pine (*Pinus
sylvestris*). Here have been introduced countless exotics
– a huge collection of camellias, shrubs such as
hoherias and clethras, and Exbury azaleas in lollipop
colours. The Muckross estate is beautifully cared for
and makes a marvellous place for a long walk with
frequent stops to admire exceptional plants.

NATIONAL BOTANIC GARDENS

County Dublin

Glasnevin, Dublin 9
N of the city centre
Tel: 01 837 4388
Fax: 01 836 0080

Owner:
The Office of Public Works

Open: Daily except 25 Dec,
summer 9–6; winter
10–4.30; Sun opens 11).
48 acres

THE DEPTH of historic interest, the charms of the
site and its buildings, and the very large range of
plants combine to make this one of the most attractive
of all botanic gardens. Its history goes back to 1795
when the first part of the site was acquired and Dr
Walter Wade laid out the first garden. Today, the
collection of plants at Glasnevin includes over 20,000
different species and cultivars. Several 19th-century
glasshouses provide striking ornaments – in particular
the Curvilinear Range and the magnificent Great Palm
House. The soil here is alkaline, so this is no place for
ericaceous plants although a few are cultivated in
artificial pockets of acid soil. Trees are arranged by

genus, with large collections of maples, rowans, cedars, cherries and several others. Features of specifically horticultural interest include a rose garden, a demonstration of different lawn grasses, a display of annuals and a vegetable garden. There is an immense amount to stimulate the mind – but it is also just a wonderful place.

POWERSCOURT GARDENS

County Wicklow

Enniskerry
20km S of Dublin by N11
Tel: 01 286 7676
Fax: 01 286 3561

Owner: Powerscourt Estate

Open: Mar to Oct, daily
9.30–5.30; Nov to Feb, daily
9.30–5.30. 47 acres

NOT ALL showpieces are necessarily attractive to visitors but Powerscourt seduces from the moment you arrive. The drive curves through beautiful parkland studded with magnificent 200-year-old beeches. From the 17th century the estate belonged to the Wingfield family, who became the Viscounts Powerscourt and built a great Palladian house in the 1740s. The central part of the house, and almost all its contents, were destroyed by fire in 1974. The formal gardens behind the house had their origins in 1840 when the 6th Viscount commissioned Daniel Robertson to lay out a giant paved terrace south of the house. The Italian Gardens on the slopes below were added from the late 1850s – a formal garden descending in great terraces to a vast pool at the bottom, guarded by two leaping winged horses (the Wingfield crest) and with a single immense water jet at its centre. The whole layout is centred on the peak of the Sugar Loaf Mountain in the lovely Wicklow Hills to the south. The banks of the lake are well wooded and rich in exceptional trees dating back to the 19th century, especially such conifers as Monterey cypress (*Cupressus macrocarpa*), the incense cedar (*Calocedrus decurrens*), monkey puzzles (*Araucana araucaria*) and Douglas fir (*Pseudotsuga menziessii*). Hidden in the woods on one side of the lake is a pretty Japanese garden, laid out in 1908. The walk about the banks of the lake, at upper or lower level, offers delicious views of both the formal gardens and the notable trees which are disposed all about.

PRIMROSE HILL

County Dublin

Lucan
12km W of Dublin by N4
Tel: 01 628 0373

Owner: Mrs Cicely Hall
and Mr Robin Hall

Open: Feb, mid Jun to mid Aug, daily 2–6; also by appointment. 6 acres

THE HOUSE at Primrose Hill is a delightful Regency villa and the garden, with its winding paths and nooks and crannies, is like a glorified cottage garden – 'glorified' because of the range and distinction of the plants used. For example, here is the pretty cottage-garden double-flowered buttercup but here also is the aristocratic and very beautiful *Paeonia suffruticosa* sbsp. *rockii*. Mrs Hall came here in the 1950s and she and her son Robin are fastidious connoisseurs of plants. There is a marvellous collection of snowdrops (hence the February opening), several cultivars which originated here (such as the lobelias 'Pink Elephant' and 'Spark'), the lovely scarlet *Lilium chalcedonicum* and much else. But this is not merely a plant-spotter's garden for there is much artistry in the planting – the conical *Picea glauca* var. *albertiana* 'Conica' emerging from a wave of aquilegias, pink-brown *Dicentra* 'Stuart Boothman' among variegated astrantia and, more simply, a wave of Solomon's seal under an apple tree.

ROWALLANE

County Down

Saintfield,
Ballynahinch BT24 7LH
11m SE of Belfast by A7
Tel: 01238 510721
Fax: 01238 511242

Owner: The National Trust

Open: Nov to Mar, daily
except Sat and Sun 9–5; Apr
to Oct daily 10.30–6
(weekends 2–6). 20 acres

THE DRIVE leading up to Rowallane passes through dense woodland with mossy rocks pressing in on either side and mysterious conical cairns of rounded stones. The garden was made by Hugh Armytage Moore, who came here in 1903. He was particularly interested in woody plants, especially rhododendrons which he planted in the undulating ground in bold clumps and belts, as though they were the ingredients of a landscape garden. Many of his plantings were raised from seed collected by the great plant hunters of the early 20th century – such as Wilson, Forrest and Kingdon-Ward. The microclimate is very benign, as the many species from the southern hemisphere show – olearias from Australia, the orange-flowered *Desfontainea spinosa* from Chile, and *Pseudowintera colorata*, with curiously variegated foliage, from New Zealand. The character of the garden is essentially informal but in the walled garden beds have excellent shrub roses and the National Collection of large-flowered penstemons.

TYPES OF GARDENS AND GARDEN FEATURES

Aboreta
Batsford Arboretum
Bedgebury National
    Arboretum
Birr Castle
Borde Hill
Bradenham Hall Garden
Castlewellan National
    Arboretum
Dawyck Botanic Garden
Dunloe Castle Gardens
Exbury Gardens
Fota Arboretum
Hergest Croft
The Sir Harold Hillier
    Arboretum
J.F. Kennedy Arboretum,
    The
Malahide Demesne
Mount Congreve
Mount Usher
Muckross Gardens and
    Arboretum
National Botanic Gardens
Ness Garden
Powerscourt Gardens
Royal Botanic Garden,
    Edinburgh
Savill Garden
Scone Palace
Stone Lane Gardens
Thorp Perrow
Valley Garden
Wakehurst Place
Westonbirt

Especially Good Borders
Anglesey Abbey
Arley Hall
Ballymaloe Cookery School
Benington Lordship
Blickling Hall
Bradenham Hall Garden

Clare College
Cottesbrooke Hall
Crathes Castle
Dillon Garden, The
Falkland Palace
Great Dixter
Hardwick Hall
House of Pitmuies
Kellie Castle
Leith Hall
Loseley Gardens
Newby Hall
Old Vicarage Garden, The
Parham
Powis Castle
The Priory

Botanic Gardens
Cambridge University
    Botanic Garden
Chelsea Physic Garden
Dawyck Botanic Garden
Harlow Carr Botanical
    Gardens
Logan Botanic Garden
National Botanic Gardens
Oxford Botanic Garden
Royal Botanic Garden,
    Edinburgh
Royal Botanic Garden, Kew
Younger Botanic Garden
    Benmore

Demonstration Gardens
Cabbages & Kings
Capel Manor
Harlow Carr
National Botanic Gardens
Rosemoor
Ryton Organic Gardens
Wisley Garden
Yalding

Herb Gardens
Gunby hall
Hardwick Hall
Herb and Heather Centre
Hexham Herbs
Holdenby Hall Gardens
Hollington Herb Garden
Iden Croft
Poyntzfield Herb Nursery
Sissinghurst Castle

Japanese Gardens
Capel Manor
Compton Acres
Heale Garden
Kyoto Garden
Powerscourt Gardens
Tatton Park

Kitchen Gardens
Barnsley House
Barrington Court
Bourton House Garden
Calke Abbey
Creagh Gardens
Edmondsham House
Felbrigg Hall
Glenveagh Castle
Glin Castle
Helmingham Hall
Lismore Castle
Upton House
West Dean

Landscape Gardens
Antony House
Audley End
Blaise Castle
Blenheim Palace
Boughton House Park
Bowood
Chatsworth
Claremont
Duncombe Park
Euston Hall
Farnborough Hall
Gibside
Hackfall Wood
Hawkstone Park
Hermitage, The
Hestercombe
Larchill Arcadian Garden
Mount Edgcumbe
Osterley Park
Painshill
Painswick Rococo Garden
Petworth
Prior Park
Rievaulx Terrace
Royal Botanic Garden, Kew
Scotney Castle
Sheffield Park
Shugborough
Stourhead

Stowe
Studley Royal
Wrest Park

Rock Gardens
Cragside House
Glen Chantry
Killerton House
Muckross Gardens
Murrel Garden, The
Newby Hall
Royal Botanic Garden,
  Edinburgh
Sizergh Castle
Wisley Garden

Rose Gardens
Bradenham Hall Garden
Broughton Castle
Butterstream Garden
Castle Howard
Cliveden
Gardens of the Rose, The
Haddon Hall
Helmingham Hall
Hodges Barn
Hyde Hall
Kiftsgate Court
Loseley Gardens
Malleny House
Mannington Hall
Mottisfont Abbey
Polesden Lacey
Renishaw Hall
Sissinghurst Castle
Sudeley Castle
Warwick Castle

Water and Bog Gardens
Annes Grove
Buscot Park
Beth Chatto Gardens
Birr Castle
Coleton Fishacre
Docton Mill
Forde Abbey
Hermitage, The
Hodnet Hall
Kilfane Glen
Larchill Arcadian Garden
Longstock Water Gardens
Marwood Hill Gardens
Minterne

Mount Usher
Sezincote
Stapeley Water Gardens
Westbury Court

Woodland Gardens
Abbotsbury Sub-tropical
  Gardens
Achamore
Altamont
Annes Grove
Antony Woodland Garden
Arbigland
Ardnamona
Arduaine
Birr Castle
Bodnant
Brodick Castle
Caerhays Castle
Castle Howard
Castlewellan National
  Arboretum
Craigieburn Garden
Crarae Garden
Creagh Gardens
Dawyck Botanic Garden
Emo Court Garden
Exbury Gardens
Fairhaven Garden Trust
Fernhill
Furzey Gardens
Glenveagh Castle
High Beeches, The
Holker Hall
Inverewe
Kilfane Glen
Killerton House
Knightshayes Court
Leonardslee
Minterne
Mount Congreve
Mount Usher
Muckross Gardens
Muncaster Castle
Penjerrick
Rowallane
Savill Garden
Scotney Castle
Sheffield Park
Stone Lane Gardens
Trebah
Trengwainton
Trewithen

NURSERIES FOR SPECIFIC KINDS OF PLANTS

Alpines
Abriachan Nurseries
Ardfearn Nursery
Christie's Nursery
Edrom Nursery
Glen Chantry
Holden Clough Nursery
W.E.Th. Ingwersen
Inshriach Nursery
Mead Nursery, The
Norden Alpines
Old Court Nurseries
Padlock Croft
Perhill Nurseries
Potterton & Martin
Rookhope Nurseries

Aquatic Plants
Rowden Gardens
Stapeley Water Gardens

Box
Langley Boxwood Nursery

Bulbs
Jacques Amand Ltd
Avon Bulbs
Broadleigh Gardens
The Monocot Nursery
Paradise Centre

Camellias
Burncoose Nurseries
Coghurst Nursery
Marwood Hill Garden
Starborough Nursery

Campanulas
Bernwode Plants
Padlock Croft
W.E.Th. Ingwersen
Norden alpines
Wootten's Plants

Citrus Fruit
Reads Nursery

Clematis
Caddicks Clematis Nursery
Fisk's Clematis Nursery
Great Dixter

Colchicums
Broadleigh Gardens
W.E.Th. Ingwersen
The Moncot Nursery

Daylilies
Apple Court

Delphiniums
Blackmore & Langdon

Ferns
Fibrex Nurseries
Spinners

Fruit Trees
Bernwode
Brogdale
Deacons Nursery
Reads Nursery

Fuchsias
B. and H.M. Baker

Geraniums
Bernwode Plants
Crûg Farm Plants
East Lambrook Manor
Glebe Cottage Plants
Hall Farm Nursery
Rushfields of Ledbury

Grasses
Apple Court
Hoecroft Plants
Rushfields of Ledbury

Hellebores
Avon Bulbs
Blackthorn Nursery
Fibrex Nurseries
Rushfields of Ledbury
Washfield Nursery

Herbaceous Perennials
Blackthorn Nursery
Blooms of Bressingham
Bosvigo House
Bernwode Plants
Cally Garden
Beth Chatto Garden
Christie's Nursery
Church Hill Cottage
  Garden
Cotswold Garden Flowers
Cottage Garden Plants
Crûg Farm Plants
East Lambrook Manor
Eastgrove Cottage Gardens
Foxgrove Plants
Gannock Growers
Glen Chantry
Green Farm Plants
Hadspen Garden
Hall Farm Nursery
The Hannays of Bath
Merriments Gardens
Monksilver Nursery
Old Court Nurseries
Perhill Nurseries
Perry's Plants
Pleasant View Nursery
Rowden Gardens
Rushfields of Ledbury
Stillingfleet Lodge Nursery
Washfield Nursery
Waterwheel Nursery
Wootten's Plants

Herbs
Herb and Heather Centre
Hollington Herb Garden
Iden Croft
Poyntzfield Herb Nursery

Hostas
Apple Court
Hadspen Garden
Park Green Nurseries

Ivy
Fibrex Nurseries

Magnolias
Burncoose Nurseries
Spinners
Starborough Nursery

Maples
Mallet Court Nursery
Spinners
Starborough Nursery

Meconopsis
Craigieburn Garden

Pelargoniums
Fibrex Nurseries Ltd
Wootten's Plants

Peonies
Kelways

Pinks
Bernwode Plants
Glebe Cottage Plants
W. E.Th. Ingwersen
Kingstone Cottages

Primulas
Abriachan Nurseries
Christie's Nursery
Cluny House
Edrom Nurseries
Glebe Cottage
W. E. Th. Ingwersen
Inshriach Nursery
Monksilver Nursery
Norden Alpines
Paradise Centre
Rowden Gardens

Rhododendrons
Burncoose Nurseries
Lea Gardens
G. Reuthe
Spinners
Starborough

Roses
David Austin
Peter Beales Roses
Cottage Garden Roses
Cranborne Manor
Perryhill Nurseries

Salvias
Pleasant View Nursery

Shrubs
Bluebell Nursery

Burncoose Nurseries
Duchy of Cornwall
  Nursery
Hopley's Plants
Spinners
Waterwheel Nursery

Snowdrops
Avon Bulbs
Foxgrove Plants

Trees
Bluebell Nursery
Mallet Court Nursery
Pantiles Plant Centre
Spinners

Tulips
Jacques Amand
Broadleigh Gardens
W. E. Th. Ingwersen

Violas and Pansies
W. E. Th. Ingwersen
Norden Alpines

Water Lilies
Stapeley Water Gardens

GARDENS BY FAMOUS DESIGNERS

Sir Reginald Blomfield
(1856–1942)
Mellerstain
Sulgrave Manor

Charles Bridgeman
(d. 1738)
Claremont
Rousham Hall
Stowe
Wimpole Hall
Wolterton Park

Lancelot 'Capability' Brown
(1716–83)
Audley End
Berrington Hall
Blenheim Palace
Bowood
Castle Ashby
Chatsworth
Claremont
Euston Hall
Harewood House
Ickworth
Petworth
Sheffield Park
Stowe
Warwick Castle
Wimpole Hall
Wrest Park

Percy Cane
(1881–1976)
Dartington Hall
Falkland Palace

Dame Sylvia Crowe
(1901–97)
Cottesbrooke Hall
'Penicillin Garden' (Oxford Botanic Garden)

William Emes
(1730–1803)
Belton House
Erddig

Beatrix Farrand
(1872–1959)
Dartington Hall

W.S. Gilpin
(1762–1843)
Audley End
Scotney Castle

Gertrude Jekyll
(1843–1932)
Broughton Castle
Hestercombe
Knebworth
Lindisfarne Castle
Manor House (Upton Grey)

Sir Geoffrey Jellicoe
(1900–96)
Cliveden
Cottesbrooke Hall
Mottisfont Abbey

William Kent
(1685–1748)
Claremont
Euston Hall
Rousham House
Stowe

George London
(d. 1714)
Chatsworth
Hanbury Hall
Petworth

Sir Robert Lorimer
(1864–1929)
Hill of Tarvit House
Kellie Castle

Sir Edwin Lutyens
(1869–1944)
Castle Drogo
Hestercombe
Heywood
Knebworth

Thomas Mawson
(1861–1933)
Wightwick Manor

W.A. Nesfield
(1793–1881)
Castle Howard
Harewood House
Witley Court

Russell Page
(1906–85)
Leeds Castle
Port Lympne

Sir Joseph Paxton
(1803–65)
Chatsworth
Somerleyton
Tatton Park

Harold Peto
(1854–1933)
Buscot Park
Heale House
Iford Manor
Ilnacullin
West Dean Gardens

Humphry Repton
(1752–1818)
Antony House
Blaise Castle
Bowood
Plas Newydd
Sheffield Park
Sheringham Park
Tatton Park
Wimpole Hall

William Robinson
(1838–1935)
Emmetts
Gravetye Manor
Killerton House
Nymans
Shrubland Gardens

Lanning Roper
(1912–83)
Broughton Castle
Claverton Manor
Glenveagh Castle

Penshurst Place
Scotney Castle

Edward Weir Schultz
(1860–1951)
Cottesbrooke Hall

F. Inigo Thomas
(1866–1950)
Athelhampton

Sir John Vanbrugh
(1644–1726)
Blenheim Palace
Claremont
Seaton Delaval Hall

Sir Clough Williams-Ellis
(1883–1978)
Plas Brondanw
Portmeirion

NATIONAL COLLECTIONS OF PLANTS

The National Council for the Protection of Plants and Gardens (NCCPG) has set up National Collections of groups of plants. Most of these are not normally accessible to the public, but some are held by gardens and nurseries described in this book. They are as follows:

abelias
  Pleasant View Nursery
agapanthus
  Bicton College
alders
  Stone Lane Gardens
apples
  Brogdale
astilbes
  Holehird Gardens
  Marwood Hill Gardens
begonias
  Stapeley Water Gardens
birches
  Hergest Croft
  Stone Lane Gardens
box
  Langley Boxwood
  |Nursery
bromeliads
  Stapeley Water Gardens
campanulas
  Padlock Croft
celandines
  Rowden Gardens
cistus
  Chelsea Physic Garden
colchicums
  Felbrigg Hall
conifers (dwarf)
  Valley Garden
cotoneasters
  Sir Harold Hillier Garden
crab-apples
  Hyde Hall

crocosmias
Lanhydrock
daylilies
Antony House
dogwoods
Sir Harold Hillier Garden
Newby Hall
Rosemoor
erythroniums
Greencombe
euphorbias
Bernwode Plants
Oxford Botanic Garden
ferns (hardy)
Savill and Valley Gardens
ferns (polystichum)
Greencombe
Holehird
figs
Reads Nursery
foxgloves
The Botanic Nursery
fritillaries (European species)
Cambridge University Botanic Garden
geraniums
Cambridge University Botanic Garden
East Lambrook Manor
galeobdolon
Monksilver Nursery
hollies
Rosemoor
Valley Garden
hostas
Apple Court
Harewood House
hydrangeas
Holehird Gardens
ivy
Erddig
junipers
Bedgebury National Pinetum
kniphofias
Barton Manor
lamiums
Monksilver Nursery
lavenders
Norfolk Lavender
Lawson cypresses
Bedgebury National

Pinetum
magnolias
Bodnant
Valley Garden
Wentworth Castle
mahonias
Valley Garden
maples (excluding Acer japonicum *and* A palmatum *cultivars)*
Hergest Croft
(Acer japonicum)
Westonbirt
meconopsis
Craigieburn Garden
Michaelmas daisies
Old Court Nurseries
mints
Iden Croft
oaks
Sir Harold Hillier Garden
origanums
Iden Croft
penstemons
Kingston Maurward College
Rowallane
Threave Garden
peonies
Branklyn Garden
periwinkles
Monkilver Nursery
pieris
The High Beeches
Valley Garden
pinks (old garden varieties)
Kingstone Cottages
pittosporum
Bicton College
planes
Mottisfont Abbey
polygonums
Rowden Gardens
primulas (Asiatic species)
Cluny House
pulmonarias
Stillingfleet Lodge Nurseries
rhododendron (species)
Valley Garden
Wentworth Castle
roses (pre 1900)
Mottisfont Abbey

roses (19th-century)
Malleny House
salvias
Pleasant View Nursery
santolinas
Herb and Heather Centre
snowdrops
Wisley Garden
stewartias
The High Beeches
styracaceae
Holker Hall
thymes
Hexham Herbs
tulips (species and primary hybrids)
Cambridge University Botanic Garden
viburnums
Hyde Hall
willows (lowland species)
Westonbirt Arboretum
yews
Bedgebury National Pinetum
zelkovas
Hergest Croft

INDEX